W9-BVA-152

WILLIAM SHAKESPEARE

WILLIAM SHAKESPEARE

Other titles in the
People Who Made History series:

PEOPLE WHO MADE HISTORY

WILLIAM SHAKESPEARE

Laura Marvel, *Book Editor*

Daniel Leone, *President*
Bonnie Szumski, *Publisher*
Scott Barbour, *Managing Editor*
David M. Haugen, *Series Editor*

GREENHAVEN
PRESS®

THOMSON

GALE

San Diego • Detroit • New York • San Francisco • Cleveland
New Haven, Conn. • Waterville, Maine • London • Munich

© 2004 by Greenhaven Press. Greenhaven Press is an imprint of The Gale Group, Inc., a division of Thomson Learning, Inc.

Greenhaven® and Thomson Learning™ are trademarks used herein under license.

For more information, contact
Greenhaven Press
27500 Drake Rd.
Farmington Hills, MI 48331-3535
Or you can visit our Internet site at http://www.gale.com

Cover credit: © Stock Montage
Library of Congress, 20, 36, 118, 177

LIBRARY OF CONGRESS CATALOGING-IN-PUBLICATION DATA

William Shakespeare / Laura Marvel, book editor.
    p. cm. — (People who made history)
    Includes bibliographical references and index.
    ISBN 0-7377-0901-4 (lib. : alk. paper) — ISBN 0-7377-0900-6 (pbk. : alk. paper)
    1. Shakespeare, William, 1564–1616. 2. Shakespeare, William, 1564–1616—Influence. 3. Shakespeare, William, 1564–1616—Appreciation. 4. Shakespeare, William, 1564–1616—Film and video adaptations. 5. Shakespeare, William, 1564–1616—Stage history—1950– . 6. Dramatists, English—Early modern, 1500–1700—Biography. I. Marvel, Laura. II. Series.
    PR2894.W555 2004
    822.3'3—dc21
                                              2002045478

Printed in the United States of America

CONTENTS

ments that concentrate on the passions of Shakespeare's characters have proven the most successful.

Chapter 4: Shakespeare Permeates Popular Culture

"Bardfests." Nevertheless, a chance encounter with the poetry itself can still offer a transformative experience.

Foreword

In the vast and colorful pageant of human history, a handful of individuals stand out. They are the men and women who have come variously to be called "great," "leading," "brilliant," "pivotal," or "infamous" because they and their deeds forever changed their own society or the world as a whole. Some were political or military leaders—kings, queens, presidents, generals, and the like—whose policies, conquests, or innovations reshaped the maps and futures of countries and entire continents. Among those falling into this category were the formidable Roman statesman/general Julius Caesar, who extended Rome's power into Gaul (what is now France); Caesar's lover and ally, the notorious Egyptian queen Cleopatra, who challenged the strongest male rulers of her day; and England's stalwart Queen Elizabeth I, whose defeat of the mighty Spanish Armada saved England from subjugation.

Some of history's other movers and shakers were scientists or other thinkers whose ideas and discoveries altered the way people conduct their everyday lives or view themselves and their place in nature. The electric light and other remarkable inventions of Thomas Edison, for example, revolutionized almost every aspect of home-life and the workplace; and the theories of naturalist Charles Darwin lit the way for biologists and other scientists in their ongoing efforts to understand the origins of living things, including human beings.

Still other people who made history were religious leaders and social reformers. The struggles of the Arabic prophet Muhammad more than a thousand years ago led to the establishment of one of the world's great religions—Islam; and the efforts and personal sacrifices of an American reverend named Martin Luther King Jr. brought about major improvements in race relations and the justice system in the United States.

Each anthology in the People Who Made History series begins with an introductory essay that provides a general overview of the individual's life, times, and contributions. The group of essays that follow are chosen for their accessibility to a young adult audience and carefully edited in consideration of the reading and comprehension levels of that audience. Some of the essays are by noted historians, professors, and other experts. Others are excerpts from contemporary writings by or about the pivotal individual in question. To aid the reader in choosing the material of immediate interest or need, an annotated table of contents summarizes the article's main themes and insights.

Each volume also contains extensive research tools, including a collection of excerpts from primary source documents pertaining to the individual under discussion. The volumes are rounded out with an extensive bibliography and a comprehensive index.

Plutarch, the renowned first-century Greek biographer and moralist, crystallized the idea behind Greenhaven's People Who Made History when he said, "To be ignorant of the lives of the most celebrated men of past ages is to continue in a state of childhood all our days." Indeed, since it is people who make history, every modern nation, organization, institution, invention, artifact, and idea is the result of the diligent efforts of one or more individuals, living or dead; and it is therefore impossible to understand how the world we live in came to be without examining the contributions of these individuals.

INTRODUCTION: SHAKESPEARE'S LIFE AND LEGACY

Although over a hundred historical records survive documenting William Shakespeare's birth, marriage, children, business transactions, and death, his personal life remains a bit of a mystery. What inspired the son of the Stratford mayor, a young man with a wife and three children, to go to London and join a company of players? How did a man with a grammar-school education write plays that have prompted four centuries of admiration and controversy? What happened to the manuscripts of these immortal plays? Why did Shakespeare say nothing about his plays, poems, or books in his last will and testament? Such questions as these have led some readers and scholars to doubt that the man from Stratford was actually the author of the famous plays attributed to him, and speculations about who may have written the plays and used the pseudonym *Shakespeare* have arisen periodically during the last two centuries. Other readers and scholars find the historical record satisfactory evidence of Shakespeare's authorship. Another group finds discussion of Shakespeare's personal life irrelevant to the legacy he left behind, the plays and poems. Still others enjoy the opportunity that the authorship controversy affords and respond to it by playing creatively with plausible motivations for the mysterious Mr. William Shakespeare.

Recently Marc Norman and Tom Stoppard imagined Shakespeare's early life in London in their Academy Award–winning film *Shakespeare in Love.* Although this creative envisioning of Shakespeare's character does not solve the mystery, it deftly interweaves two central themes that frame the controversy: the art of writing and the necessity of making money. Set against a backdrop of financial crisis in the theaters, the interwoven themes are epitomized in a wager: If Will Shakespeare is able to convince Queen Elizabeth that a play can "show us the very truth and nature of love,"[1] then he will receive from the fictional Lord Wessex 50 British pounds, which will buy him a partnership in the Chamberlain's Men. In the film, Shakespeare creates *Romeo and Juliet* as both a reflection of his love for the fictional Viola de Lesseps and a mirror of his desires for and fears about the relationship. The film concentrates on the way Will and Viola's developing relationship influences the play that Will is writing and how the play influences their relationship. Like Romeo and Juliet, Will and Viola consummate their love, then lose one another. Unlike Romeo and Juliet, Will and Viola do not die. In fact, they each realize their professional desires before they are parted. Viola performs onstage, as Juliet; Will plays Romeo and wins the wager. At the close of the film, Viola travels to the New World as Lord Wessex's wife, and we understand that Will will become a partner in the Chamberlain's Men and will honor Queen Elizabeth's request for a new play by Twelfth Night.

The creation of art that holds a mirror up to nature and the use of art to make a living not only help clarify what scholars know about the man Shakespeare but also point to central themes in the body of his plays. Shakespeare is both a creative artist and an astute businessman.

THE BIRTH AND GROWTH OF THE ARTIST

Official records document William Shakespeare's baptism at Holy Trinity Church, Stratford, Warwickshire, on April 26, 1564, and his burial fifty-two years later in the same church on April 25, 1616. Since the memorial monument records the day of Shakespeare's death as April 23, and since infants were commonly christened three days after birth, William Shakespeare's birth and death are traditionally celebrated on April 23. This date holds particular significance in England as St. George's Day, a feast day honoring the patron saint of England.

William Shakespeare was the third of eight children born to John and Mary Arden Shakespeare. At the time of William's birth, John was a glover and Mary, the daughter of a gentleman farmer, possessed a considerable inheritance. The year after William's birth, John was elected alderman, and several years later he became bailiff (mayor) of Stratford.

Although the Stratford Grammar School attendance records no longer exist, there is no reason to doubt that Shakespeare attended school. John Shakespeare's status as an alderman of Stratford entitled his children to free education at the excellent local grammar school. Oxford-educated Thomas Jenkins was the Stratford schoolmaster from 1575 to 1579 and would have taught the boys the standard curriculum: Latin grammar and literature in Latin, including the works of Ovid, Virgil, Plautus, Terence, and Seneca.

Although Shakespeare probably finished his formal schooling at the usual age, fifteen or sixteen, he must have pursued his education actively and independently throughout his lifetime. His works reveal familiarity with Latin and French language and literature, ancient history (notably Plutarch), English history (primarily from Rafael Holinshed's *Chronicles*), Italian literature, and English literature from Geoffrey Chaucer to his contemporaries. The plays also reveal Shakespeare's considerable practical knowledge about English courtly life, the trades, the army, and the church. As scholar Harry Levin explains, Shakespeare's "frame of reference is so far-ranging, and he is so concretely versed in the tricks of so many trades, that lawyers have written to prove he was trained in the law, sailors about his expert seamanship, naturalists upon his botanizing, and so on through the professions."[2]

At the age of eighteen, Shakespeare was married to twenty-six-year-old Anne Hathaway. On November 27, 1582, a marriage license was issued for the couple, and in May 1583 their daughter Susanna was born. Two years later twins, Hamnet and Judith, completed the Shakespeare family. No records exist to document Shakespeare's life between the birth of the twins in 1585 and the snarling reference of playwright Robert Greene to Shakespeare as the upstart actor and playwright in London in 1592, but scholars have speculated at length about Shakespeare's probable reasons for pursuing a career as an actor and playwright.

Perhaps the performances of traveling troupes of actors inspired Shakespeare's interest in theater when he was still a child. Stratford records indicate performances by two traveling theatrical troupes, the Queen's Men and the Earl of Worcester's Men, as early as 1568, when Shakespeare was a boy of five. Theatrical troupes continued to make periodic visits to Stratford during Shakespeare's boyhood and adolescence, and in 1586 the Earl of Leicester's Men played in Stratford. "This fact has prompted speculation that the young Shakespeare joined them at this time and returned with them to London to begin his career, although no evidence supports this proposition,"[5] remarks Charles Boyce in his encyclopedic work *Shakespeare A to Z.* Perhaps, as scholar Francois Laroque suggests, Shakespeare actually joined the Queen's Men after it had lost one of its players, William Knell, in a brawl with a fellow actor while the troupe was performing in Stratford in June 1587. "The young Shakespeare could easily have stepped in to his shoes, as experience was not required. Actors learned on the job."[4] Since there is no evidence that traveling troupes actually recruited when on the road, these speculations cannot be proven; it may well be that Shakespeare's fascination with traveling productions and the need for money to support his growing family inspired him to go to London on his own to try his luck in the theater.

THE MATURING ARTIST AND BLOSSOMING BUSINESSMAN

Whether Shakespeare joined a theatrical troupe, then made his way to London, or whether he went to London to make money to support his growing family, as a man of the theater, Shakespeare was splendidly successful. By 1592 he had already written the three parts of *Henry VI* and was popular enough to provoke at least one rival playwright's venom. Robert Greene, a Cambridge-educated playwright, scorned Shakespeare's lack of a university education and his quick popularity when he attacked Shakespeare in his pamphlet *Groatsworth of Wit.*

Between 1592 and 1594 the plague spread through London, so the lord mayor closed the theaters in the interest of public health. During this period Shakespeare concentrated on writing poetry; his two long poems, *Venus and Adonis* and *The Rape of Lucrece,* were composed and printed in 1593 and 1594. These are the only works whose publication was probably supervised by Shakespeare himself. Shakespeare does not appear to have been interested in preserving an authoritative text of any of his plays for future readers. As a practical man of the theater, he was perhaps more interested in the performance and the box office than in preserving his works for posterity. In addition, as editor G. Blakemore Evans explains, "once a dramatist had completed a play and sold it to an acting company, he ceased to have any personal rights in it, the play becoming the property of the company, which thus controlled the uses to which the play could be put, including its publication."[5]

By 1594, when the theaters reopened, Shakespeare was a charter member of a theatrical company called the Chamberlain's Men, which in 1603 became the royal company, called the King's Men. As a permanent member of the company, Shakespeare worked with the great English actors of the time: Richard Burbage (renowned for his performances as a tragic hero), Henry Condell, John Heminge, Will Kemp (famous for his comic roles), and William Sly. Shakespeare himself is listed as an actor for the company when it performed two comedies for Queen Elizabeth during the Christmas season of 1594, and he was named a chief actor in Ben Jonson's play *Every Man in His Humour*, which was performed by the Chamberlain's Men in 1598. Beginning in 1599, this company acted at the Globe Theatre.

THE GLOBE THEATRE

From contemporary evidence one can surmise that the Globe accommodated two to three thousand spectators. Scholar David Bevington explains the particulars of the public theaters:

> The public playhouses were essentially round, or polygonal, and open to the sky, forming an acting arena approximately 70 feet in diameter; they did not have a large curtain with which to open and close a scene, such as we see today in opera and some traditional theater. A platform measuring approximately 45 feet across and 27 feet deep . . . projected into the yard. . . . The roof . . . above the stage and supported by two pillars, could contain machinery for ascents and descents. . . . Above this roof was a hut. . . . The underside of the stage roof, called the heavens, was usually richly decorated with symbolic figures of the sun, the moon, and the constellations. That platform stage stood at a height of 5½ feet or so above the yard, providing room under the stage for otherworldly effects. A trapdoor . . . gave access to the space below. The structure at the back of the platform . . . known as the tiring-house because it was the actor's attiring (dressing) space, featured at least two doors. . . . [A] gallery above the doors . . . extends across the back and evidently contains spectators. On occasions when the action "above" demanded the use of this space, as when Juliet appears at her "window," the gallery seems to have been used by the actors.[6]

Shakespeare held a one-eighth interest in the Globe Theatre. No other Elizabethan dramatist is known to have shared in the ownership of a theater and therefore been entitled to a share of the profits. Scholar Sylvan Barnet asserts, "From his acting, his play writing, and his share in the playhouse, Shakespeare seems to have made considerable money,"[7] but it is for the plays themselves that Shakespeare, in rival playwright Ben Jonson's words, reveals himself as the "Soul of the Age."[8]

PHENOMENAL SUCCESS AS A LONDON PLAYWRIGHT

In the first decade of his London playwriting career, 1590 to 1600, Shakespeare concentrated on history plays and comedies. His two tetralogies of English history plays were enormously popular. The first group of four history plays, *Henry VI*, parts 1, 2, and 3 and *Richard III*, focuses on the Wars of the Roses, the thirty-year dynastic struggle (1455–1485) between two branches of the Plantagenet family for the English throne.

The second group of four history plays that Shakespeare wrote, *Richard II, Henry IV*, parts 1 and 2, and *Henry V*, focuses on the period of English history just prior to the Wars of the Roses. A much more mature sequence of plays, this second tetralogy explores the genesis of the Wars of the Roses. Shakespeare, following his source of history, *Holinshed's Chronicles*, identified the deposing of King Richard II by his cousin, the Lancastrian Henry IV, as the event that precipitated the ensuing struggle. Henry IV's reign, marked by political rebellions and troubled by the antics of his son, the rebellious Prince Hal, forms the subject of the two *Henry IV* plays. Although Prince Hal enjoys playing thief with his tavern companions, especially the fat knight Falstaff, whose lies, laziness, and agile wit are strong temptations, Hal determines to assume his responsibilities as heir apparent by the close of *Henry IV, Part 1*. Upon his father's death, Prince Hal is crowned King Henry V, and in the play that bears his name, he successfully unites the warring factions in England, renews the Hundred Years' War against France, and defeats the powerful French army against impossible odds at the Battle of Agincourt. Although the English triumph over France is short-lived, and the Wars of the Roses will tear England apart when Henry V's son, Henry VI, takes the throne, the last play in the second tetralogy celebrates Henry V's military success, patriotic rhetoric, and personal charm. When he courts Katherine, the king of France's daughter, Henry V shows himself a witty lover worthy of a place in the comedies that Shakespeare was writing during this period.

The comedies of the 1590s, including *The Taming of the*

Shrew, A Midsummer Night's Dream, and *The Merchant of Venice,* as well as *Much Ado About Nothing, As You Like It,* and *Twelfth Night,* which follow at the turn of the century, all share a focus on the forms and fun of love. In addition, they reveal Shakespeare's interest in money, upward mobility, roles, and role-playing. The witty heroines of these comedies match and at times outmatch their male counterparts. As David Bevington writes in his introduction to *The Complete Works of Shakespeare,*

> Several critical terms have been used to suggest the special quality of Shakespeare's comedies during this period of the later 1590s. "Romantic comedy" implies first of all a story in which the main action is about love, but it can also imply elements of the improbable and miraculous. . . . "Philosophical comedy" emphasizes the moral and sometimes Christian idealism underlying many of these comedies of the 1590s: the quest for deep and honest understanding between men and women in *Much Ado About Nothing,* the awareness of an eternal and spiritual dimension to love in *The Merchant of Venice,* and the theme of love as a mysterious force able to regenerate a corrupted social world from which it has been banished in *As You Like It.* "Love-game comedy" pays particular attention to the witty battle of the sexes that we find in several of these plays.[9]

During the second decade of his playwriting career, 1600 to 1611, Shakespeare concentrated on tragedies, among them *Hamlet, Othello, King Lear,* and *Macbeth,* and the late romances, including *The Winter's Tale* and *The Tempest.* Shakespeare's tragedies of this period are richly charged with exploration of the depths of melancholy as well as the possibilities of individual achievement. Order and the threat of disorder, the validity of the Christian faith, and the problem and nature of evil are also thematically central. Popular scholar Norrie Epstein clarifies the dimensions of Shakespearean tragedy:

> Shakespearean tragedy exposes those dark impulses that lie below life's smooth surface: the well-regulated Danish court in *Hamlet* hides something rotten; the charming and loyal Iago [in *Othello*] is a psychopath. . . . The heroes of Shakespeare's tragedies are pushed to the limits of human endurance: a young prince is compelled to avenge the murder of his father; an exiled king wanders homeless on a stormy heath; a husband strangles his wife on their marriage bed; a loyal subject murders his king. . . . Shakespeare's greatest tragic figures are fierce absolutists who find compromise impossible. . . . Macbeth sees the creature he has become but he cannot change.

Lear divides his kingdom; Hamlet swears vengeance; Othello believes Iago's lies—their fates are sealed.[10]

Shakespeare's mature tragedies reveal both soul-searching exploration and doubt; the romances, on the other hand, intimate the possibility of harmonious reconciliation following years of suffering and learning. In *The Winter's Tale* Leontes, the jealous husband, mourns sixteen years before the wife he thought dead and his daughter are returned to him. In *The Tempest* Prospero, whose brother has usurped his dukedom, spends twelve years on an unnamed island before his enemies are accidentally brought to the island, tested, taught, and reconciled. While Prospero's "Our revels now are ended" speech is often read as Shakespeare's own farewell to the stage, the speech is perhaps equally important as an evoca-

William Shakespeare

tion of Shakespeare's vision of theater—its importance and its limitations. The art of the dramatist creates illusions as insubstantial as dreams yet as potentially transforming as a journey into a new world.

FINANCIAL SUCCESS IN STRATFORD

During his residence in London, from about 1590 to 1610, Shakespeare's association with Stratford remained strong. In 1596 his father applied for and was awarded a coat of arms, which officially made him a gentleman and which was presumably paid for with William's earnings. Sadly, in 1596 Shakespeare's only son and heir, Hamnet, died at the age of eleven. In the years that followed, Shakespeare's successes outstripped his sorrows. In 1597 Shakespeare bought the Stratford mansion New Place for his family, and in 1598 he is recorded as a leading owner of grain in the town. In 1601, when his father died, Shakespeare inherited his parents' home. In 1602 and 1605 he made further investments in Stratford and bought additional property. The marriage of his daughter Susanna to Dr. John Hall in 1607 and the birth of their daughter, Elizabeth, in 1608 strengthened Shakespeare's ties and position in Stratford. Because of various entries in local records and diaries, many scholars believe that Shakespeare spent much more of his time in Stratford between 1608 and 1612. By 1613 Shakespeare appears to have retired completely to Stratford. He purchased a house in Blackfriars, London, in 1613, but there is no indication that he ever lived there.

SHAKESPEARE'S LAST WILL AND POSTHUMOUS TESTAMENTS TO HIS ACHIEVEMENTS

On March 25, 1616, Shakespeare revised and signed his last will and testament. Scholar David Bevington explains the contents of the will:

> This will disposes of all the property of which Shakespeare is known to have died possessing, the greater share of it going to his daughter Susanna. His recently married daughter Judith received a dowry, a provision for any children that might be born of her marriage, and other gifts. Ten pounds went to the poor of Stratford; Shakespeare's sword went to Mr. Thomas Combe; twenty-six shillings and eight pence apiece went to Shakespeare's fellow actors Hemings, Burbage, and Condell to buy them mourning rings; and other small bequests went to various other friends and relatives. An interlineation contains the bequest of Shakespeare's "second best bed with the furniture," that is, the hangings, to his wife.[11]

Although Shakespeare's small bequest to his wife has led to much provocative conjecture concerning their marriage, Shakespeare certainly did not leave his wife destitute. By law a third of Shakespeare's estate would go to his surviving wife, so there was no need to mention this in the will.

Shakespeare died about a month after revising his will, on April 23, 1616. By 1623, seven years after his death, two substantial monuments to his memory had been established. An elaborate limestone bust, designed by stonemason Gheerart Janssen, and presumably commissioned by Shakespeare's family, was erected in Holy Trinity Church, Stratford, sometime between 1616 and 1622. Since Janssen, a Dutch stone carver, had established his business near the Globe Theatre, some scholars think he may actually have known Shakespeare, and they therefore believe that the bust provides a satisfactory likeness of the man. In 1623 a second monument to Shakespeare's memory was established when two of Shakespeare's fellow actors, Henry Condell and John Hemings, published the First Folio. It is the earliest published collection of Shakespeare's thirty-six plays and contains eighteen plays that had not been previously printed in separate quarto editions. The First Folio is a priceless tribute to the professional achievements of Shakespeare as a playwright.

THE AUTHORSHIP CONTROVERSY

According to Bevington, "Beginning in the late eighteenth century, and especially in the mid-nineteenth century, a few admirers of Shakespeare began to be troubled by the scantiness of information about England's greatest author."[12] No record of his schooling has survived; no acknowledgement of his experience with kings and queens, soldiers, lawyers, and doctors has survived; no manuscripts of his plays have been preserved. However, many records of his success as a businessman do survive. As a result, skeptics have supposed that some other more "reputable Elizabethan writer with connections at court and considerable cultural attainments"[13] must be the "real" author of the plays. Various names, from Sir Francis Bacon and Queen Elizabeth to Christopher Marlowe and Edward de Vere, the seventeenth earl of Oxford, have been suggested, and the theory of an elaborate hoax to protect the identity of the true author has been presented in conjunction. Recently, supporters of Edward de Vere have claimed considerable media coverage, though most teachers, actors, and scholars remain unconvinced.

COMMERCIAL SUCCESS ONSTAGE IN THE EIGHTEENTH CENTURY

Although the authorship controversy continues to rage, the bulk of respondents in the last four centuries have been amazed by the adaptability of Shakespeare's plays and his continuing appeal as a great artist. The success of Shakespeare's plays in his own time, and through much of the four centuries since, can be attributed not only to their intrinsic worth but also to their adaptability. The plays were written to be performed by a small, exceptionally versatile company of men and boy actors. They performed in elaborate costumes, but with little scenery, on a broad apron stage in open daylight. The plays have, however, proven remarkably adaptable to subsequent changes in theater company organization, physical theater spaces, and literary and public tastes.

During the late seventeenth and eighteenth centuries, Shakespeare was regarded as a natural but untutored ge-

nius. Language had grown more courtly and wit more refined; as a result, editors of Shakespeare, such as Alexander
Pope, felt free to improve Shakespeare's ignorant errors. The
select theater-going public expected sophisticated performances from prominent director/manager/leading actors
and, for the first time, actresses in the elegant indoor theaters. The literary taste for classical decorum encouraged
productions that observed the classical "unities" of time,
place, and action and revealed a balanced, symmetrical
structure in which poetic justice was observed. As a result,
Shakespeare's plays were radically rewritten to suit both
new physical space and new literary tastes. The most popular adaptations were those that already featured large roles
for the leading actor. Adapters then eliminated minor characters, created new "counter plots" to increase symmetry of
structure and to provide more substantial roles for the leading actresses; endings also were sometimes changed to support poetic justice. Nahum Tate's adaptation of *King Lear* in
1681 is perhaps the best known of this period. The play focuses on the title character; minor characters like "the Fool"
were eliminated; Cordelia's role was expanded and made
parallel to Lear's in that she, too, wanders about the heath
during a storm and is attacked by the evil Edmund before
being rescued by the good Edgar. In addition, the ending is
changed. Cordelia is not executed, and Lear does not die.
Rather, the good are rewarded as poetic justice requires:
Lear regains his throne and Cordelia marries Edgar.

The most well known of the manager/director/actor/
adapters was David Garrick, who dominated the London
stage from 1741 to 1776. He not only rewrote several of
Shakespeare's plays, but he also performed the leading roles,
directed the productions, and managed the Drury Lane Theater. Garrick established himself as the definitive Hamlet in
1742, and in subsequent years he cultivated the view that he
was Shakespeare's chosen heir. In 1769 Garrick planned a
three-day celebration of Shakespeare in Stratford, the Stratford Jubilee. Garrick, the master of ceremonies, presented
the town of Stratford with a statue of Shakespeare designed
to look like the ghost of Hamlet's father. Playing Hamlet,
Garrick eloquently recited the "Ode" he had prepared for the
occasion, directly addressing the statue.

Not surprisingly, with its interest in spectacle and adaptations, the eighteenth century is noted for the initial opera

treatments of Shakespeare's plays, including Sir William Davenant's *Macbeth,* John Dryden's *The Tempest,* John Christopher Smith's *The Fairies* (based on *A Midsummer Night's Dream*), and many settings of *Romeo and Juliet.*

NINETEENTH-CENTURY READERS AND SCHOLARS FOCUS ON CHARACTER

During the late eighteenth and nineteenth centuries, literary taste shifted away from classical precepts, and Shakespeare was celebrated as a creative genius. Character analysis became a central preoccupation of literary critics such as Maurice Morgann and Samuel Taylor Coleridge, and perhaps predictably then, Romantic and Victorian critics and writers valued Shakespeare on the page rather than Shakespeare adapted for the stage. The desire to probe character required deep philosophical contemplation of this profound artist, a luxury not encouraged by the staged performances that had become so elaborate and so dependent on spectacular visual effects that the plays were cut drastically to allow time for scene changes.

The intensive study of Shakespeare's characters in the nineteenth century led to a parallel interest in the character of the genius who had created such memorable dramatic characters. Edward Dowden, a lecturer at Trinity College, Dublin, established the dating of Shakespeare's plays and was, as a result, able in 1875 to publish his vision of the progress of Shakespeare the man from a vivacious, clever young man delighted with beauty who enjoyed existence (and who wrote the comedies); to a more mature man who understood the world of history (and wrote the histories); to a man willing to delve "into the darkest and saddest parts of human life," including "the great mystery of evil" (in the tragedies); to the older man who could envision the world with philosophical calm (in the romances).[14]

Academic interest in Shakespeare led to the printing of the Cambridge edition of the complete plays, which included scholarly apparatus and the popular Globe edition without the footnotes. Advances in the printing industry made inexpensive editions of individual plays available, and expurgated editions of the plays were printed for women and children. By the close of the nineteenth century, Shakespeare was an established school and university subject, and all educated people were expected to be familiar with his plays.

General acquaintance with Shakespeare is assumed by writers who allude to or respond directly to his works. Jane Austen, Charlotte Brontë, John Keats, Charles Dickens, Matthew Arnold, Robert Browning, and George Bernard Shaw in England; Emily Dickinson, Herman Melville, escaped slave Frederick Douglass, and Mark Twain, among many others, in America; Fyodor Dostoyevsky in Russia; and Johann Wolfgang von Goethe in Germany all assume reader familiarity with Shakespeare.

Musical settings of Shakespeare's plays flourished during the nineteenth century. Opera settings include Giuseppe Verdi's *Macbeth, Otello,* and *Falstaff.* Overtures include Felix Mendelssohn's overture to *A Midsummer Night's Dream* and Pyotr Ilich Tchaikovsky's *Romeo and Juliet* fantasy overture.

SHAKESPEARE IN THE TWENTIETH CENTURY

Stage adaptations made Shakespeare a commercial success in the late seventeenth and eighteenth centuries, and attentiveness to the written works, especially to individual dramatic characters, made Shakespeare the subject of serious scholarly study during the late eighteenth and nineteenth centuries. During the twentieth century the process of commercial adaptation continued and the critical appreciation of Shakespeare as an artist continued as well.

During the first half of the twentieth century, academics embraced historical criticism; they rejected the nineteenth-century focus on character and concentrated instead on theatrical conventions that arise out of a specific historical period—Shakespeare's dramatic predecessors as well as his contemporaries—and the ways in which Shakespeare responds to the philosophical, political, scientific, and cosmological ideas of his age. The new critics of the 1930s, 1940s, and 1950s reacted against what they saw as the historicists' overemphasis on Shakespeare's cultural and theatrical environment and insisted instead on close readings of Shakespeare's words and images. Psychological criticism, myth criticism, and Christian interpretations of Shakespeare emerged near the middle of the century.

While different critical schools were offering students a variety of ways to interpret Shakespeare's works, Laurence Olivier was establishing himself as the preeminent Shakespearean actor/director/producer/film star. Olivier's performances as Henry V, Hamlet, and Richard III sealed his reputation as England's premier interpreter of Shakespeare on stage and in film. In America, Cole Porter's *Kiss Me, Kate* (1948) and Leonard Bernstein's *West Side Story* (1957) revealed how successfully *The Taming of the Shrew* and *Romeo and Juliet* could be adapted as musicals. Perhaps the most remarkable translation of Shakespeare into film during this period is Akira Kurosawa's *Throne of Blood* (1957). Kurosawa reworks *Macbeth* to reflect the history and folklore of his native Japan.

The book *Shakespeare Our Contemporary* (1966), by Polish intellectual Jan Kott, marks a turning point in the relationship between scholarly evaluation of the intrinsic value of Shakespeare's art and commercial adaptation of Shakespeare's work. Kott finds in Shakespeare's works a universality that seems free of absolutist ideological positions, a body of work that is for all times precisely because each age sees mirrored in the works its own experiences, anxieties, and sensibilities. For instance, Kott sees in Shakespeare's *Hamlet* the alienation, fear, and vision of politics as madness so central to his own experience of daily life under Stalinism in post–World War II Poland. Kott's book inspired numerous theater productions in England and America, most notably Peter Brook's production of *King Lear* starring Paul Scofield. Literary critic Martin Esslin explains the importance of the Brook *King Lear:*

> In that production a play which had been regarded as unactable for many generations came to life with tremendous impact, and as a highly contemporary statement of the human condition. And this because it was presented not as a fairy tale of a particularly stubborn story-book king, but as an image of aging and death, the waning of power, the slipping away of man's hold on his environment: a great ritual poem on evanescence and mortality, on man's loneliness in a storm-tossed universe.[15]

The interrelationship of intellectual discussions of Shakespeare's works and commercial productions of them has continued throughout the latter half of the twentieth century. New historicist, feminist, poststructuralist, and cultural interpretations of Shakespeare's works have suggested new angles for productions. Shakespearean repertory companies in London, Stratford, Stratford (Ontario), Stratford (Connecticut), Cleveland, Ashland (Oregon), New York's Central Park, as well as in Germany, Scandinavia, Hong Kong, Japan, and Taiwan, thrive, and late twentieth-century productions have been made in the image of the century. Many creative feminist and poststructuralist transformations of Shakespeare's texts, including plays like Tom Stoppard's *Rosencrantz and Guildenstern Are Dead* and Ann-Marie MacDonald's *Goodnight Desdemona, (Good Morning Juliet)* and novels like John Wideman's *Philadelphia Fire* and Jane Smiley's *A Thousand Acres,* reflect contemporary theories and invigorate contemporary Shakespeare studies. Alternately, commercially filmed versions of Shakespeare's plays have inspired a new subfield of academic study: Shakespeare on film.

SHAKESPEARE IS EVERYWHERE

Franco Zeffirelli successfully popularized Shakespeare on film during the 1960s with his productions of *Taming of the Shrew* and *Romeo and Juliet.* Roman Polanski's *Macbeth,* Laurence Olivier's *King Lear,* and Akira Kurosawa's *Ran* (based on *King Lear*) followed during the 1970s and 1980s, but the Shakespeare film boom occurred during the 1990s. It actually began in 1989 with Kenneth Branagh's *Henry V.* By the close of 1996 Zeffirelli's *Hamlet,* starring Mel Gibson; Gus Van Sant's *My Own Private Idaho;* Branagh's *Much Ado About Nothing; Renaissance Man,* starring Danny DeVito; Ian McKellen's *Richard III;* Lawrence Fishburn's *Othello;* Branagh's *Hamlet;* Al Pacino's *Looking for Richard;* Trevor Nunn's *Twelfth Night;* Baz Luhrmann's *William Shakespeare's Romeo and Juliet;* and Marc Norman and Tom Stoppard's *Shakespeare in Love* had together launched Shakespeare's new notoriety. In the December 30, 1996/January 6, 1997, issue of *Newsweek,* Shakespeare was proclaimed "Dead White Male of the Year." "He's gone Hollywood. He's on the Web. He's got theme parks and teenage fans,"[16] announced David Gates, the author of the article. Other headlines explain, "It's the 90s, so the Bard Is Back" and "Moviemakers Can't Get Enough of Shakespeare." In the twenty-first century, the Shakespeare-on-film boom continues. In fact, *Shakespeare Quarterly* devoted its entire Summer 2002 issue to "Screen Shakespeare." Shakespeare's commercial value has never been stronger, and critical discussion of Shakespeare's works continues to flourish.

While some may consider the recent boom in Shakespeare films a sellout, in the pejorative sense, there is no denying that Shakespeare films during the 1990s sell out not only because they are so popular but also because they have inspired the interest of teenagers, young adults, teachers, and scholars.

Shakespeare was both a creative genius and an astute businessman. Since his death, interest has alternated between focusing on Shakespeare's artistry and efforts to make money by adapting his works for an ever-changing popular audience. In the twenty-first century both the controversy and admiration that have marked Shakespeare's impact on others from his time to ours will no doubt continue.

NOTES

1. Marc Norman and Tom Stoppard, *Shakespeare in Love: A Screenplay.* New York: Miramax Film and Universal Studios, 1998, p. 95.

2. Harry Levin, introduction to *The Riverside Shakespeare*, 2nd ed., ed. G. Blakemore Evans. Boston: Houghton and Mifflin, 1997, p. 3.

3. Charles Boyce, *Shakespeare A to Z: The Essential Reference to His Plays, His Poems, His Life and Times, and More.* New York: Facts On File, 1990, p. 365.

4. Francois Laroque, *The Age of Shakespeare.* New York: Harry N. Abrams, 1993, p. 39.

5. Quoted in Evans, *The Riverside Shakespeare*, p. 56.

6. David Bevington, ed., *The Taming of the Shrew.* New York: Bantam Books, 1998, p. xxxiv.

7. Sylvan Barnet, "Shakespeare: An Overview," in *The Taming of the Shrew.* New York: Signet, 1986, p. xi.

8. Ben Jonson, "To the Memory of My Beloved, the Author Mr. William Shakespeare," prefixed to the Shakespeare First Folio of 1623.

9. David Bevington, *The Complete Works of Shakespeare*, 4th ed. New York: HarperCollins, 1992, p. lxvii.

10. Norrie Epstein, *The Friendly Shakespeare.* New York: Viking, 1993, p. 304.

11. Bevington, *The Complete Works of Shakespeare*, p. lxxvi.

12. Bevington, *The Complete Works of Shakespeare*, p. lxi.

13. Bevington, *The Complete Works of Shakespeare*, p. lxi.

14. Quoted in Gary Taylor, *Reinventing Shakespeare.* Oxford, UK: Oxford University Press, 1989, p. 177.

15. Martin Esslin, introduction to *Shakespeare Our Contemporary*, by Jan Kott. New York: Anchor Books, 1966, p. xxi.

16. David Gates, "Return of the Bard," *Newsweek*, December 30, 1996/January 6, 1997, p. 82.

CHAPTER 1

SHAKESPEARE, THE MAN

 **WILLIAM SHAKESPEARE**

Shakespeare's Life and Work

David Bevington

Based on over one hundred official documents and about fifty contemporary allusions to Shakespeare and his works, scholars are able to construct a reasonably accurate biography of William Shakespeare. In this selection from his introduction to *The Complete Works of Shakespeare*, University of Chicago professor David Bevington outlines Shakespeare's life and career, drawing from the evidence available to scholars. He includes references to Shakespeare's family and education; he traces Shakespeare's career as an actor, playwright, and shareholder in the theater company The Lord Chamberlain's Men; and he documents Shakespeare's growing prosperity as a property owner. Bevington also quotes contemporary opinion of Shakespeare to reveal the development of his reputation as a poet and playwright.

In addition to editing *The Complete Works of Shakespeare* and *Medieval Drama*, Bevington is author of several studies of medieval, Tudor, and Shakespearean drama, including *From Mankind to Marlowe, Action Is Eloquence, Tudor Drama and Politics*, and *Politics of the Stuart Court Masque.*

Our first substantial records of the [Shakespeare] family begin with Richard Shakespeare, who was, in all probability, Shakespeare's grandfather, a farmer living in the village of Snitterfield four miles from Stratford. He was a tenant on the property of Robert Arden of Wilmcote, a wealthy man with the social status of gentleman. Richard Shakespeare died about 1561, possessed of an estate valued at the very respectable sum of thirty-eight pounds and seventeen shillings.

His son John made a great step forward in the world by

his marriage with Mary Arden, daughter of his father's landlord. John Shakespeare had some property of his own and
through his wife acquired a good deal more. He moved from
Snitterfield to Stratford at some date before 1552. He rose to
great local importance in Stratford and bought several
houses, among which was the one on Henley Street traditionally identified as Shakespeare's birthplace. William
Shakespeare was born in 1564 and was baptized on April 26.
The exact date of his birth is not known, but traditionally we
celebrate it on April 23, the feast day of St. George, England's
patron saint. (The date is at least plausible in view of the
practice of baptizing infants shortly after birth.)...

SHAKESPEARE IN SCHOOL

Nicholas Rowe, who published in 1709 the first extensive biographical account of Shakespeare, reports the tradition that
Shakespeare studied "for some time at a Free-School." Although the list of students who actually attended the King's
New School at Stratford-upon-Avon in the late sixteenth century has not survived, we cannot doubt that Rowe is reporting
accurately. Shakespeare's father, as a leading citizen of Stratford, would scarcely have spurned the benefits of one of Stratford's most prized institutions. The town had had a free
school since the thirteenth century, at first under the auspices
of the Church. During the reign of King Edward VI (1547–
1553), the Church lands were expropriated by the crown and
the town of Stratford was granted a corporate charter. At this
time, the school was reorganized as the King's New School,
named in honor of the reigning monarch. It prospered. Its
teachers, or "masters," regularly held degrees from Oxford
during Shakespeare's childhood and received salaries that
were superior to those of most comparable schools.

Much has been learned about the curriculum of such a
school. A child would first learn the rudiments of reading
and writing English by spending two or three years in a
"petty" or elementary school. The child learned to read from
a "hornbook," a single sheet of paper mounted on a board
and protected by a thin transparent layer of horn, on which
was usually printed the alphabet in small and capital letters
and the Lord's Prayer. The child would also practice an ABC
book with catechism. When the child had demonstrated the
ability to read satisfactorily, the child was admitted, at about
the age of seven, to the grammar school proper. Here the day

was a rigorous one, usually extending from 6 A.M. in the summer or 7 A.M. in the winter until 5 P.M. Intervals for food or brief recreation came at midmorning, noon, and mid-afternoon. Holidays occurred at Christmas, Easter, and Whitsuntide (usually late May and June), comprising perhaps forty days in all through the year. Discipline was strict, and physical punishment was common.

Latin formed the basis of the grammar school curriculum. The scholars studied grammar, read ancient writers, recited, and learned to write in Latin. A standard text was the *Grammatica Latina* by William Lilly or Lyly, grandfather of the later Elizabethan dramatist John Lyly. The scholars also became familiar with the *Disticha de Moribus* (moral proverbs) attributed to Cato, *Aesop's Fables*, the *Eclogues* of Baptista Spagnuoli Mantuanus or Mantuan (alluded to in *Love's Labor's Lost*), the *Eclogues* and *Aeneid* of Virgil, the comedies of Plautus or Terence (sometimes performed in Latin by the children), Ovid's *Metamorphoses* and other of his works, and possibly some Horace and Seneca.

Shakespeare plentifully reveals in his dramatic writings an awareness of many of these authors, especially Plautus (in *The Comedy of Errors*), Ovid (in *A Midsummer Night's Dream* and elsewhere), and Seneca (in *Titus Andronicus*). Although he often consulted translations of these authors, he seems to have known the originals as well. He had, in Ben Jonson's learned estimation, "small Latin and less Greek"; the tone is condescending, but the statement does concede that Shakespeare had some of both. He would have acquired some Greek in the last years of his grammar schooling. By twentieth-century standards, Shakespeare had a fairly comprehensive amount of training in the ancient classics, certainly enough to account for the general, if unscholarly, references we find in the plays.

SHAKESPEARE'S MARRIAGE AND CHILDREN

When Shakespeare was eighteen years old, he married Anne Hathaway, a woman eight years his senior. (The inscription on her grave states that she was sixty-seven when she died in August of 1623.) The bishop's register of Worcester, the central city of the diocese, shows for November 27, 1582, the issue of a bishop's license for the marriage of William Shakespeare and Anne "Whately"; the bond of sureties issued next day refers to her as "Hathaway." She has been identified with all reasonable probability as Agnes (or Anne) Hathaway, daughter of the then recently deceased Richard Hathaway of the hamlet of Shottery, a short distance from Stratford. . . .

The actual record of the marriage in a parish register has not survived, but presumably the couple were married shortly after obtaining the license. They may have been married in Temple Grafton, where Anne had relatives. The couple took up residence in Stratford. Anne was already pregnant at the time of the marriage, for she gave birth to a daughter, Susanna, on May 26, 1583. . . .

On February 2, 1585, Shakespeare's only other children, the twins Hamnet and Judith, were baptized in Stratford Church. The twins seem to have been named after Shakespeare's friends and neighbors, Hamnet Sadler, a baker, and his wife, Judith. . . .

SHAKESPEARE'S ARRIVAL IN LONDON

Because of the total absence of reliable information concerning the seven years from 1585 to 1592, we do not know how Shakespeare got his start in the theatrical world. He may have joined one of the touring companies that came to Stratford and then accompanied the players to London. Edmund Malone offered the unsupported statement (in 1780) that Shakespeare's "first office in the theater was that of prompter's attendant." Presumably, a young man from the country would have had to begin at the bottom. Shakespeare's later work certainly reveals an intimate and practical acquaintance with technical matters of stagecraft. In any case, his rise to eminence as an actor and a writer seems to have been rapid. He was fortunate also in having at least one prosperous acquaintance in London, Richard Field, formerly of Stratford and the son of an associate of Shakespeare's father. Field was a printer, and in 1593 and 1594 he published two handsome editions of Shakespeare's first serious poems, *Venus and Adonis* and *The Rape of Lucrece*.

The first allusion to Shakespeare after his Stratford days is a vitriolic attack on him. It occurs in *Greene's Groats-worth of Wit Bought with a Million of Repentance*, written by Robert Greene during the last months of his wretched existence (he died in poverty in September of 1592). A famous passage in this work lashes out at the actors of the public theaters for having deserted Greene and for bestowing their favor instead on a certain upstart dramatist. The passage warns three fellow dramatists and University Wits, Christopher Marlowe, Thomas Nashe, and George Peele, to abandon the writing of plays before they fall prey to a similar ingratitude. The diatribe runs as follows:

> . . . Base minded men all three of you, if by my misery you be not warned. For unto none of you (like me) sought those burs to cleave—those puppets, I mean, that spake from our mouths, those antics garnished in our colors. Is it not strange that I, to whom they all have been beholding, is it not like that you, to whom they all have been beholding, shall (were ye in that case as I am now) be both at once of them forsaken? Yes, trust them not. For there is an upstart crow, beautified with our feathers, that with his "Tiger's heart wrapped in a player's hide" supposes he is as well able to bombast out a blank verse as the best of you, and, being an absolute *Johannes Factotum*, is in his own conceit the only Shake-scene in a country.

The "burs" here referred to are the actors who have forsaken Greene in his poverty for the rival playwright "Shake-scene"—an obvious hit at Shakespeare. The sneer at a *"Johannes Factotum"* suggests another dig at Shakespeare for being a Jack-of-all-trades—actor, playwright, poet, and theatrical handyman in the directing and producing of plays. The most unmistakable reference to Shakespeare, however, is to be found in the burlesque line, "Tiger's heart wrapped in a player's hide," modeled after "O tiger's heart wrapped in a woman's hide!" from *3 Henry VI* (1.4.137). Shakespeare's success as a dramatist had led to an envious outburst from an older, disappointed rival. . . .

SHAKESPEARE'S CAREER DURING ELIZABETH'S REIGN

By the year 1594, Shakespeare had already achieved a considerable reputation as a poet and dramatist. We should not be surprised that many of his contemporaries thought of his nondramatic writing as his most significant literary achievement. Throughout his lifetime, in fact, his contemporary fame rested, to a remarkable degree, on his nondramatic poems, *Venus and Adonis, The Rape of Lucrece,* and the *Sonnets* (which were circulated in manuscript prior to their unauthorized publication in 1609). . . .

Yet Shakespeare's plays were also highly regarded by his contemporaries, even if those plays were accorded a literary status below that given to the narrative and lyrical poems. Francis Meres insisted, in 1598, that Shakespeare deserved to be compared not only with Ovid for his verse but also with Plautus and Seneca for his comedies and tragedies:

> As the soul of Euphorbus was thought to live in Pythagoras, so the sweet, witty soul of Ovid lives in mellifluous and honey-tongued Shakespeare: witness his *Venus and Adonis,* his *Lucrece,* his sugared sonnets among his private friends, etc.

> As Plautus and Seneca are accounted the best for comedy and tragedy among the Latins, so Shakespeare among the English is the most excellent in both kinds for the stage: for comedy, witness his *Gentlemen of Verona,* his *Errors,* his *Love's Labor's Lost,* his *Love's Labor's Won,* his *Midsummer Night's Dream,* and his *Merchant of Venice;* for tragedy, his *Richard the II, Richard the III, Henry the IV, King John, Titus Andronicus,* and his *Romeo and Juliet. . . .*

SHAKESPEARE'S RISING PROSPERITY

During the years from 1594 to 1601, Shakespeare seems to have prospered as an actor and writer for the Lord Chamberlain's men. Whether he had previously belonged to Lord Strange's company or to the Earl of Pembroke's company, or possibly to some other group, is uncertain, but we know that he took part in 1594 in the general reorganization of the companies, out of which emerged the Lord Chamberlain's company. In 1595, his name appeared, for the first time, in the accounts of the Treasurer of the Royal Chamber as a member of the Chamberlain's company of players, which had presented two comedies before Queen Elizabeth at Greenwich in the Christmas season of 1594. This company usually performed at the Theatre, northeast of London, from 1594 until 1599, when they moved to the Globe playhouse south of the Thames. They seem to have been the victors in the intense economic rivalry between themselves and the Lord Admiral's company at the Rose playhouse under Philip Henslowe's management. Fortunately for all the adult companies, the boys' private theatrical companies were shut down during most of the 1590s. Shakespeare's company enjoyed a phenomenal success, and in short time it became the most successful theatrical organization in England.

The nucleus of the Chamberlain's company in 1594 was the family of Burbage. James Burbage, the father, was owner of the Theatre, Cuthbert Burbage was a manager, and Richard Burbage became the principal actor of the troupe. Together the Burbages owned five "shares" in the company, entitling them to half the profits. Shakespeare and four other principal actors—John Heminges, Thomas Pope, Augustine Phillips, and Will Kempe—owned one share each. Not only was Shakespeare a full sharing actor, but also he was the principal playwright of the company. He was named as a chief actor in the 1616 edition of Ben Jonson's *Every Man in His Humor*, performed by the Chamberlain's company in 1598. Later tradition reports, with questionable reliability, that Shakespeare specialized in "kingly parts" or in the roles of older men, such as Adam in *As You Like It* and the Ghost in *Hamlet*. Shakespeare was more celebrated as a playwright than as an actor, and his acting responsibilities may well have diminished as his writing reputation grew. The last occasion on which he is known to have acted was in Jonson's *Sejanus* in 1603.

Shakespeare acted in many of his own and his contemporaries' plays. Here he performs before Queen Elizabeth and her court.

His prosperity appears in the first record of his residence in London. The tax returns, or Subsidy Rolls, of a Parliamentary subsidy granted to Queen Elizabeth for the year 1596 show that Shakespeare was a resident in the parish of St. Helen's, Bishopsgate, near the Theatre, and was assessed at the respectable sum of five pounds. By the next year, Shakespeare had evidently moved to Southwark, near the

Bear Garden, for the returns from Bishopsgate show his taxes delinquent. He was later located and the taxes paid.

In 1596, Shakespeare suffered a serious personal loss: the death of his only son Hamnet, at the age of eleven. Hamnet was buried at Stratford in August.

Shakespeare acquired property in Stratford during these years, as well as in London. In 1597 he purchased New Place, a house of importance and one of the two largest in the town. Shakespeare's family entered the house as residents shortly after the purchase and continued there until long after Shakespeare's death. The last of his family, his granddaughter, Lady Bernard, died in 1670, and New Place was sold.

Shakespeare was also interested in the purchase of land at Shottery in 1598. He was listed among the chief holders of corn and malt in Stratford that same year and sold a load of stone to the Stratford corporation in 1599.

No less suggestive of Shakespeare's rapid rise in the world is his acquisition of the right to bear arms, or, in other words, his establishment in the rank and title of gentleman. The Herald's College in London preserves two drafts of a grant of arms to Shakespeare's father, devised by one William Dethick and dated October 20, 1596. Although we may certainly believe that the application was put forward by William Shakespeare, John Shakespeare was still living, and the grant was drawn up in the father's name. . . .

SHAKESPEARE'S CAREER DURING JAMES I'S REIGN

Upon the death of Queen Elizabeth in 1603 and the accession to the throne of King James I, Shakespeare's company added an important new success to their already great prosperity. According to a document of instruction from King James to his Keeper of the Privy Seal, dated May 19, 1603, and endorsed as "The Players' Privilege," the acting company that had formerly been the Lord Chamberlain's men now became the King's company. The document names Shakespeare, Richard Burbage, Augustine Phillips, John Heminges, Henry Condell, Will Sly, Robert Armin, Richard Cowley, and Lawrence Fletcher—the last, an actor who had played before the King and the Scottish court in 1599 and 1601. These players are accorded the usual privileges of exercising their art anywhere within the kingdom and are henceforth to be known as the King's company. The principal members of the troupe were also appointed to the honorary rank of Grooms of the Royal Chamber. We therefore find them duly recorded in the Accounts of the Master of the Wardrobe on March 15, 1604, as recipients of the customary grants of red cloth, so that they, dressed in the royal livery, might take part in the approaching coronation procession of King James. The same men are mentioned in these grants as in the Players' Privilege. Shakespeare's name stands second in the former document and first in the latter. In a somewhat similar manner, the King's players, as Grooms of the Royal Chamber, were called in attendance on the Spanish ambassador at Somerset House in August 1604.

The Revels Accounts of performances at court during the winter season of 1604–1605 contain an unusually full entry, listing several of Shakespeare's plays. The list includes *Othello, The Merry Wives of Windsor, Measure for Measure,* "*The play of Errors,*" *Love's Labor's Lost, Henry V,* and *The Merchant of Venice.* The last play was "again commanded by the King's majesty," and so was performed a second time. This list also sporadically notes the names of "the poets which made the plays," ascribing three of these works to "Shaxberd." (Probably the final *d* is an error for *e,* since the two characters are easily confused in Elizabethan handwriting; the word represents "Shaxbere" or "Shaxpere.") The entire entry was once called into question as a possible forgery but is now generally regarded as authentic.

A number of records during this period show us glimpses of Shakespeare as a man of property. On May 1, 1602, John and William Combe conveyed to Shakespeare one hundred and seven acres of arable land, plus twenty acres of pasture in the parish of Old Stratford, for the sizable payment of three hundred and twenty pounds. The deed was delivered to Shakespeare's brother Gilbert and not to the poet, who was probably at that time occupied in London. On September 28th of the same year, Shakespeare acquired the title to "one cottage and one garden by estimation a quarter of an acre," located opposite his home (New Place) in Stratford. . . .

Shakespeare's greatness is, by this time, taken for granted. Anthony Scoloker, for example, in his epistle prefatory to *Diaphantus, or The Passions of Love* (1604), attempts to describe an excellent literary work in this way:

> It should be like the never-too-well read *Arcadia* . . . or to come home to the vulgar's element, like friendly Shake-

speare's tragedies, where the comedian rides, when the trage-
dian stands on tip-toe. Faith, it should please all, like Prince
Hamlet.

The antiquarian William Camden includes Shakespeare's
name among his list of England's greatest writers in his *Remains of a Greater Work Concerning Britain* (1605):

> These may suffice for some poetical descriptions of our an-
> cient poets. If I would come to our time, what a world could I
> present to you out of Sir Philip Sidney, Edmund Spenser,
> Samuel Daniel, Hugh Holland, Ben Jonson, Thomas Cam-
> pion, Michael Drayton, George Chapman, John Marston,
> William Shakespeare, and other most pregnant wits of these
> our times, whom succeeding ages may justly admire. . . .

THE LATE YEARS: 1608–1616

In the summer of 1608, Shakespeare's acting company
signed a twenty-one-year lease for the use of the Blackfriars
playhouse, an indoor and rather intimate, artificially lighted
theater inside the city of London, close to the site of St. Paul's
cathedral. . . .

Shakespeare's last plays, written with a view to Blackfriars and the court, as well as to the Globe, are now usually
called "romances" or "tragicomedies," or sometimes both.
The term "romance" suggests a return to the kind of story
Robert Greene had derived from Greek romance: tales of ad-
venture, long separation, and tearful reunion, involving
shipwreck, capture by pirates, riddling prophecies, children
set adrift in boats or abandoned on foreign shores, the illusion of death and subsequent restoration to life, the revela-
tion of the identity of long-lost children by birthmarks, and
the like. The term "tragicomedy" suggests a play in which
the protagonist commits a seemingly fatal error or crime, or
(as in *Pericles*) suffers an extraordinarily adverse fortune to
test his patience; in either event, he must experience agonies
of contrition and bereavement until he is providentially delivered from his tribulations. The tone is deeply melancholic
and resigned, although suffused also with a sense of gratitude for the harmonies that are mysteriously restored. . . .

Shakespeare's reputation among his contemporaries was
undiminished in his late years, even though [Francis] Beaumont and [John] Fletcher were the new rage at the Globe and
Blackfriars. Among those who apostrophized Shakespeare
was John Davies of Hereford in *The Scourge of Folly* (entered
in the Stationers' Register in 1610):

To our English Terence, Mr. Will Shakespeare.

Some say, good Will, which I, in sport, do sing:
Hadst thou not played some kingly parts in sport,
Thou hadst been a companion for a king,
And been a king among the meaner sort.
Some others rail. But, rail as they think fit,
Thou hast no railing, but a reigning, wit.
And honesty thou sow'st, which they do reap,
So to increase their stock which they do keep. . . .

SHAKESPEARE'S WILL AND MONUMENT

In January of 1615 or 1616, Shakespeare drew up his last will and testament with the assistance of his lawyer Francis Collins, who had aided him earlier in some of his transactions in real estate. On March 25, 1616, Shakespeare revised his will in order to provide for the marriage of his daughter Judith and Thomas Quiney in that same year. Shakespeare's three quavering signatures, one on each page of this document, suggest that he was in failing health. The cause of his death on April 23 is not known. An intriguing bit of Stratford gossip is reported by John Ward, vicar of Holy Trinity in Stratford from 1662 to 1689, in his diary: "Shakespeare, Drayton, and Ben Jonson had a merry meeting, and it seems drank too hard, for Shakespeare died of a fever there contracted." The report comes fifty years after Shakespeare's death, however, and is hardly an expert medical opinion.

The will disposes of all the property of which Shakespeare is known to have died possessing, the greater share of it going to his daughter Susanna. His recently married daughter Judith received a dowry, a provision for any children that might be born of her marriage, and other gifts. Ten pounds went to the poor of Stratford; Shakespeare's sword went to Mr. Thomas Combe; twenty-six shillings and eight pence apiece went to Shakespeare's fellow actors Heminges, Burbage, and Condell to buy them mourning rings; and other small bequests went to various other friends and relatives.

An interlineation contains the bequest of Shakespeare's "second best bed with the furniture," that is, the hangings, to his wife. Anne's name appears nowhere else in the will. Some scholars, beginning with Edmund Malone, have taken this reference as proof of an unhappy marriage, confirming earlier indications, such as the hasty wedding to a woman who was William's senior by eight years and his prolonged residence in London for twenty years or more seemingly without his family. The evidence is inconclusive, however. Shakespeare certainly supported his family handsomely, acquired much property in Stratford, and retired there when he might have remained still in London. Although he showed no great solicitude for Anne's well-being in the will, her rights were protected by law; a third of her husband's estate went to her without having to be mentioned in the will. New Place was to be the home of Shakespeare's favorite daughter Susanna, wife of the distinguished Dr. John Hall. Anne Shakespeare would make her home with her daughter and, with her dower rights secured by law, would be quite as wealthy as she would need to be.

The date of Shakespeare's death (April 23, 1616) and his age (his fifty-third year) are inscribed on his monument. This elaborate structure, still standing in the chancel of Trinity Church, Stratford, was erected some time before 1623 by the London stonecutting firm of Gheerart Janssen and his sons. Janssen's shop was in Southwark, near the Globe, and may have been familiar to the actors. The bust of Shakespeare is a conventional sort of statuary for its time. Still, it is one of the only two contemporary likenesses we have. The other is the Droeshout engraving of Shakespeare in the Folio of 1623.

The epitaph on the monument reads as follows:

Iudicio Phylium, genio Socratem, arte Maronem;
Terra tegit, populus maeret, Olympus habet.
Stay passenger. Why goest thou by so fast?
Read, if thou canst, whom envious Death hath placed
Within this monument: Shakespeare, with whom
Quick Nature died, whose name doth deck this tomb
Far more than cost, sith all that he hath writ
Leaves living art but page to serve his wit.

Obiit anno domini 1616,
Aetatis 53, die 23 April.

These lines, of which the beginning Latin couplet compares Shakespeare with Nestor (King of Pylos) for wise judgment, Socrates for genius, and Virgil (Maro) for poetic art, and avers that the earth covers him, people grieve for him, and Mount Olympus (that is, heaven) has him, indicate the high reputation he enjoyed at the time of his death.

Gaps in the Biography Provoke Questions About Shakespeare's Authorship

Diana Price

Scholar Diana Price argues in the following selection from her book *Shakespeare's Unorthodox Biography* that the biographical evidence does not confirm that Shakespeare, the man from Stratford, was the author of the plays attributed to him. According to Price, no evidence exists to prove that he was a skilled writer, let alone a literary genius. The evidence instead identifies Shakespeare as a shrewd businessman who invested well and became prosperous. In this selection, Price spells the name of the businessman from Stratford "Shakspere" to distinguish him from the famous playwright "Shakespeare."

Among Price's other scholarly works are articles on the authorship question, including "What's in a Name" and "Reconsidering Shakespeare's Monument," as well as several contributions to the *Shakespeare Newsletter.*

The biography of William Shakspere is deficient. It cites not one personal *literary* record to prove that he wrote for a living. Moreover, it cites not one personal record to prove that he was *capable* of writing the works of William Shakespeare. In the *genre* of Elizabethan and Jacobean literary biography, that deficiency is unique. While Shakspere left over seventy biographical records, not one of them tells us that his occupation was writing. In contrast, George Peele's meager pile of twenty-some personal biographical records includes at least nine that are literary. John Webster, one of the least documented writers of the day, left behind fewer than a dozen personal biographical records, but seven of them are literary.

Scholars do not identify this most glaring of deficiencies in Shakspere's biography—the absence of contemporaneous personal literary paper trails. Those who express dismay at the paucity of evidence nevertheless imply that there is *some* legitimate literary peg on which to hang Shakspere's biographical skeleton. There is no such literary peg. One can make a case for Shakspere as a shareholder, actor, moneylender, broker, entrepreneur, real estate investor, or commodity trader, but one cannot make a case, based on the biographical evidence, for Shakspere as a writer.

CONTRADICTIONS IN STANDARD BIOGRAPHIES

Although the documented facts about Shakspere are nonliterary, they present a coherent and consistent character. Those same facts lose their coherence when combined with other facts that emerge from the literary works themselves. When biographers try to fit the two sets of facts together, they find them incompatible. Their solution has been to put the conflicting information into the same book, but into different chapters.

Few biographers have attempted a life story of Shakspere that unfolds in strict chronological order. Most segregate theatrical activities and Stratford business dealings into separate chapters, regardless of the chronological sequence. [Biographer Samuel] Schoenbaum admitted that the greatest Shakespearean biographers were unable to construct a coherent narrative for the life of the dramatist. . . .

Louis Untermeyer understated the case when he wrote that the Shakespeare of biography "seems to have lived a life of complex paradox. Never in the history of literature has there been so strange a union of genius and businessman, of the superlatively natural creator, the accommodating workman, and the small-town citizen". [Biographer E.A.J.] Honigmann put his finger on another inherent contradiction: "For, having stumbled through the mists of sentimentality and tradition, we discover that the sign-posts always point two ways at once. Some thought him a hoarding miser, others 'open, and free'".

Indeed, scholars have crammed the world's greatest dramatic genius inside a straitjacket named William Shakspere, constraining him with the known facts of an unintellectual life. The constraints have forced biographers to create an abnormal noncharacter with no discernible personality. What is known of Shakspere's character is canceled out by the attempt to splice his life onto Shakespeare's literary output. The manipulation of data to obscure or rationalize the more flagrant contradictions reduces the Shakespeare of biography to an amorphous nonentity.

In fact, the playwright of biography makes no sense as a human being. Shakspere deserted his family whenever he was in London, yet biographers picture him "raising a family" or suppose he was committed to strong family values. This supposed paragon of literacy let his children grow up functionally illiterate, while he himself was a man of no recorded education. He left no trace of having been a precocious student, and legend tells us that he dropped out of grammar school. According to Schoenbaum, "almost everyone seems to have thought well of Shakespeare", but the first time he turned up in print, he was lambasted as the untrustworthy and arrogant "upstart Crow". The *Parnassus* authors called him "shrewd", that is, calculating. The Shakspere of record was obsessed with financial self-interest and was accused of being a callous skinflint, yet we are told he was "gentle Will". We are also told that this mild-mannered "Shakespeare lived quietly, unobtrusively, for the most part", or that he was "a relaxed and happy man, almost incapable of taking offense", but the historical records show that he was accused of assault in 1596, that he hauled people into court to recover debts, and that he hoarded grain during famine. Ben Jonson seems to have considered him a thief, a man who liked to hear himself talk, and, at times, a laughingstock.

Playwriting paid far less than did Shakspere's documented activities, yet we are told that he wrote plays to make money. As far as we know, nobody paid him to write anything. He was supposedly the leading light of "his" theatre company, but business records show that his primary roles with the acting company were that of financier and entrepreneur. Moreover, he was in Stratford, not London, during certain performance seasons and lucrative holiday assignments at court, so he could not always have been present with the company. This man with a head for money and an ambition for social status then turned his back on the opportunity of his life, when James I assumed patronage of the King's Men. Alvin Kernan cited the 1603 warrant for the letters patent that elevated the Lord Chamberlain's Men to the King's Men:

> With this warrant, the resident playwright of the King's Men, William Shakespeare, also became official playwright to the prince. . . . The social status of Shakespeare's acting company escalated greatly when its members became grooms of the chamber and servants to his majesty.

The statement that Shakespeare became "the official playwright to the prince" is an extreme one for which there is no evidence. Nevertheless, if Shakspere really was a playwright with an exceptional nose for opportunity, why did he shift his attentions away from the theatre profession and toward business investments in Stratford, when he was at the height of his supposed London career? His 1602 purchase of the Stratford freehold property had already placed him "among the local landed gentry and . . . in the position of landlord to many tenant farmers"; his 1605 purchase of tithes, while lucrative, required additional work to administer the numerous subleases.

It was not the only time he walked away from opportunities offering real social advancement. In *The Norton Shakespeare*, we are told that "in Elizabethan England, aristocratic patronage, with the money, protection, and prestige it alone could provide, was probably a professional writer's most important asset". We are told by another biographer that Shakespeare "was a professional in constant search for aristocratic buttering on his bread". But the records suggest otherwise. Despite the importance of literary patronage, Shakespeare, whoever he was, apparently gave up looking for patrons after just two dedications. . . .

SHAKSPERE LEAVES NO LITERARY FOOTPRINTS

The two writers whom historians most closely associate with Shakespeare—[Ben] Jonson and [Michael] Drayton—never wrote about him by name during his lifetime. Shakespeare, whose sensitivity to human relationships and conflicts is the marvel of every playgoer, apparently had *no* literary friends—or enemies—or if he did, as far as we know, they inexplicably failed to invite him to contribute commendatory verses, never exchanged letters with him, and never mentioned him as though they knew him.

Traditional biographers rarely inquire into the temperament of the creative genius, but if they did, Shakspere of Stratford would not fit the mold. Certainly no contemporary described him as an artist driven by his Muse. The play-

MARK TWAIN COMMENTS ON SHAKESPEARE'S BIOGRAPHY
In this selection from his 1909 essay, "Is Shakespeare Dead?," American humorist Mark Twain comments on the gaps in Shakespeare's biography, which force historians into remarkable conjectures and surmises.

Shakespeare pronounced *Venus and Adonis* "the first heir of his invention," apparently implying that it was his first effort at literary composition. He should not have said it. It has been an embarrassment to his historians these many, many years. They have to make him write that graceful and polished and flawless and beautiful poem before he escaped from Stratford and his family—1586 or '87—age, twenty-two, or along there; because within the next five years he wrote five great plays, and could not have found time to write another line.

It is sorely embarrassing. If he began to slaughter calves, and poach deer, and rollick around, and learn English, at the earliest likely moment—say at thirteen, when he was supposably wrenched from that school where he was supposably storing up Latin for future literary use—he had his youthful hands full, and much more than full. He must have had to put aside his Warwickshire dialect, which wouldn't be understood in London, and study English very hard. Very hard indeed; incredibly hard, almost, if the result of that labor was to be the smooth and rounded and flexible and letter-perfect English of the *Venus and Adonis* in the space of ten years; and at the same time learn great and fine and unsurpassable literary *form*.

However, it is "conjectured" that he accomplished all this and more, much more: learned law and its intricacies; and the complex procedure of the law courts; and all about soldiering, and sailoring, and the manners and customs and ways of royal courts and aristocratic society; and likewise accumulated in his one head every kind of knowledge the learned then possessed, and every kind of humble knowledge possessed by the lowly and the ignorant; and added thereto a wider and more intimate knowledge of the world's great literatures, ancient and modern, than was possessed by any other man of his time—for he was going to make brilliant and easy and admiration—compelling use of these splendid treasures the moment he got to London. And according to the surmisers, that is what he did. Yes, although there was no one in Stratford able to teach him these things, and no library in the little village to dig them out of. His father could not read, and even the surmisers surmise that he did not keep a library.

Mark Twain, *1601, and Is Shakespeare Dead?* New York: Oxford University Press, 1996.

wright was surely a man of consuming passion and artistic compulsion, yet Shakspere supposedly stopped writing abruptly at the top of his career. Then this presumed towering intellectual deserted literary London at the height of his powers to return to the illiterate environs of Stratford. Commentators suppose that he was just plain tired, or that Shakspere, the "family man", wanted to retire to his hometown.

Shakspere was supposedly a skilled writer, but his will was utterly unliterary, and his handwriting was practically illegible. Shakespeare the poet believed his verses were powerful enough to outlive marble, yet Shakspere, a man of documented self-interest, did nothing to ensure their accurate preservation through supervised publishing. Schoenbaum accepted the incompatible attitudes without blinking: "If Shakespeare was indifferent to the ultimate fate of the plays that immortalized him, he showed no similar nonchalance about assembling and passing down intact his estate". Schoenbaum further speculated that Shakspere died without knowing, and "possibly not caring" whether his plays would be preserved in print. Shakspere, the parsimonious operator, was supposedly nonchalant even when the Shakespeare plays were published surreptitiously, despite the fact that piracy hit him and his fellow shareholders in the pocketbook.

Shakespeare's poetry had earned him considerable fame and respect, yet not one writer of the day noted Shakspere's death in 1616. The Stratford bust and epitaph supposedly represent the best anyone could produce at the time to memorialize an eminent poet and dramatist. Some biographers even swallow the idea that England's greatest dramatist wrote doggerel for his own tombstone.

Instead of highlighting these outrageous conflicts in schedule, temperament, activity, and so on, biographers attempt to put credible spins on them all. They romanticize hard facts, avoid the worst of the information, separate inherently conflicting material into different chapters, and then manipulate Shakspere's motives, personality, and presumed creative flow to manufacture a synthetic literary biography. In so doing, they neutralize or contradict the solid information found in Shakspere's historical dossier. Harold Bloom, author of *The Western Canon*, would undoubtedly be horrified to think that he reflected a nonconformist's view:

> It is as though the creator of scores of major characters and hundreds of frequently vivid minor figures wasted no imagi-

native energy in inventing a persona for himself. At the very center of the Canon is the least self-conscious and least aggressive of all the major writers we have known.

There is an inverse ratio, a little beyond our analytical skills, between Shakespeare's virtual colorlessness and his preternatural dramatic powers.

Similarly, Park Honan's Shakespeare "seems to have flourished with a certain annihilation of the sense of himself".

AN ASTUTE BUSINESSMAN, NOT A WRITER

Shakspere's documentary records are not those of a literary genius but those of a man with financial acumen and a mediocre intellect. If all the Shakespeare plays had been published anonymously, *nothing* in William Shakspere's documented biographical trails would remotely suggest that he wrote them. Shakspere of Stratford is not, in fact, a viable authorship candidate, and if he were discovered today as a new contender, his candidacy would not be taken seriously.

Who, then, was William Shakspere of Stratford? The records tell us. The uncontested documentation proves that he was a successful businessman who invested shrewdly and made a lot of money. . . .

In fact, an intensive examination of the Stratford-based records led [author Robert] Bearman to a bourgeois Shakspere whose records bore almost no resemblance to the poet of legend. In these records, Bearman found "little, if anything, to remind us that we are studying the life of one who in his writings emerges as perhaps the most gifted of all time in describing the human condition. Here in Stratford he seems merely to have been a man of the world, buying up property, laying in ample stocks of barley and malt and, when others were starving, selling off his surpluses and pursuing debtors in court, and conniving, as it seems, at the Welcombe enclosures [the process of fencing in common land, which often resulted in the expelling of tenants]". Shakspere was lampooned early in his career as a miserly Ant, greedy for gain, and his documentary records are consistent with that portrayal.

Shakspere's last will vividly exhibits his preoccupation with the physical trappings of the newly gentrified. Its terms show that he was primarily concerned with preserving his real estate empire for a future male heir. His mean streak is found in his most infamous bequest, that of the second-best bed to his wife. Whereas most wills of the day made bequests to well-beloved wives, or appointed them as executors, Shakspere humiliated his wife from beyond the grave. The provision of the second-best bed is not even in the body copy; it is an interlineation stuck in at the end of the section in which Shakspere bequeathed all his real estate holdings to his daughter and son-in-law. The bed is Shakspere's one and only bequest to his wife, whom he did not even mention by name. Many biographers assure their readers that Shakspere was confident that his wife would be sufficiently provided for under a law that automatically granted widows one third of the estate. However, the authors of *Playhouse Wills* found that "there is, inconveniently, no evidence that [the law] was observed in Warwickshire". Therefore, upon Shakspere's demise, his widow became a dependent, tenant, or enforced guest in her own home. Nor did he leave anything to anyone on her side of the family, leaving clothes to his sister and bequests to other blood relatives. Nor could he remember the name of his own sister's son; the will shows a blank space where the name was to be written.

Shakspere's predilection for moneylending at interest filtered down into his last wishes. He specified that a 10% penalty be levied should the bequests to his two daughters not be paid in a timely fashion. Since Susanna was one of the executors, Shakspere "in effect ordered one daughter to pay interest to the other". It is difficult to sustain a case for Shakspere the gentle family man in the face of such cold, impersonal, and incontrovertible evidence.

Most of the legatees named in the will, Shakspere's "inner circle", were upwardly mobile wealthy landowners or business associates. Shakspere left bequests to William Reynolds "gent.", who owned property in Welcombe and became "one of the largest landowners in Stratford"; Anthony Nashe "gent.", who witnessed some of Shakspere's property transactions, was involved in the tithes that Shakspere bought, would obtain a coat of arms in 1619, and was "one of the wealthiest men in Stratford"; Anthony's brother, John, who managed and farmed the tithes that Shakspere had leased from the Hubaud family; Thomas Russell, "Esquire", an extremely wealthy landowner who bought a manor in nearby Droitwich after an unsuccessful attempt to purchase Clopton House in Stratford; and Francis Collins, "gent.", Shakspere's attorney. Shakspere left his sword to Thomas, the nephew of moneylender John Combe. He also named neighbor Hamnet Sadler, baker and money collector, and, as a witness, Julius Shaw, wool trader and maltster. As we have seen, Shakspere left small bequests to three of his London colleagues, Burbage, Heminges, and Condell, but he remembered no one in the literary profession.

All the documentary evidence shows that Shakspere was a shrewd negotiator at the bargaining table, manipulative, sometimes involved in shady deals, and pretentious. Those characteristics are amply reinforced by the satirical allusions that biographers reluctantly introduce, only to drop like hot potatoes. Again and again, the satirical portraits deliver the same bombastic operator with an overblown opinion of himself, but none of them points to a writer. . . .

LOOKING FOR SHAKESPEARE THE PLAYWRIGHT

No biographer has successfully integrated the life of Shakspere with the works of Shakespeare. Although the synthesis of what we know about the writer is the antithesis of what we know about the man from Stratford, biographers nevertheless have attempted to merge these mutually incompatible entities, forcing a marriage of convenience filled with chronological disorders. What we know of Shakspere's business activities encroaches too much on his presumed playwriting time, and what we do *not* know of his education and cultural enlightenment precludes his having gotten the necessary preparation. If Shakspere had acquired the education and cultural experiences to write the plays, he would have left at least a few footprints behind to prove it. Shakspere's extant records are not only devoid of personal literary evidence, they point *away* from a literary career and toward other vocations. The footprints that he did leave lead to a literary dead end.

The contradictory and incompatible evidence has prompted anti-Stratfordians to search for an alternative author. When the hard evidence is examined, what emerges is an overwhelming weight of probability that William Shakspere of Stratford did *not* write the plays of William Shakespeare, and an equally overwhelming weight of probability that a gentleman of rank did. The idea that "William Shakespeare" was the pen name of an Elizabeth aristocrat is ultimately less fanciful than ascribing to an alleged grammar school dropout the most exquisite dramatic literature in the English language.

The Testimony of His Contemporaries Confirms Shakespeare's Identity

Jonathan Bate

Jonathan Bate, King Alfred Professor of English at the University of Liverpool, refutes the claim made by Oxfordians that Edward de Vere, seventeenth earl of Oxford, was the author of Shakespeare's plays. In this selection from his book *The Genius of Shakespeare* Bate explains that de Vere died in 1604 before many of Shakespeare's plays were even written. Further, he contends that the plays were written by a professional man of the theater, not an amateur aristocratic playwright like de Vere. Most importantly, Bate quotes from Shakespeare's contemporaries, who clearly link the man from Stratford with the writer of the plays.

Professor Bate has lectured on Shakespeare around the world. His other books include *Shakespeare and the English Romantic Imagination, Shakespeare and Ovid,* the new Arden edition of *Titus Andronicus,* and a novel, *The Cure for Love.*

There is a mystery about the identity of William Shakespeare. The mystery is this: why should anyone doubt that he was William Shakespeare, the actor from Stratford-upon-Avon?

It is the first question which the professional Shakespearean is always asked in casual conversation outside the walls of the academy—who wrote the plays? When told of the hard core of evidence that the man from Stratford did so, people are surprised. Sometimes it is suspected that the academics are covering up a scandal: it is said that *we do not*

Jonathan Bate, *The Genius of Shakespeare.* New York: Oxford University Press, 1998. Copyright © 1998 by Jonathan Bate. Reproduced by permission.

know who wrote the plays attributed to Shakespeare. Every now and then—it has been happening for over a hundred years—an amateur literary sleuth comes forward and, amidst a flurry of publicity, claims to have *solved the mystery.* The professors are likened to the plodding Inspector Lestrade; the truth can only be revealed by some unacknowledged Sherlock Holmes. . . .

Most academic Shakespeareans are as dismissive of the large and colourful army of Anti-Stratfordians as Lestrade is of Holmes. But I have taken an interest in the authorship question ever since, at the age of fourteen, I fell under the influence of a brilliant but eccentric Greek master. He tried to persuade me that the plays were written by the Earl of Oxford. He was so convinced of this himself that he changed his name by deed poll to Edward, in honour of Edward de Vere, the author of 'Shake-speare'. He triumphantly drew my attention to phrases in the sonnets. 'That every word doth almost sel my name' (Sonnet 76): 'every', he said, almost sells or tells or spells 'e-vere', which was proof positive.

Admittedly, I began to become sceptical when I discovered that the original proponent of de Vere's claim was an Edwardian schoolmaster who rejoiced in the name of J. Thomas Looney. It was also more than a little unfortunate that de Vere died in 1604. *Macbeth* could not have been composed before the Gunpowder Plot of 1605; *The Winter's Tale* was licensed by Sir George Buc, who only began licensing plays for performance in 1610; *The Tempest* was impelled by a voyage which took place in 1609; and *Henry VIII* was described by at least two witnesses as a 'new play' in 1613. How de Vere managed to write these plays from beyond the grave is a profound mystery indeed. But I persevered in my interest until I had examined all the evidence, and I remain fascinated by the mystery of the persistence of the Anti-Stratfordian position. It has something of the power of a myth, and myths are fictions from which there are always truths to be learned.

THE PLAYS WERE WRITTEN BY A PROFESSIONAL MAN OF THE THEATRE

Henry VIII was one of Shakespeare's three collaborations with John Fletcher, who subsequently took over as house dramatist of the King's Men. Fletcher had intimate links with Shakespeare's fellow-actors, but no connection with Oxford's circle. If there is one thing we can say for certain about Shakespeare's plays it is that they were written by a man of the theatre. An early play like *Titus Andronicus* was composed under the influence of the hit plays of the late 1580s, notably Thomas Kyd's *The Spanish Tragedy* and Christopher Marlowe's *The Jew of Malta;* a middle play like *Hamlet* was intricately bound up with the rivalry between the adult and children's acting companies around 1600; the late plays were responsive to Fletcher's innovations in the writing of tragicomic romance and the King's Men's purchase of the lease on the indoor playhouse at Blackfriars. Countless technicalities of staging in every one of the plays reveal that only a professional theatrical insider could have written them.

Amateur aristocrats such as the Earl of Oxford did write plays, but these were static and rarefied things in comparison with the mobile mingle-mangle of the public drama, with its mix of kings and clowns that so offended purists like Sir Philip Sidney. The difference between popular stage drama and aristocratic 'closet' drama may be instantly apprehended by anyone who takes the trouble to read, say, Shakespeare's *Antony and Cleopatra* in conjunction with the neoclassical version of *Antony* that was Englished by Sir Philip's sister, the Countess of Pembroke. For reasons that will be discussed later . . . , a motley collection of writers has been seduced by the . . . Looney hypotheses. But a much more striking fact is that no major actor has ever been attracted to Anti-Stratfordianism. That is because actors know from the inside that the plays must have been written by an actor.

Insofar as Looney and later Oxfordians address the problem of chronology at all, they have to argue that the later plays were written before 1604, kept in manuscript, and subsequently revised by the players with topical allusions to post-1604 events added in. But this argument is fatally flawed in the cases of *Macbeth* and *The Tempest:* the former does not merely allude to the Gunpowder Plot, it is a Gunpowder play through and through, while the latter could only have been written after the publication of Florio's translation of Montaigne in 1603 and the tempest that drove Sir George Somers' ship to Bermuda in 1609.

Nor can Oxfordians provide any explanation for the manifest stylistic differences between Shakespeare's Elizabethan and his Jacobean plays, or the technical changes attendant upon the King's Men's move to the Blackfriars theatre four years after their candidate's death. Unlike the Globe, the Blackfriars was an indoor playhouse; it therefore depended on artificial lighting; candles would not burn unattended for the full length of a play, so act-divisions were introduced, during which they could be trimmed or replaced (the audience, meanwhile, was entertained with music). The plays written after Shakespeare's company began using the Blackfriars in 1608, *Cymbeline* and *The Winter's Tale* for instance, have what most of the earlier plays do not have: a carefully planned five-act structure. No Oxfordian has addressed this difficulty for their faith. Presumably they would say that Oxford wrote a batch of five-act plays just in case the King's Men one day happened to acquire an indoor playhouse and that he gave instructions on his deathbed for these plays to be kept in a closet until such a day arrived. That there is no record of Oxford ever having had any contact with any of the King's Men has not deterred Oxfordians in the past and will not deter them in the future.

THE EVIDENCE LINKING SHAKESPEARE TO STRATFORD

Since the theory that William Shakespeare of Stratford did not write the works of Shakespeare still retains a strong hold on the popular imagination and is bolstered by a steady trickle of television programmes and magazine articles, it is worth making a simple statement of the evidence that William Shakespeare of Stratford did write the works of Shakespeare. The Anti-Stratfordian position begins from incredulity at the idea of a provincial grammar-school boy being the greatest artistic genius the world has ever seen. Some reasons for that incredulity will be discussed later, as will the history of the idea of a great artistic genius. For now, I want to remain with bare facts.

Only a few of the Anti-Stratfordians deny that the William Shakespeare who was born and died in Stratford-upon-Avon spent much of his life as an actor in London. John Shakespeare of Stratford, William's father, was granted a coat of arms in 1596; that same coat of arms appears on the monument to William Shakespeare which was erected in the Stratford parish church some time between his death in 1616 and the publication of the First Folio of the collected plays in 1623. In 1602 a member of the College of Heralds complained about his colleagues having granted arms to a number of supposedly unworthy persons, among them 'Shakespear the

Player'. Shakespeare of Stratford must therefore have been Shakespeare the Player. Furthermore, in his will the Stratford man left money to buy mourning rings to 'my fellows, John Heminges, Richard Burbage and Henry Condell'. This establishes beyond doubt that he was the same William Shakespeare who was a sharer with those actors in the company of the Lord Chamberlain's (later King's) Men.

The more widespread Anti-Stratfordian argument is that the actor was merely a front man and that the true author of the plays was someone else who for some reason could not reveal himself (or herself) as the true author. This is usually imagined to be an aristocrat unwilling to stigmatize his name by attaching it to something so undignified as a play. There is, however, not a single example of any aristocrat of the sixteenth or seventeenth centuries having expressed regret publicly or privately at not being able to write plays. As I have said, many of them, including the Earl of Oxford, did write plays—only not for public performance. The last thing an aristocrat would have wanted was his work being exposed to the garlic-breathed multitude. There is but one record of an aristocrat penning comedies for the common players, and it sounds more like malicious gossip than fact—it occurs in an informer's letter. The aristocrat in question was not Oxford, but William Stanley, the Earl of Derby. Since Stanley had the Christian name 'William', qualifying him to write the phrase 'my name is *Will*' (Sonnet 136), it is surprising that the case for him as the author of Shakespeare has never had the popularity of that for Oxford. Where Oxford's problem is that he died too soon to have written half Shakespeare's plays, Stanley's is that he lived long enough to have written all Beaumont and Fletcher's as well. He did not die until 1641.

The supposed 'fact' on which all Anti-Stratfordian arguments rest is the claim that there is no hard evidence to link the Stratford man to the *writing*, as opposed to the acting, of the plays. But this is not a fact at all: several contemporaries explicitly make the link.

Above all, there is the testimony of Ben Jonson. He knew Shakespeare intimately. He spoke about him privately and wrote about him publicly. He knew him as both an actor—Shakespeare was in the cast of at least two of Jonson's plays—and a writer. He remarked upon his fellow-dramatist's compositional practices. In his poem in praise of his 'beloved' friend, . . . he christened him 'Sweet Swan of Avon'. There is the decisive link with Stratford-upon-Avon.

Then there is Francis Beaumont. He co-wrote plays with Shakespeare's collaborator, John Fletcher. Beaumont penned some famous verses celebrating the wits who drank at the Mermaid Tavern. When in 1613 'William Shakespeare of Stratford upon Avon in the County of Warwick gentleman' bought a gatehouse in Blackfriars, one of the trustees he named in the purchase deed was William Johnson, the owner of the Mermaid. The obvious inference is that William Shakespeare of Stratford-upon-Avon, gentleman and actor, knew Johnson well because he was a regular customer at the Mermaid and thus a drinking companion of Beaumont. Now, in a manuscript verse-letter addressed to Jonson, Beaumont specifically praised Shakespeare for writing his best lines 'by the dim light of Nature', without 'Learning'. Beaumont thus knew Shakespeare the actor and spoke of him as a writer. Furthermore, his statement that Shakespeare achieved poetic greatness without the benefit of advanced learning precisely refutes the foremost claim of all the Anti-Stratfordians, namely that the plays could only have been written by someone who had benefited from a better formal education than Shakespeare's.

Then there is William Camden. He was both Jonson's schoolmaster and an officer in the College of Heralds. In 1602, he co-wrote with William Dethick a reply to the complaint of another heraldic officer that they had demeaned the profession by granting coats of arms to base-born persons such as 'Shakespear the Player'. Camden and Dethick replied that Shakespeare's father was a magistrate in Stratford-upon-Avon, a justice of the peace who had married a daughter and heir of the highly respectable Arden family, that he 'was of good substance and habelité', and therefore thoroughly merited the grant of arms. The following year Camden completed his *Remains of a greater Work concerning Britain*, in which he listed William Shakespeare, together with his fellow-dramatists Ben Jonson, George Chapman, and John Marston, among 'the most pregnant wits of these our times'. Within the space of a year, then, Camden describes Shakespeare as a leading writer and answers the complaint about granting a coat of arms to the player by delineating Shakespeare's Stratford pedigree. The writer therefore has to be the player. . . .

FURTHER TESTIMONY

Then there is Leonard Digges. He was an Oxford don who had connections with Stratford-upon-Avon and knew the London literary scene. His stepfather, Thomas Russell, was an overseer of Shakespeare's will. In a manuscript note written during Shakespeare's lifetime Digges, like Camden, affirmed what the proponents of Bacon, de Vere, and others have continually denied—the Stratford man's authorship of the plays. Digges' note was a memorandum to himself on the flyleaf of a book. He remarked that Lope de Vega was admired in Spain as both a dramatist and a poet just as Shakespeare was admired in England for both his plays and his sonnets. Since Digges was brought up by his stepfather in a village on the outskirts of Stratford-upon-Avon in the 1590s, his note's reference to 'our Will Shakespeare' establishes a firm link between his home town and the author of the sonnets and plays. Furthermore, as a manuscript note scribbled for his own personal use, not intended for publication, this evidence cannot be dismissed as part of a 'conspiracy' to pass off Shakespeare as the author of the plays, which is what the Anti-Stratfordians assume of the prefatory material to the First Folio by Digges, Jonson, and others.

Digges' commendatory poem for the Folio refers to the dramatist's 'Stratford monument'. The inscription on that monument gives the highest imaginable praise to Shakespeare's writing, just as the inscription on the grave of his daughter, Susanna, speaks of her inheriting her father's 'wit'. . . . Wit, in the sense of verbal facility, was what William Shakespeare was especially known for in his own lifetime. Proponents of the Looney hypothesis, on the other hand, always regard the Stratford actor as a kind of Tony Lumpkin, an illiterate rustic clown.

Then there is Francis Meres. . . . He was close enough to Shakespeare to know that in the 1590s the dramatist circulated unpublished sonnets 'among his private friends'; he had no doubts about ascribing both the sonnets and the plays to Shakespeare. The sonnets were not intended for publication. A pseudonym to disguise the authorship of published works is one thing, but if a writer circulates a batch of his poems in manuscript among his personal friends and includes in one of those poems the phrase 'for my name is *Will*', one has to be something of a Looney to conclude that his name was in fact Edward (de Vere) or Francis (Bacon). In addition, proponents of de Vere's claim have long been embarrassed by the fact that Meres' list of contemporary dramatists includes the names of both Shakespeare and Edward, Earl of Oxford—if Oxford wrote plays under his own name, why did he also have to do so under Shakespeare's? . . .

Anti-Stratfordians like to say that none of William Shakespeare's letters survive. This is also false. Letters addressed by William Shakespeare to Henry Wriothesley, the Earl of Southampton, may be read at the beginning of the texts of *Venus and Adonis* and *The Rape of Lucrece* in any complete edition of his works. The letter prefixed to *Venus and Adonis* is couched in the servile language which low-born writers had no choice but to use if they aspired to the patronage of aristocrats: 'only if your Honour seem but pleased, I account my self highly praised, and vow to take advantage of all idle hours, till I have honoured you with some graver labour'. Pride of place was so important to Elizabethan society that the idea of the mighty Earl of Oxford in the forty-third year of his life writing such words to one of Burghley's whipper-snapper wards is even more fantastic than the thought of him writing plays after his own death.

WHY THE AUTHORSHIP DOUBTS BEGAN

The list of contemporary testimonies and evidence could be considerably extended. *No one in Shakespeare's lifetime or the first two hundred years after his death expressed the slightest doubt about his authorship.* So why did people start expressing such doubts?

That nobody raised the question for two hundred years proves that there is no intrinsic reason why there should be a Shakespeare Authorship Controversy. There must therefore be extrinsic reasons for the origin and growth of the controversy. The likeliest would seem to be a change in the idea of Shakespeare, or a change in the idea of authorship, or both. . . . In the course of the eighteenth century there were indeed closely related changes in these two ideas.

There was no Shakespeare Authorship question at the beginning of the eighteenth century for two reasons. First, though Shakespeare was highly regarded, he was not sufficiently highly regarded for anybody to worry themselves about his provincial origins and lack of a university degree. For much of the century, the argument was not so much 'How could such clever plays have been written by the Stratford lad?' as 'Are the plays totally lacking in learning or just somewhat lacking in learning?' It would have been much more probable for there to have been a Jonson Authorship question: 'How could such genuinely learned plays have been written by a sometime bricklayer's apprentice who didn't go to university and who may even have left school before the sixth-form?' Secondly, the myth of the solitary author, alone with his blank sheet of paper, his thoughts springing fully-formed from his own innate genius, had not yet taken hold. As the sonnet mystery . . . was consequent upon a Romantic idea of poetry as autobiography, so the Authorship mystery is consequent upon a Romantic idea of authorial genius.

By the end of the eighteenth century, Shakespeare had been hailed as a genius, even a God. The moment a faith takes hold, heretics emerge. In a curious way, they are actually required in order to sustain the orthodoxy.

CHAPTER 2

SHAKESPEARE'S WORKS: "OF AN AGE AND FOR ALL TIME"

WILLIAM SHAKESPEARE

Shakespeare Both Imitates and Influences His Contemporaries

Martin Wiggins

Martin Wiggins, a Fellow of the Shakespeare Institute at the University of Birmingham, argues in this selection that Shakespeare was not a great dramatic innovator, like Christopher Marlowe, George Chapman, and John Marston. Instead, Wiggins contends that Shakespeare saw the possibilities in the innovations of his contemporaries and perfected them. For instance, he learned from Marlowe the power of characters who violate established hierarchies, then created his own female versions of this defiant anti-authoritarianism. Shakespeare, in turn, influenced his contemporaries, Wiggins explains. Shakespearean plots, scenes, lines, and jokes were parodied, appropriated, and re-used in numerous plays by his contemporaries and immediate successors. Wiggins asserts that Shakespeare's success in perfecting the innovations of others makes his plays superb, but the pre-eminence of his plays also inhibited narrative and dramatic originality in the plays of immediate successors.

In addition to *Shakespeare and the Drama of His Time*, Martin Wiggins has written *Journeyman in Murder: The Assassin in English Renaissance Drama* and he has edited and introduced *Four Jacobean Sex Tragedies*.

In 1592, [playwright] Robert Greene ended a dissolute life, his mind and pen swinging deliriously between self-pitying repentance and his usual jealous resentment of writers who had met with better fortune than he. In one of his deathbed writings, he warned his fellow playwrights, [Christopher]

Marlowe, [Thomas] Nashe, and [George] Peele, to beware of actors, 'those puppets . . . that speak from our mouths, those antics garnished in our colours'. Making a vain effort to foment the London theatre's first demarcation dispute, he pointed out that they were getting above themselves, writing their own plays and so taking work away from the professional dramatists; some of them may even have been committing plagiarism. His spleen was directed most of all at one relative newcomer: 'there is an upstart crow, beautified with our feathers, that with his "tiger's heart wrapped in a player's hide" supposes he is as well able to bombast out a blank verse as the best of you; and being an absolute *Johannes fac totum* [jack-of-all-trades], is in his own conceit the only Shake-scene in a country.' It was an offensive outburst against Shakespeare—Henry Chettle, who saw the book through the press after Greene's death, was forced to apologize a few months afterwards—and it was typical of Greene's attitude to younger talents: four years earlier, he had been similarly rude about Marlowe, attacking the immorality of the *Tamburlaine* plays whilst also producing his own catchpenny imitation, *Alphonsus, King of Aragon* (1587–8). Yet if we lay aside our distaste for Greene's tone and our customary reverence for his target, it is possible that he may have had a sustainable perception, not about whether actors have the right to be dramatists, but about the kind of talent Shakespeare possessed.

The principal vehicle of Greene's attack is one of Shakespeare's characters: Queen Margaret from the *Henry VI* plays. In *Part 2*, she contributes to the virtuous Lord Protector's downfall, and so to England's slide into civil war, with an accusation of treacherous deceit: 'Seems he a dove? His feathers are but borrowed, | For he's disposèd as the hateful raven'. And in *Part 3*, when she taunts the captured Duke of York with a handkerchief soaked in the blood of his murdered son, he replies with a powerful aria of pain and recrimination, which includes the play's best remembered line, then and now: 'O tiger's heart wrapped in a woman's hide'. Greene's taunting misquotation, and his central conceit of the feather thief, both derive from crucial moments when the Queen takes a hand in the demise of powerful men. His point takes its force from Shakespeare's emphasis on her violation of established hierarchies and gender roles, which make her a literal embodiment of the anarchy that is engulfing the kingdom. Her treatment of York shows harsh qualities supposedly alien to her sex—'Women are soft, mild, pitiful, and flexible— | Thou stern, obdurate, flinty, rough, remorseless,'—and she adopts a masculine function in leading troops on the battlefield in place of her husband the King. Similarly, in Greene's analysis, Shakespeare the actor-puppet is unjustly supplanting his university-trained betters in presuming to write his own plays.

SHAKESPEARE IS INDEBTED TO OTHERS' INNOVATIONS

Many a terrible queen stalks the tragedies and history plays of the period: the group also includes Elinor in Peele's *Edward I* (*c.* 1591) and Tamora in [Shakespeare's] *Titus Andronicus*, and the character type remained fitfully potent as late as William Rowley's *The Birth of Merlin* (1622). These are all characters most notable, like Queen Margaret, for their defiance or supplanting of male authority and their rejection of the norms of feminine behaviour. Often they involve themselves in the man's world of politics, with disastrous results. In the anonymous history play cum political farce, *Look About You* (1599?), for example, Queen Eleanor of Aquitaine is said to have committed mass murder in starting a war: she is

> The tigress that hath drunk the purple blood
> Of three times twenty thousand valiant men,
> Washing her red chaps in the weeping tears
> Of widows, virgins, nurses, sucking babes.
>
> (236–9)

It is striking, however, that the accusation is framed so that her victims include not only dead soldiers but also dead babies. These queens are portrayed as creatures of horror most of all in their deviation from the nurturing, maternal concept of womanhood: Queen Margaret is also associated with child murder (for all that some recent feminist critics have tried to reclaim her as a good mother), Tamora connives at Lavinia's rape, and the theme probably reached its ultimate pitch of *grand guignol* [drama stressing horror and sensationalism] in *Edward I* when Queen Elinor uses poisonous snakes to suckle a nursing mother's breasts—not just a deed of physical horror but also a symbolic action which strikes against motherhood in attacking the part of the female body which most defines it.

It is not known for certain which of these characters came

first (most early 1590s plays are notoriously difficult to date precisely), but the balance of probabilities favours Queen Margaret. If so, she was Shakespeare's most distinctive and original creation at the time Greene used her in his attack, a fine focus for his envy if not a very good illustration of his argument. Yet it is an originality which operates in terms already defined by an even more original recent work: as an empowered woman, Margaret is another exemplar of the fashion for hierarchical disruption which Marlowe had initiated with *Tamburlaine the Great.* In that sense, she was original but not revolutionary, and the response from other dramatists was simply to transplant her salient characteristics into other situations and other terrible queens; she did not have anything like the kind of shatteringly liberating effect of Marlowe's play. In this, as we shall eventually see, she may reflect the deeper point about Shakespeare which underlies Green's nasty little diatribe. . . .

SHAKESPEARE IS PARODIED BY HIS COMTEMPORARIES

Just as Shakespeare himself attracted gossip and anecdote when he became a known literary figure, so his plays became a focus for jokes and parodies, and none more so than *Hamlet.* It was perhaps inevitable that the authors of *Eastward Ho* [(George Chapman, John Marston, and Ben Jonson)], having given the name Gertrude to the goldsmith's daughter who makes a bad marriage, should have decided to call her footman Hamlet; and he is duly asked if he is mad when he gets angry. A year later, in *The Woman Hater,* Francis Beaumont raised an intertextual laugh when two characters discuss the disappearance of a culinary delicacy:

> LAZARELLO Speak: I am bound to hear.
> COUNT So art thou to revenge when thou shalt hear:
> The fish head is gone and we know not whither.

It is notable, however, that this is not the kind of lethal parody that was aimed at Marlowe in 1597. Both jokes work through incongruity: the mock-heroic juxtaposition of Shakespearian revenge rhetoric (from *Hamlet,* 1. 5. 6–7) with the picaresque story of a stolen meal, and the wryly inapposite naming of a tiny role after the longest and most challenging part in Shakespeare. Consequently they depend on a respect for the original play, rather than making it ridiculous as the Marlowe burlesques had done. There was never any time, from the ascendancy of Shakespeare until the closure of the London theatres in 1642, when younger dramatists successfully mocked his plays into outmoded oblivion; and this meant that those plays cast a long and not entirely comfortable shadow.

In the years leading up to Shakespeare's retirement, probably at the end of 1613, his work seems to have become the basis for what looks like a 'King's Men style': scenes and events which he created were redeployed, sometimes very ingeniously, by younger dramatists writing for the company. For example, Beaumont and Fletcher's *The Maid's Tragedy* includes a scene where the heroine, cross-dressed as a young soldier, visits the home of her ex-fiancé and has to argue with a servant in an effort to gain admittance; it is loosely based on the similar scene between Coriolanus and Aufidius' servants in Shakespeare's play. Fletcher's *Valentinian* features a confrontation between a sexually undisciplined head of state and a heroine who compares her raped body with a desecrated temple, and who is told that she has no redress—'Justice shall never hear ye: I am justice'—with the same chilling simplicity of Angelo's 'Who will believe thee, Isabel?' in *Measure for Measure.* And the strangled heroine of Webster's *The Duchess of Malfi* revives, like Desdemona in *Othello*, for just long enough to say a few last pathetic words. . . .

SHAKESPEARE INFLUENCES HIS IMMEDIATE SUCCESSORS

It is not altogether impossible that the dramatists hope to make their scripts more acceptable by tailoring them to fit a presumed 'house style' in the company's existing repertory, or even that Shakespeare, at this late stage in his career, liked to see plays written 'his way'. But it seems far more likely that the influence operated, at least in part, at a less conscious level, not so much in the individual playwrights as in the play-writing culture to which they belonged: that ways of imagining events and scenes were increasingly determined by the practice of the most senior author still working in the theatre. This seems to be borne out by the way Shakespeare's imaginative hold tightened as he personally receded into history.

A good example of the extent of that influence is [Thomas] Middleton and [William] Rowley's *The Changeling*, one of the most powerful tragedies written during the decade after Shakespeare's death. Middleton, who wrote the main plot, found in his source, a crime novella by John Reynolds, a bald story of a beautiful murderess named Beatrice-Joanna who employs an admirer, Deflores, to rid herself of an unwanted suitor, and ends up committing adultery with him. The character's name was soon worn down to Beatrice, at least in the authors' stage directions and speech prefixes, and one reason for this was probably that, in developing the story, Middleton began to think of her in terms of Shakespeare's Beatrice in *Much Ado About Nothing*. Both Beatrices are initially characterized in terms of an exaggerated antipathy for a man, Benedick and Deflores respectively, who is eventually to become her sexual partner; each has unwillingly to suffer his company as a result of an errand, in *Much Ado* when Beatrice is sent to fetch Benedick in to dinner and in *The Changeling* when Deflores is sent to tell Beatrice-Joanna that her fiancé has arrived; each Beatrice wants murder done and wishes she were a man, and each is reluctant to give the task to her preferred lover, respectively Benedick and Alsemero. Both plots also feature crucial moments which turn on the substitution of maidservant for mistress, though in somewhat different circumstances.

Middleton was further influenced by another Shakespeare play, which left its traces in the incongruous fact that the murder victim has told everyone that he has gone off in a gondola even though the play is set in Spain, and in another character's nautical description of making a pass at a woman: 'Yonder's another vessel, I'll board her; if she be lawful prize, down goes her topsail'. Middleton was obviously thinking of Iago on Othello's marriage: 'Faith, he tonight hath boarded a land-carrack. | If it prove lawful prize, he's made forever'. As often with the better writers of the time, Shakespeare included, precise verbal echoes like this are the stigmata of a deeper imaginative influence, pinpricks that let through the light. The development of Deflores from the personable young man in the novella to the play's cunning, obsessive villain was evidently via *Othello*'s 'honest' Iago: Middleton's character attracts the same ironically inappropriate epithet, and shares Iago's views, expressed to Roderigo, about the unlikelihood of female constancy. But Middleton's central transformation was to make him physically repellent: thus Beatrice-Joanna is made 'To fall in love with what she feared to look on', as Brabantio says of Desdemona's affair with Othello. All these elements from Shakespeare are deeply embedded in the imaginative process which created the play's distinctive tragic situation; and it is possible to chart a similar enabling Shakespearian presence in the roots of other tragedies of the time, such as John Ford's *The Broken Heart* (1629) and *'Tis Pity She's a Whore* (1630). . . .

The quarter-century of Shakespeare's career was a period of extraordinary creativity in English drama, and the perceived pre-eminence of his plays, reflecting the effortless superiority of a dead author, placed frustrated yet admiring younger dramatists in a double bind:

> Thy Muse's sugared dainties seem to us
> Like the famed apples of old Tantalus:
> For we, admiring, see and hear thy strains,
> But none I see or hear, those sweets attains.
>
> [Thomas Bancroft]

Shakespeare set a standard of excellence which their own work could not hope to reach, but by which it would nevertheless be judged. The result was a drama with a broad streak of nostalgia and a noticeable dependence on recycled materials.

In plays of the post-Shakespearian period you will find, among many others: a comic scene with a gravedigger, which contemporaries recognized as a lift from *Hamlet* (in Thomas Randolph's *The Jealous Lovers*); a father who affects disapproval of his daughter's low-born suitor, but, like Simonides in *Pericles*, communicates his true feelings to the audience in asides (Ford's *Perkin Warbeck*); a husband who is tempted by a villainous schemer into believing his wife has been unfaithful (Ford's *Love's Sacrifice*), and another who becomes insanely jealous after his wife seems to have disposed of one of his love-gifts (Philip Massinger's *The Emperor of the East*); a plot centred on lovers from rival families (Thomas May's *The Heir*); a queen whose husband irrationally accuses her of adultery with a court favourite whom she has praised (Richard Brome's *The Queen and Concubine*); characters who pretend to be statues and are reanimated by supposedly magical means (Massinger's *The City Madam*); a murderer who cannot wash his hands clean of blood which only he can see (*The Jews' Tragedy*); a clown who asks for guerdon and remuneration (Alexander Brome's *The Cunning Lovers*); and a group of artisans who are to perform before royalty, with a leading actor who wants to play all the parts (Thomas Rawlins's *The Rebellion*). (In case anyone has not guessed all the unspecified Shakespearian originals, look at: *Othello; Romeo and Juliet;* Hermione and the statue scene in *The Winter's Tale; Macbeth;* Costard in *Love's Labours Lost;* and Bottom and company in *A Midsummer Night's Dream.*) These examples include plots, events, lines of dialogue, jokes and comic set-pieces, spectacular scenes, and modes of human behaviour: Shakespeare's imaginative influence was pervasive.

My point is not the old and discredited one that post-Shakespearian drama lacks artistic integrity: recent criticism has, on the contrary, emphasized its seriousness and its deep engagement with the political crisis of its period. However, it is obvious that its narrative and dramatic horizons were substantially determined by the plays of the recent past, including not only Shakespeare but also some of his younger contemporaries like Jonson and [John] Webster. . . .

Shakespeare did not open out new and influential modes of drama in the way that Marlowe and Chapman and Marston had done, enabling later writers to exercise their own creativity in different ways; he only provided them with a treasure-house of new source material. In that sense, his was essentially a secondary talent (by which I do not mean a second-rate one): he was a great completer, maximizing the potential of other men's innovations and thereby, perhaps, beautifying himself with their feathers. The plays so adorned, seen in themselves, were among the greatest glories of English drama. Seen as part of a historical process, they were also its curse.

Shakespeare Is Enshrined As Britain's National Poet in the Eighteenth Century

Michael Dobson

In the introduction to his book *The Making of the National Poet*, Indiana University professor Michael Dobson focuses on the genesis of "bardolatry" (the idolizing of Shakespeare) in the eighteenth century, and he outlines the process by which Shakespeare emerged as Britain's national poet by 1789. Shakespeare died in 1616, but several of his plays were performed until 1642 when Britain's theaters were closed. By 1660 when Charles II was crowned king and the theaters were reopened, Shakespeare had been dead for over forty years and his plays had not been performed for nearly twenty years.

According to Dobson, many of our modern conceptions of Shakespeare spring from the eighteenth century when all but one of Shakespeare's plays were revived. Although nearly all were substantially rewritten to suit the tastes of the theater-going public, the plays, as adapted and interpreted, were viewed as venerable classics. Dobson explains that the author was formally enshrined as Britain's national poet at the Stratford Jubilee in 1769.

With Stanley Wells, Michael Dobson has also edited *The Oxford Companion to Shakespeare*.

Then comes the 'resurrection'—on speculation. Betterton the player, and Rowe the writer, make a selection from a promiscuous heap of plays found in a garret, nameless as to authorship. . . . 'I want an author for this selection of plays!' said Rowe. 'I have it!' said Betterton; 'call them Shakespeare's!' And

Michael Dobson, *The Making of the National Poet*. New York: Oxford University Press, 1992. Copyright © 1992 by Michael Dobson. Reproduced by permission.

Rowe, the 'commentator,' commenced to puff them as 'the bard's', and to write a history of his hero in which there was scarcely a word that had the foundation of truth to rest upon.

This is about the sum and substance of the manner of setting up Shakespeare.   [Colonel Joseph C. Hart]

In 1660, after all, at the start of [veteran actor Thomas] Betterton's career in the theatre, Shakespeare's plays had not been reprinted in a collected edition since the Second Folio appeared in 1632; very few living actors had any experience of performing them, and that experience dated from twenty years earlier, before the Civil Wars, at which time the number of Shakespeare plays still in the repertory had already dwindled to perhaps five—*Hamlet, Othello, Julius Caesar, The Merry Wives of Windsor*, and *1 Henry IV*. By 1769, when almost every national newspaper and magazine reprinted [Nicholas] Rowe's biography as part of their coverage of David Garrick's Stratford Jubilee, readers of Shakespeare might have consulted collected editions not only by Rowe but by an illustrious succession of prestigious writers including Alexander Pope, Sir Thomas Hanmer, and Samuel Johnson, and any actor in the employ of the Theatres Royal would have needed a working familiarity with at least twenty-four of Shakespeare's plays, revivals of which accounted for more than one in six of all dramatic performances given in London. . . .

ORIGINS OF MODERN CONCEPTIONS OF SHAKESPEARE

This book aims to describe how this extraordinary change in Shakespeare's status came about, attempting in the process to replace Hart's conspiracy theory of the 'setting up' of Shakespeare (a type of explanation to which discussions of Shakespeare's canonicity are especially prone) with what I hope will be a more persuasive account of how Shakespeare came to occupy the centre of English literary culture between the restoration of the monarchy [in 1660] and the Stratford Jubilee [in 1769].

This process deserves close scrutiny, not least because so many of the conceptions of Shakespeare we inherit date not from the Renaissance but from the Enlightenment. It was this period, after all, which initiated many of the practices which modern spectators and readers of Shakespeare would generally regard as normal or even natural: the performance of his female roles by women instead of men (instigated at a revival of *Othello* in 1660); the reproduction of his works in scholarly editions, with critical apparatus (pioneered by Rowe's edition of 1709 and the volume of commentary appended to it by Charles Gildon the following year); the publication of critical monographs devoted entirely to the analysis of his texts (an industry founded by John Dennis's *An Essay upon the Writings and Genius of Shakespeare*, 1712); the promulgation of the plays in secondary education (the earliest known instance of which is the production of *Julius Caesar* mounted in 1728 'by the young Noblemen of the Westminster School'), and in higher education (first carried out in the lectures on Shakespeare given by William Hawkins at Oxford in the early 1750s); the erection of monuments to Shakespeare in nationally symbolic public places (initiated by Peter Scheemakers' statue in Poets' Corner, Westminster Abbey, unveiled in 1741); and the promotion of Stratford-upon-Avon as a site of secular pilgrimage (ratified at Garrick's Jubilee in 1769). The fact that these ways of presenting and representing Shakespeare have endured for so long has tended to make their specifically Enlightenment origins and interests virtually invisible—to the extent that until comparatively recently, histories of Shakespeare's reception, especially his critical reception, have characteristically identified the eighteenth century as the period which simply 'rediscovered' Shakespeare and restored him to his natural pre-eminence in English culture. . . .

EIGHTEENTH-CENTURY ADAPTATIONS OF SHAKESPEARE'S PLAYS

For historians primarily interested in stage interpretations of Shakespeare, the period has been conspicuous for a very different series of innovations: to cite only a handful, the first conflation of two Shakespeare plays into one (*The Law Against Lovers*, created by Sir William Davenant from *Measure for Measure* and *Much Ado About Nothing* in 1662); the first *Troilus and Cressida* in which Cressida commits suicide to prove her innocence (John Dryden's *Troilus and Cressida, or, Truth Found Too Late*, first acted in 1679); the first *Henry V* in which the protagonist is pursued to France by his scorned ex-mistress Harriet, disguised as a page (Aaron Hill's *King Henry the Fifth, or, The Conquest of France by the English*, 1723); the first *As You Like It* to betroth Celia to Jaques and include *Pyramus and Thisbe* (Charles Johnson's *Love in a Forest*, performed in the same year); and the first *Cymbeline* to observe the unities of time and place (prepared

by William Hawkins in 1759). To the embarrassment and
perplexity of students of Shakespeare's reputation, precisely
the same period which at some time saw the revival of every
single play in the Shakespeare canon (excepting only *Love's
Labour's Lost*) also saw the substantial rewriting of every
single play in the Shakespeare canon (excepting only *Othello*
and *1 Henry IV*), and although numbers of these adaptations
never established themselves in the repertory, many of the
plays upon which Shakespeare's reputation as the supreme
dramatist of world literature is now most squarely based—
including *Macbeth, The Tempest, King Lear, Coriolanus,
Richard III, Romeo and Juliet,* and *The Winter's Tale*—were in
practice only tolerated in the theatre in heavily revised versions, even while that very reputation was being established.

This coexistence of full-scale canonization with whole-
sale adaptation, of the urge to enshrine Shakespeare's texts
as national treasures with the desire to alter their content,
has long been regarded as a quaint paradox, the rewritten
versions of the plays generally being dismissed as at best a
bizarre cul-de-sac of literary history, inessential to the 'real'
story of Shakespeare's reception. This view, I would argue,
has seriously distorted our understanding of Shakespeare's
changing roles in Augustan culture, and by implication—
since the social and cultural forces which converged over
that period to establish his supremacy have preserved it ever
since—of his continuing presence in our own. I hope to
show over the course of this study that adaptation and canonization, so far from being contradictory processes, were
often mutually reinforcing ones: that the claiming of Shakespeare as an Enlightenment culture hero both profited from,
and occasionally demanded, the substantial rewriting of his
plays. In this light I shall be examining the adaptations produced during the crucial century from the 1660s to the 1760s
alongside the prodigious numbers of other texts produced
about Shakespeare during the same period ('legitimate' and
otherwise) as complementary aspects of the extensive cultural work that went into the installation of Shakespeare as
England's National Poet. . . .

"BARDOLATRY" BECOMES A NATIONAL RELIGION

Although to use the term 'Bardolatry' at all may seem pa-
tronizing, I have no intention, either, of disparaging the Enlightenment's enthusiasm for Shakespeare; however flip-

pantly the term may have been coined (by George Bernard Shaw), its implication that the author-cult of Shakespeare has functioned, and continues to function, as a kind of religion is one which few cultural anthropologists would dispute. It is with Bardolatry's rise to orthodoxy as a *national* religion that I shall be especially concerned here. Writing in the 1630s, Ben Jonson was careful to distinguish his own high regard for Shakespeare from profane adulation ('I lov'd the man, and doe honour his memory (on this side Idolatry) as much as any'), but by the middle of the next century this distinction had all but vanished from many English writings on Shakespeare. At the climax of his Jubilee in 1769, David Garrick gesticulated towards a graven image of the Bard with the words, "'Tis he! 'tis he! | "The god of our idolatry!'", (words which, characteristically, adapt and appropriate some of Shakespeare's own, from the balcony scene of *Romeo and Juliet*); and even before this apogee of canonization Shakespeare had often been recognized as occupying a position in British life directly analogous to that of God the Father. In 1739 the playwright Thomas Cooke, in the epilogue to his play *The Mournful Nuptials*, identifies Shakespeare as one of the faiths of the ruling class, dividing Britain between 'They who are born to taste' and 'The tasteless vulgar', the former hailed as staunch believers in Shakespeare and the Church of England, the latter derided as schismatic followers of Harlequin and John Wesley. Similarly, Arthur Murphy, in an essay addressed to the sceptical Voltaire in 1753, links Bardolatry with both Anglicanism and Little-Englandism, remarking that 'with us islanders *Shakespeare* is a kind of established religion in poetry'.

From their time onwards, Shakespeare has been as normatively constitutive of British national identity as the drinking of afternoon tea, and it is now probably as hard for any educated Briton to imagine not enjoying the former as it would be to imagine forgoing the latter. This analogy may be less trivializing than it appears: the national habit of Shakespeare, after all, and the national habit of tea have their origins in exactly the same period of expanding trade abroad and vigorous nationalism at home—both rise from being novelties with Pepys in the 1660s to being addictions with Dr Johnson in the 1760s. That Shakespeare was declared to rule world literature at the same time that Britannia was declared to rule the waves may, indeed, be more than a coincidence. As Edward Capell points out, dedicating his edition of the Complete Plays to the Duke of Grafton just after the colonial victories of the Seven Years War, to reproduce Shakespeare in the manner he deserves is to participate in an export industry which has cornered all world markets, contributing thereby to the nation's cultural capital. . . .

SHAKESPEARE BECOMES A NATIONAL TREASURE

The ensuing pages chart, in essence, the emergence between the 1660s and the 1760s of a shared sense of the national importance of Shakespeare and a general agreement about the broader contours of his authorial image, if not about what specific local positions his plays endorse or in what adapted or re-edited forms they should be presented. I have divided the century over which this development takes place into four successive phases, corresponding broadly to four different sets of strategies by which both Shakespeare-as-author and the texts that make up the Shakespeare canon are rewritten and repositioned—loosely speaking, 1660–78, 1678–88, 1688–1735, and 1735–69.

During the first phase, . . . Shakespeare is imagined at worst as an artless rustic, at best as an archaic father-king: the rewritings which attempt to finish and update his works for a sceptical present (most successfully the William Davenant–John Dryden version of *The Tempest*, 1667) place their quasiroyal author at the mercy of contemporary politics, whether theatrical, governmental, or familial.

In the second phase, . . . which coincided with the constitutional crises of the 1670s and 1680s, Shakespeare's plays are rewritten sometimes to court such immediate topicality but more often to avoid it: their author is presented more than ever as a king (and is even brought onto the stage in the likeness of King Hamlet's ghost to introduce Dryden's version of *Troilus and Cressida* in 1679), but his dominion is now primarily over the private realm of the passions.

Revived in prologues as a disembodied author, Shakespeare, from the Glorious Revolution [in 1688] through the 1730s, is rewritten as such, his plays increasingly purged of their grosser, fleshlier comic details as he becomes a proper, and proprietary, Augustan author. From this period onwards, Shakespeare's texts are no longer simply modernized but are instead retrospectively and unobtrusively corrected, his antiquated style imitated by adaptors as they strive to polish his now venerable works into native classics. . . . Adaptation and canonization become ever more mutual processes at this time, as biographers and panegyrists of Shakespeare attempt to construct an author worthy of the Complete Plays, and adaptors—and indeed editors—attempt in their turn to make the plays worthy of their author.

From the early eighteenth century forwards, adaptation diminishes in importance alongside other means of appropriating and promoting Shakespeare's authority. . . . [I consider] especially the covert rewriting of the national past in which [David] Garrick's own adaptations participate, examining the mid-eighteenth century's preferred stage versions of, in particular, *The Winter's Tale*, *The Taming of the Shrew*, and *Cymbeline* in the context of a number of other contemporary texts—pamphlets, lectures, poems, prefaces—which despite virulent disagreements between themselves assimilate Shakespeare to a common agenda of domestic virtue at home and colonial warfare abroad. By this stage in the rise of Bardolatry, with Shakespeare enshrined as the transcendent personification of a national ideal, even his unadapted texts seem virtually irrelevant to popular conceptions of his 'essential' British greatness. . . .

Garrick's Stratford festivities [in 1769], explicitly choosing Shakespeare to be Britain's national deity, provide a fitting end to this account, and a fitting point from which to review its implications for the subsequent progress of his cult, on both sides of the Atlantic. While I would not wish to argue that anything about Shakespeare was settled once and for all by this extraordinary cultural event, it may well be that even now, over two centuries later, what is most striking about its traces is not their kitsch strangeness but their unnerving familiarity. To a surprising degree, the Jubilee encoded in itself the history to date of the Bardolatry it proclaims—'the sum and substance of the manner of setting up Shakespeare', to return to Colonel Hart's formulation—and it may furthermore have substantially predicted the form in which, with however many signs of strain, it still survives. If less avid for souvenir cuttings of the mulberry tree allegedly planted by Shakespeare in his garden at New Place than our eighteenth-century forebears, in our continuing promotion of Shakespeare-dominated literary studies as a nationally vital academic discipline able to subsume law, theology, and even medicine, offering a stable antidote to all mere intellectual fads, we are perhaps still voices in the chorus Garrick's ballads led in 1769, enthusiastic participants in the same triumphal procession:

> With learning and knowledge the well-lettered birch
> Supplies Law and Physic and grace for the Church.
> But Law and the Gospel in Shakespeare we find,
> And he gives the best physic for body and mind.
>   All shall yield to the Mulberry Tree, *etc.*
> •   •   •   •   •   •   •   •
> Then each take a relic of this hallowed tree,
> From folly and fashion a charm let it be.
> Fill, fill to the planter, the Cup to the brim,
> To honour your country do honour to him.
>   All shall yield to the Mulberry Tree,
>
>   Bend to thee,
>   Blest Mulberry,
>   Matchless was he
>   Who planted thee,
>   And thou like him immortal be!

Drums, fifes, and bells ring.
They all exit in a hurry, going to see the
Pageant.

Shakespeare Is "Alive" and Thriving in the Twentieth Century

Joseph Papp and Elizabeth Kirkland

In this selection from their book *Shakespeare Alive!* Joseph Papp, founder of the New York Shakespeare Festival, and Elizabeth Kirkland, Harvard graduate and Rhodes Scholar, consider the mystery of Shakespeare's continuing popularity in America and around the world. They conclude that Shakespeare's universal themes, the sources of his plots, his language, and his vibrant characters contribute to his universal appeal, but they assert that the re-creation of the plays on stages across the globe truly keeps Shakespeare alive today.

Joseph Papp has directed or produced nearly all of Shakespeare's plays at the New York Shakespeare Festival's permanent home, The Public Theater, on and off Broadway, in Central Park, and in numerous schools. He has also written the forewords for each of the individual editions of Shakespeare's plays published by Bantam Books. Elizabeth Kirkland has been a producer, publicity manager, stage manager, and performer; she also worked with Papp at the New York Shakespeare Festival.

Although Shakespeare may have made his home in Stratford, he has obviously found a home in every corner of the world since then. Even during his lifetime, his plays were performed by Catholic recusants in the north of England, on a ship off of Sierra Leone, and in the cities of Elbing and Gdansk in eastern Europe. In the subsequent four centuries Shakespeare's plays seem to have gone everywhere else as well; each nation has annexed him and made him its own by translating, adapting, and performing his plays. . . .

A Frenchman [Henri Fluchère] declared that Shakepeare is "part and parcel of our literary consciousness." One observer at the . . . China Shakespeare Festival commented that [as J. Kynge reports] "the Chinese love Shakespeare so much that in a few years time they will say the bard was Chinese."

He might just as well have said Indian, or Japanese, or Polish. Every nation pats itself on the back for keeping Shakespeare alive; and every nation finds itself in Shakespeare. A German will look at Hamlet and see the mirror of the German soul; a native of India will make Hamlet an Indian, like the writer [quoted by R.G. Shahari] who scrawled, "What are we Indians, but pale Hamlets, sick with too much thinking and chattering?" A provincial Scottish troupe in the eighteenth century reached an impasse when every actor insisted on playing Hamlet, and only Hamlet—the company settled it by abandoning the play.

To some, Shakespeare is a provider of endless delight and entertainment; the empress of Russia, Catherine the Great, translated and reworked *The Merry Wives of Windsor* and *Timon of Athens* along Russian lines. To others, Shakespeare is a source of inspiration in times of hardship or turmoil. The French performed his plays during the German occupation of Paris in World War II, when English books were banned. The Armenians, engaged in a struggle for political autonomy, are said to have taken courage from the struggles of King Lear, Macbeth, Shylock, and Othello. And in 1916, though they were in the middle of World War I, the people of Yugoslavia took time out to organize a ceremony for the three hundredth anniversary of Shakespeare's death, basing their celebration on the same premise that our observer in China stated—that Shakespeare truly belongs to all nations.

SHAKESPEARE IN AMERICA

Perhaps he does, but Americans would like to believe that he is just a little more at home in the United States than anywhere else. Shakespeare has made frequent cameo appearances in the chronicles of American history, and he's meant many different things to people at various times in the life of the republic. Early American citizens loved him for his tales of swashbuckling and romance; early American statesmen looked to him for examples of political wisdom and moral courage. He also provided journalists and cartoonists with endless material to use in their commentaries on the state of the union.

The first presidents were lovers of Shakespeare. George Washington's boyhood home contained six volumes of Shakespeare's plays, and several signers of the Declaration of Independence owned Shakespeare volumes. John Adams got up at four o'clock on a winter morning to answer a letter about *Hamlet* and to "commune with a lover and worthy representative of Shakespeare upon the glories of this immortal bard." Abraham Lincoln carried a copy of *Macbeth* (his favorite) with him as he rode the law circuits in Illinois. Later, when he was president, a copy of Shakespeare sat on the White House desk (along with the Bible and the U.S. Statutes). Art, religion, and society—what else did one need for a full understanding of the achievement and genius of humankind but these three books?

Both sides enlisted Shakespeare's help in the American Revolution. Writers revised and revamped Hamlet's famous question to dramatize the conflicting impulses within the rebelling colony. A Tory loyalist [quoted by Moses C. Tyler in *The Literary History of the American Revolution*] lambasted the rebels by asking,

> To sign or not to sign!—That is the question:
> Whether 't were better for an honest man
> To sign—and so be safe . . .

or to risk the consequences of loyalty by refusing to sign the oath of rebellion against Britain. A Boston newspaper pondered the taxation question similarly [as E.C. Dunn reports in *Shakespeare in America*]:

> Be taxt or not be taxt—that is the question.
> Whether 'tis nobler in our minds to suffer
> The sleights and cunning of deceitful statesmen
> Or to petition 'gainst illegal taxes
> And by opposing, end them? . . .

Although the United States won its political independence in 1776, theatrical independence was a longer time in coming. The American stage tended to mimic whatever was going on in London; the famous English actor David Garrick's huge success with *Richard III* was a surefire guarantee that it would be popular in America. Moreover, many English actors crossed over to tour in the ex-colonies, either because they hadn't been able to make it on the London stage or because they hoped for financial gain. Such imported actors as the flamboyant G.F. Cooke, the fiery Edmund Kean, and the elegant and eloquent William Charles Macready were tremendously popular with American audiences (although Edmund Kean was never forgiven for refusing to perform for a Boston audience he considered too small, and Macready was plagued by anti-British prejudices).

Gradually, though, America began to develop an acting tradition of its own, led by such native-born actors as J.H. Hackett, the first major American actor to perform in England; the towering Edwin Forrest, whose rivalry with the British Macready culminated in a bloody riot in New York City that left thirty-one people dead; the great nineteenth-century actress Charlotte Cushman, who dazzled London with her performance as Romeo; and Edwin Booth, the best-loved actor of nineteenth-century America, most famous for his quiet and graceful Hamlet.

While city audiences were oohing and aahing English productions and actors were refining Shakespeare on stately stages in wealthy old cities, out on the frontier people were just having a good old time. Rough, rugged, and rowdy themselves, they responded heartily to Shakespeare's melo-drama, spectacle, bloodshed, and oratory; plays that exem-plified these virtues—*Richard III, Hamlet, Othello,* and *Julius Caesar*—were performed over and over again in sa-loons and mining camps, in billiard halls and village halls, and on Mississippi riverboats and wagon trains plodding West. And in the 1840s, a band of Seminole Indians gave a new twist to frontier Shakespeare: they attacked a traveling company in Florida, appropriated their costumes, and were later taken into custody wearing the costumes of *Othello, Hamlet,* and *Julius Caesar!*

Frontier people especially loved Shakespeare's rhetoric— the force and power of shouted passages, the grandeur of ac-cumulated phrases, the patterns of the speeches. They weren't put off by his vocabulary because they themselves used a lot of tall talk and often created words with suffixes and prefixes—"bodacious," "monstropolous," and "exflunc-tificate." They weren't alone in this; speechmaking had been a way of life in American politics even before Patrick Henry uttered his famous one-liner, "Give me liberty or give me death!" Oratory was practically a national pastime and made Americans all the more receptive to Shakespeare on the stage. . . .

SHAKESPEARE ON THE MODERN STAGE

Shakespeare has been just as successful on the modern stage as he was in the Globe. His plays have attracted such American actors as Meryl Streep, Raul Julia, Martin Sheen, Kevin Kline, James Earl Jones, and Elizabeth McGovern, all of whom have graced the stage in New York Shakespeare Festival productions.

As in previous ages, the staging of Shakespeare in the twentieth century reflects the tenor of the times. Orson Welles depicted Julius Caesar as a fascist dictator in 1937; Hamlet appeared as an inspiring man of action in a 1945 production given for American G.I.'s. The 1960s saw a burlesque version of *Macbeth* making fun of American politics, called *Macbird;* and in a production by Jewish senior citizens in a Brooklyn old folks home, an eighty-two-year-old Romeo turned to a seventy-year-old Juliet and asked, "You Jewish?"

There have been all-black, all-male, and all-female stagings of Shakespeare. The first recorded black acting company in America opened in lower Manhattan with *Richard III* in 1821. Over a century later, in 1936, Orson Welles produced his "voodoo" *Macbeth* at the Lafayette Theater in Harlem with a cast of one hundred blacks. Set in Haiti, with real witch doctors, jungle drums, and cackling voodoo priestesses, it was an eerie spectacle and a huge hit. In 1979, the New York Shakespeare Festival assembled an all-black company that performed *Julius Caesar* and *Coriolanus. As You Like It* was staged in the late 1960s with an all-male cast in modern dress. Recently, *The Taming of the Shrew* was performed by a cast of women in an interpretation intended to highlight what they saw as the play's now-outmoded expressions of chauvinism. And in 1986, at the Belasco Theater on Broadway, a company of Afro-American, Hispanic, and Asian-American actors performed Shakespeare's plays for New York City high-school students, under the auspices of the New York Shakespeare Festival.

In our century, when the director has taken on a much greater role in interpreting and guiding a play, there are as many different approaches to Shakespeare's work as there are people to think them up. Hamlet may be an adolescent in the grip of an unresolved Oedipal complex or a resolute man of action; *The Comedy of Errors* takes place in Edwardian England on one stage and in the American West among cowhands and ranchers on another stage. Whatever the interpretation, it seems that Shakespeare's plays are so expansive and flexible that they can accommodate any race, creed, color, gender, or directorial approach. Not all versions work equally well, but together they illustrate how one writer's plays can mean such very different things to different people.

THE MYSTERY OF SHAKESPEARE'S UNIVERSAL APPEAL

The real mystery is *why.*

How is it that Shakespeare can continue to entertain, inspire, and instruct people all around the world? Is it the themes he addresses? Is it that the human dilemmas he explores transcend specific centuries and particular civilizations? As a British soldier wrote from the trenches in World War I [according to Lucy Collison-Morley in *Shakespeare in Italy*], "There is no hardship or terror or doubt that happens out here that Shakespeare does not touch on or give advice for"; a copy of *Henry V* was found on his body when he died. The terrible randomness of suffering, the conflict of justice and mercy, the nature of power and the individual, life within a family, the transforming magic of love—Shakespeare works and reworks these themes in all of his plays. Such concerns don't go away; they are an eternal part of the human condition. Is *this* what keeps Shakespeare alive?

Or does it have something to do with the wide range of his sources? Shakespeare plundered legends and stories from many cultures, and in rewriting them for the theater gave them new and enduring life. And, of course, he himself became a source that subsequent artists would quarry, using him as he used his predecessors, as a springboard for their own creativity. Is *this* what keeps Shakespeare alive?

Perhaps it's the language his characters speak. Although some of Shakespeare's vocabulary has become archaic and his syntax and grammar obsolete, the rhythms of his lines and the sounds of his words retain their extraordinary power and remarkable emotional expressiveness. As one fan [M. Morgann in *An Essay on the Dramatic Character of Sir John Falstaff*] enthused in the late 1700s, "In his native tongue he shall roll the genuine passions of nature." Is *this* what keeps Shakespeare alive?

Maybe it's his astonishing characters, so full of vitality that they practically jump off the page. Each of them seems to have a life elsewhere, which the play glimpses only momentarily. And yet so real and vibrant are they that one Victorian author was inspired to invent biographies of the childhoods of Rosalind, Celia, Portia, Desdemona, and all of Shakespeare's heroines, leading up to the point where the plays begin.

But though they may seem to have lives elsewhere, they *truly* come to life only on the stage. Shakespeare's characters are creatures of the theater; they exist not to be dissected and psychoanalyzed but to be performed. Falstaff couldn't exist without an audience to show off for and a stage to prance and play on; Cleopatra craves a theater for her melodramatic histrionics; and where would Richard III be if he couldn't confide in us?

This insistent vitality isn't just expressed by major characters like Falstaff, Cleopatra, Hamlet, Rosalind, or Richard; Shakespeare breathes life into even the most insignificant of his stage creatures—the spear carriers, the servants, the children, and the minor courtiers. Think of the prisoner Barnardine in *Measure for Measure,* who throws a monkey wrench into the duke's plot by refusing to die at the convenient time; the Capulets' servant Peter in *Romeo and Juliet,* who grieves profoundly at Juliet's supposed death; and the nameless servant of Gloucester in *King Lear* who runs to fetch flax and egg whites to soothe his blinded master's bleeding face.

All of Shakespeare's characters, from talkative Hamlet to the lowliest one-line speaker, are both *of* life and larger than life. And they will continue to hold on to that life as long as they have a theater somewhere. Is *this* what keeps Shakespeare alive?

The answer to the question, of course, is all of the above. Shakespeare's universal themes and human concerns, his rhythmic language and great stories, as well as his lively theatrical characters, are all part of what keeps Shakespeare alive.

And yet, centuries of change might easily have killed him off. Our language and vocabulary, as well as our world view and our understanding of religion; the rights accorded to women and minorities; our standard of living; our understanding of the ways and values of other nations; the behavior of the family; the way our theaters are organized, equipped, and run; the tastes and preferences of the audience—all these things are drastically different from what Shakespeare knew in sixteenth-century England.

In spite of these changes he continues to speak to us—

from the wings of the theater. The comic effect of the scene in *Love's Labor's Lost* where each of the four young men eavesdrop on the next, till they are four deep listening to each other's confessions of love, is difficult for us to visualize as readers. Likewise, the cold-blooded cruelty of Goneril and Regan comes across in all its horrific barbarity only when we *see* the blinding of old Gloucester carried out in front of our eyes. The funny business of the frightened jester Trinculo creeping under the long gaberdine of the monster Caliban in *The Tempest* is less vivid when it's not seen onstage. And the utter comedy of Falstaff's cowardice in the theater renders pointless all armchair analyses of his personality by critics. As a German poet [Hugo von Hoffmansthal] said early in the twentieth century, "the true readers of Shakespeare and also those in whom Shakespeare is truly alive are those who carry within them a stage."

No doubt Shakespeare would be astonished to discover that his plays are still being performed, let alone read, and are widely hailed as the greatest dramatic works of all time. After all, he dashed them off, two a year, with little thought beyond the next day's takings at the Globe, and whether or not they would be enough to pay the rent. They were temporary, transient pieces of entertainment, conceived and written to satisfy the particular tastes of a particular audience in a particular time and place, and definitely *not* sacred works of art to be enshrined.

This is the paradox of it all: the quickly-vanishing medium for which Shakespeare wrote—the theater—is precisely what keeps him alive and well today. In adapting his sources, his language, his characters for the stage, he transformed them into something immortal. The plays, the dramatic events that thrilled and delighted Elizabethan audiences nearly four hundred years ago, live on in the twentieth century, re-created every time an actor steps up to the footlights and begins to utter the lines of Hamlet. For as long as the theater continues, and as long as actors, directors, and producers remain committed to putting the works of the world's greatest playwright on the stage where they belong—so, too, will Shakespeare stay alive.

CHAPTER 3

SHAKESPEARE'S LEGACY

WILLIAM SHAKESPEARE

Shakespeare Revolutionized the Concept of Character

Harold Bloom

In his book *Shakespeare: the Invention of the Human*, Yale University professor Harold Bloom attributes to Shakespeare the creation of characters with comprehensive human personalities. Unlike the cartoons and caricatures used by his contemporaries, Shakespeare's characters possess vitality, inwardness, and individualized styles of speaking. Shakespeare's most popular characters in his own time and today, Hamlet and Falstaff, possess a comprehensiveness and heroic vitality, which allow both to embody life's largeness. As such, they become universal figures, Bloom asserts, who influence humanity's vision of itself. Bloom contends that our understanding of human nature, our insights into family relationships and love, our skepticism about language, our ability to laugh at ourselves, and our recognition of womanly wisdom are profoundly enlarged by such Shakespearean characters as Hamlet, Falstaff, Rosalind, and Cleopatra.

Harold Bloom is Sterling Professor of Humanities at Yale University, Berg Professor of English at New York University, and former Charles Eliot Norton Professor at Harvard. He is the author of more than twenty books including *The Anxiety of Influence*, *The Western Canon*, and *The Book of J*.

If any author has become a mortal god, it must be Shakespeare. Who can dispute his good eminence, to which merit alone raised him? Poets and scholars revere Dante; James Joyce and T.S. Eliot would have liked to prefer him to Shakespeare, yet could not. Common readers, and thankfully we

Harold Bloom, *Shakespeare: The Invention of the Human.* New York: Riverhead Books, 1998. Copyright © 1998 by Harold Bloom. Reproduced by permission of the publisher.

still possess them, rarely can read Dante; yet they can read and attend Shakespeare. His few peers—Homer, the Yahwist [the author of the oldest strand of the Pentateuch (the five books of Moses)], Dante, Chaucer, Cervantes, Tolstoy, perhaps Dickens—remind us that the representation of human character and personality remains always the supreme literary value, whether in drama, lyric, or narrative. I am naïve enough to read incessantly because I cannot, on my own, get to know enough people profoundly enough. Shakespeare's own playgoers preferred Falstaff and Hamlet to all his other characters, and so do we, because Fat Jack and the Prince of Denmark manifest the most comprehensive consciousnesses in all of literature, larger than those of the biblical J Writer's Yahweh, of the Gospel of Mark's Jesus, of Dante the Pilgrim and Chaucer the Pilgrim, of Don Quixote and Esther Summerson, of Proust's narrator and Leopold Bloom. Perhaps indeed it is Falstaff and Hamlet, rather than Shakespeare, who are mortal gods, or perhaps the greatest of wits and the greatest of intellects between them divinized their creator.

SHAKESPEARE INVENTS PERSONALITY

What do Falstaff and Hamlet most closely share? If the question can be answered, we might get inside the man Shakespeare, whose personal mystery, for us, is that he seems not at all mysterious to us. Setting mere morality aside, Falstaff and Hamlet palpably are superior to everyone else whom they, and we, encounter in their plays. This superiority is cognitive, linguistic, and imaginative, but most vitally it is a matter of personality. Falstaff and Hamlet are the greatest of charismatics: they embody the Blessing, in its prime Yahwistic sense of "more life into a time without boundaries" (to appropriate from myself). Heroic vitalists are not larger than life; they are life's largeness. Shakespeare, who seems never to have made heroic or vitalistic gestures in his daily life, produced Falstaff and Hamlet as art's tribute to nature. More even than all the other Shakespearean prodigies—Rosalind, Shylock, Iago, Lear, Macbeth, Cleopatra—Falstaff and Hamlet are the invention of the human, the inauguration of personality as we have come to recognize it.

The idea of Western character, of the self as a moral agent, has many sources: Homer and Plato, Aristotle and Sophocles, the Bible and St. Augustine, Dante and Kant, and all you might care to add. Personality, in our sense, is a Shakespearean invention, and is not only Shakespeare's greatest originality but also the authentic cause of his perpetual pervasiveness. Insofar as we ourselves value, and deplore, our own personalities, we are the heirs of Falstaff and of Hamlet, and of all the other persons who throng Shakespeare's theater of what might be called the colors of the spirit.

How skeptical Shakespeare himself may have been of the value of personality, we cannot know. For Hamlet, the self is an abyss, the chaos of virtual nothingness. For Falstaff, the self is everything. Perhaps Hamlet, in Act V, transcends his own nihilism; we cannot be certain, in that ambiguous slaughter that reduces the court at Elsinore to the fop Osric, a few extras, and the inside outsider, Horatio. Is Hamlet self-divested of all his ironies at the end? Why does he give his dying vote to the bully boy Fortinbras, who wastes soldiers' lives in a battle for a barren bit of ground scarcely wide enough to bury their corpses? Falstaff, rejected and destroyed, remains an image of exuberance. His sublime personality, a vast value for us, has not saved him from the hell of betrayed and misplaced affection, and yet our final vision of him, related by Mistress Quickly in *Henry V,* remains a supreme value, evoking the Twenty-third Psalm and a child at play with flowers. It seems odd to observe that Shakespeare gives his two greatest personalities the oxymoron we call "a good death," but how else could we phrase it?

Are there *personalities* (in our sense) in the plays of any of Shakespeare's rivals? [Christopher] Marlowe deliberately kept to cartoons, even in Barabas, wickedest of Jews, and Ben Jonson as deliberately confined himself to ideograms, even in Volpone, whose final punishment so saddens us. I have a great taste for John Webster, but his heroines and villains alike vanish when juxtaposed to those of Shakespeare. Scholars attempt to impress upon us the dramatic virtues of George Chapman and of Thomas Middleton, but no one suggests that either of them could endow a role with human inwardness. . . .

INWARDNESS

What made his art of characterization possible? How can you create beings who are "free artists of themselves," as [philosopher Georg Wilhelm Friedrich] Hegel called Shakespeare's personages? Since Shakespeare, the best answer might be: "By an imitation of Shakespeare." It cannot be said that Shakespeare imitated Chaucer and the Bible in the sense that he imitated Marlowe and Ovid. He took hints from Chaucer, and they were more important than his Marlovian and Ovidian origins, at least once he had reached the creation of Falstaff. There are traces aplenty of fresh human personalities in Shakespeare before Falstaff: Faulconbridge

PRINCE HAL AND SIR JOHN FALSTAFF

University of California professor Norrie Epstein explains in this selection why Sir John Falstaff is such an engaging Shakespearean character. Falstaff is the old, fat friend and surrogate father of Prince Hal in Henry IV, *parts I and II. When Hal becomes King Henry V, he rejects Falstaff and his other low-life friends.*

While the king [Henry IV] presides over the court at Westminster, Hal, his wayward heir, presides over the taverns and brothels, where he spends his time wenching and plotting escapades with low companions, chief among whom is Sir John Falstaff. Even those who have never read or seen a Shakespeare play have heard of Falstaff, Shakespeare's greatest comic figure. He *is* funny, but his character transcends comedy. Painfully touching and sad, he's like an aging music-hall comedian. Buffoon, braggart, coward, parasite, and wit, he eclipses everyone else when he's on stage. Why is this fat old man so enchanting? "Banish plump Jack, and banish all the world," he tells Hal. And Falstaff *does* represent earthly pleasures; he's the epitome of Merrie Old England, all roast beef, wenches, wassail, and ale. A Freudian would say he represents the pleasure principle; to a moralist, he's the seven deadly sins in human form. But he can't be confined to any categories, psychological or moral. He touches us with all the sad eagerness of an old man grasping at endless youth. Significantly, the first words Falstaff addresses to Hal in the play are, ". . . what time of day is it, lad?" To which Hal replies:

> Thou art so fat-witted with drinking of old sack, and unbuttoning thee after supper, and sleeping upon benches after noon, that thou hast forgotten to demand that truly which thou wouldst truly know. What a devil hast thou to do with the time of the day?

Hal basically belongs to two worlds, each a mirror of the other: the tipsy Falstaffian circus, where time is irrelevant, and the magisterial world of his father, where he must take his place in history.

Norrie Epstein, *The Friendly Shakespeare.* New York: Viking, 1993.

the Bastard in *King John,* Mercutio in *Romeo and Juliet,* Bottom in *A Midsummer's Night's Dream.* And there is Shylock, at once a fabulous monster, the Jew incarnate, and also a troubling human uneasily joined with the monster in an uncanny blend. But there is a difference in kind between even these and Hamlet, and only a difference in degree between Falstaff and Hamlet. Inwardness becomes the heart of light and of darkness in ways more radical than literature previously could sustain.

Shakespeare's uncanny power in the rendering of personality is perhaps beyond explanation. Why do his personages seem so *real* to us, and how could he contrive that illusion so persuasively? . . .

VITALITY

[Critics G.K.] Chesterton and Anthony Burgess both stressed Shakespeare's vitality; I would go a touch farther and call Shakespeare a vitalist, like his own Falstaff. Vitalism, which William Hazlitt called "gusto," may be the ultimate clue to Shakespeare's preternatural ability to endow his personages with personalities and with utterly individuated styles of speaking. I scarcely can believe that Shakespeare preferred Prince Hal to Falstaff, as most scholars opine. Hal is a Machiavel; Falstaff, like Ben Jonson himself (and like Shakespeare?), is rammed with life. So, of course, are the great Shakespearean murderous villains: Aaron the Moor, Richard III, Iago, Edmund, Macbeth. So indeed are the comic villains: Shylock, Malvolio, and Caliban. Exuberance, well-nigh apocalyptic in its fervor, is as marked in Shakespeare as it is in Rabelais, Blake, and Joyce. The man Shakespeare, affable and shrewd, was no more Falstaff than he was Hamlet, and yet something in his readers and playgoers perpetually associates the dramatist with both figures. Only Cleopatra and the strongest of the villains—Iago, Edmund, Macbeth—hold on in our memories with the staying force of Falstaff's insouciance and Hamlet's intellectual intensity. . . .

PRIMAL AMBIVALENCE

Primal ambivalence, popularized by Sigmund Freud, remains central to Shakespeare, and to a scandalous extent was Shakespeare's own invention. Memorable pain, or memory engendered through pain, ensues from an ambivalence both cognitive and affective, an ambivalence that we associate most readily with Hamlet but that is prepared by Shylock. Perhaps Shylock began as a farcical villain—I once believed this, but now I rather doubt it. The play is Portia's, and not Shylock's, but Shylock is the first of Shakespeare's internalized hero-villains, as contrasted with such external-ized forerunners as Aaron the Moor and Richard III. I take it that Prince Hal/Henry V is the next abyss of inwardness af-ter Shylock, and so another hero-villain, a pious and patri-otic Machiavel, but the piety and the kingly quality are mod-ifiers, while the hypocrisy is the substantive. Even so, the tenacious and justice-seeking Shylock essentially is a would be slaughterer, and Shakespeare painfully persuades us that Portia, another delightful hypocrite, prevents an atrocity through her shrewdness. One would hope that *The Merchant of Venice* is painful even for Gentiles, though the hope may be illusory.

What is not illusory is the frightening power of Shylock's will, his demand to have his bond. One surely can speak of the frightening power of Hal/Henry V's will, his demand to have his throne, and France, and absolute sway over every-one, including their hearts and minds. Hamlet's greatness, his transcending of the hero-villain's role, has much to do with his rejection of the will, including the will to avenge, a project he evades by negation, in him a revisionary mode that reduces every context to theater. Shakespeare's theatri-cal genius is less Iago than Hamlet. Iago is nothing if not critical, but he is, at most, a great criminal-aesthete, and his insight fails him utterly in regard to Emilia, his own wife. Hamlet is much the freer artist, whose insight cannot fail, and who converts his mousetrap into Theater of the World. Where Shylock is an obsessive, and Hal/Henry V an ingrate who fails to see Falstaff's uniqueness, and even Iago never quite gets beyond a sense of the injured self (his own passed-over military virtue), Hamlet consciously takes on the bur-den of the theater's mystery as augmented by Shakespeare's strength. Hamlet, too, ceases to represent himself and be-comes something other than a single self—a something that is a universal figure and not a picnic of selves. Shakespeare became unique by representing other humans; Hamlet is the difference that Shakespeare achieved. I am not suggesting that Hamlet's beautiful disinterestedness in Act V ever was or became one of Shakespeare's personal qualities, but rather that Hamlet's final stance personifies Shakespeare's

Negative Capability, as John Keats termed it. At the end, Hamlet is no longer a real personage condemned to suffer inside a play, and the wrong play at that. The personage and the play dissolve into each other, until we have only the cognitive music of "let be" and "Let it be.". . .

SHAKESPEARE'S EFFECT ON US

Before Hamlet taught us how *not* to have faith either in language or in ourselves, being human was much simpler for us but also rather less interesting. Shakespeare, through Hamlet, has made us skeptics in our relationships with anyone, because we have learned to doubt articulateness in the realm of affection. If someone can say too readily or too eloquently how much they love us, we incline not to believe them, because Hamlet has gotten into us, even as he inhabited [Friedrich] Nietzsche.

Our ability to laugh at ourselves as readily as we do at others owes much to Falstaff, the cause of wit in others as well as being witty in himself. To cause wit in others, you must learn how to be laughed at, how to absorb it, and finally how to triumph over it, in high good humor. Dr. [Samuel] Johnson praised Falstaff for his almost continuous gaiety, which is accurate enough but neglects Falstaff's overt desire to teach. What Falstaff teaches us is a comprehensiveness of humor that avoids unnecessary cruelty, because it emphasizes instead the vulnerability of every ego, including that of Falstaff himself.

Shakespeare's wisest woman may be Rosalind in *As You Like It,* but his most comprehensive is Cleopatra, through whom the playwright taught us how complex eros is, and how impossible it is to divorce acting the part of being in love and the reality of being in love. Cleopatra brilliantly bewilders us, and Antony, and herself. Mutability is incessant in her passional existence, and it excludes sincerity as being irrelevant to eros. To be more human in love is, now, to imitate Cleopatra, whose erotic variety makes staleness impossible, and certitude just as unlikely. . . .

SHAKESPEARE SAVES US FROM REDUCTIVENESS

A.D. Nuttall, one of my heroes of Shakespearean criticism, wonderfully tells us that Shakespeare was not a problem solver, and cleared up no difficulties. . . . Like [philosopher Søren] Kierkegaard, Shakespeare enlarges our vision of the enigmas of human nature. Freud, wrongly desiring to be a scientist, gave his genius away to reductiveness. Shakespeare does not reduce his personages to their supposed pathologies or family romances. In Freud, we are overdetermined, but always in much the same way. In Shakespeare, as Nuttall argues, we are overdetermined in so many rival ways that the sheer wealth of overdeterminations becomes a freedom. Indirect communication, the mode of Kierkegaard, so well expounded by Roger Poole, was learned by Kierkegaard from Hamlet. Perhaps Hamlet, like Kierkegaard, came into the world to help save it from reductiveness. If Shakespeare brings us a secular salvation, it is partly because he helps ward off the philosophers who wish to explain us away, as if we were only so many muddles to be cleared up. . . .

Focus on Family Relationships

To call Shakespeare a "creator of language," as [linguistic theorist Ludwig] Wittgenstein did, is insufficient, but to call Shakespeare also a "creator of characters," and even a "creator of thought," is still not enough. Language, character, and thought all are part of Shakespeare's invention of the human, and yet the largest part is the passional. Ben Jonson remained closer to Marlowe's mode than to Shakespeare's in that Jonson's personages also are cartoons, caricatures without inwardness. That is why there is no intergenerational contest in Jonson's plays, no sense of what Freud called "family romances." The deepest conflicts in Shakespeare are tragedies, histories, romances, even comedies: of blood. When we consider the human, we think first of parents and children, brothers and sisters, husbands and wives. We do not think of these relationships in terms of Homer and of Athenian tragedy, or even of the Hebrew Bible, because the gods and God are not primarily involved. Rather, we think of families as being alone with one another, whatever the social contexts, and that is to think in Shakespearean terms. . . .

Shakespeare's Characters Undergo Change

The wheel of fortune, time, and change turns perpetually in Shakespeare, and accurate perception of him must begin by viewing these turnings, upon which Shakespeare's characters are founded. Dante's characters can evolve no further; Shakespeare's, as I have noted, are much closer to Chaucer's, and seem to owe more to Chaucer's mutable visions of men

and women than to anyone's else's, including biblical por-
trayals or those of Shakespeare's favorite Latin poet, Ovid.
Tracing Ovid's effect upon Shakespeare in his study *The Gods
Made Flesh,* Leonard Barkan observes: "Many of the great
figures of Ovid's poem define themselves by their struggle to
invent new languages." Metamorphoses in Shakespeare are
almost always related to the playwright's endless quest to
find distinct language for every major and many a minor
character, language that can change even as they change,
wander even as they wander. Turning around, in Shakespeare, frequently takes on the traditional image of wheeling,
the wheel sometimes being Fortune's emblem of extrava-
gance: of roaming beyond limits.

Shakespeare's own audiences chose Falstaff as their favorite, even above Hamlet. Fortune's wheel seems to have little relevance to others; Falstaff is ruined by his hopeless,
misplaced paternal love for Prince Hal. Hamlet dies after a
fifth act in which he has transcended all his earlier identities in the play. Falstaff is thus love's fool, not fortune's, while
Hamlet can only be regarded as his own fool or victim, re-
placing his father surrogate, the clown Yorick. It is appropriate that the antithetical figures of Lear and Edmund both in-
voke the image of the wheel, but to opposite effects and
purposes. Shakespeare's plays are the wheel of all our lives,
and teach us whether we are fools of time, or of love, or of
fortune, or of our parents, or of ourselves.

Shakespeare Coined Fifteen Hundred New Words

Jeffrey McQuain and Stanley Malless

During the sixteenth and seventeenth centuries English vocabulary expanded rapidly as writers and scientists borrowed words from Latin and Greek, travelers introduced Italian words, and merchants added to the language Chinese, Spanish, and Persian words for various foreign products. Within this period of rapid lexical expansion, Shakespeare stands as one of the foremost creators of new words and phrases. In this selection from their book *Coined by Shakespeare*, Jeffrey McQuain and Stanley Malless explain Shakespeare's word-making practices, including changing nouns to verbs, adding suffixes to existing words, subtracting syllables from existing words, and deriving new words from proper nouns, sounds, and animals. Several entries from their dictionary are also included in this selection.

Jeffrey McQuain, a researcher for William Safire's *On Language* column in the *New York Times Magazine*, is also author of *Power Language*. McQuain and Stanley Malless, a professor of education at Simpson College in Iowa, have also coauthored *The Elements of English*.

William Shakespeare's reputation has never been greater. Almost four centuries after the playwright's death, his publications are thriving, his stage productions are multiplying, and films based on his plays are flourishing. Audiences today may view stagings of the Bard's works by more than 150 companies and festivals around the world, from a summer festival in Williamsburg, Virginia, to a full season at the recently rebuilt Globe Theatre in London. Beyond this planet, the moons that

Jeffrey McQuain and Stanley Malless, *Coined by Shakespeare*. Springfield, MA: Merriam-Webster Incorporated, 1998. Copyright © 1998 by Jeffrey McQuain and Stanley Malless. All rights reserved. Reproduced by permission.

circle Uranus have been given names of Shakespeare characters ranging from *Juliet* and *Ophelia* to *Oberon* and *Puck*. Underlining that universal success, a *Newsweek* headline at the end of 1996 nominated the playwright "Dead White Male of the Year," and *The Washington Post* named him "Greatest Genius of the Millennium," adding a rhetorical "Any questions?"

Scholarship about Shakespeare has similarly soared. A 1983 bibliography for *Henry V*, for instance, listed more than 2,000 studies of that single play, including works written in Ukrainian and Korean. Last year a CD-ROM released by Cambridge University Press, covering Shakespeare scholarship from 1990 to 1993, provided more than 12,000 entries, and "Shaksper," an electronic Shakespeare conference, now boasts more than 1,000 members worldwide. Here, however, is the first book ever to focus on the Bard's coinages.

WORDS COINED BY SHAKESPEARE

How many words has Shakespeare added to English? Guesses have ranged from a few hundred terms to more than 10,000, with the most likely estimate approximately 1,500 words. As the scholar Marvin Spevack has commented, "Shakespeare's was the period of the most rapid growth of vocabulary in the recorded history of the language." Other writers of the English Renaissance also added to the language; the dramatist Ben Jonson, for instance, is credited with such words as *analytic* and *antagonist*. But it is Shakespeare, employing more than 20,000 words in his plays and poems, whose inventiveness and creative wordplay have most widely enriched our daily vocabulary.

Bardophiles and Bardophobes alike tend to think of Shakespeare's language all too often as an unfamiliar hodgepodge, ranging from oaths like *gadzooks* (meaning "God's hooks" and referring to the nails used in the Crucifixion) and *zounds* ("God's wounds") to archaisms like *bodkin* (a type of dagger) and *forsooth* ("truly").

The Bard's creations, however, reach far beyond the odd and the obsolete. From *assassination* to *zany*, these words are encountered every day. Cracker Barrel restaurants, for instance, offer "*Traditional* Favorites," Pontiac boasts, "We Build *Excitement*," and a recipe in *The New York Times Magazine* offers the perfect "*hint:* it's what you do after you flour and before you simmer."

Shakespeare's words are current in business (*employer* and

manager, investment and *retirement*), as well as in law (*circumstantial* evidence and *foregone* conclusions) and politics (especially among those who *negotiate* or *petition*). The *advertising* world looks for new *designs* and *exposure*. Reporters profess familiarity with the word *reword*, if not with *misquote*, and activists actively use the Bard's best in phrases from "civil rights *protesters*" to "human rights *violations*." The most romantic embrace such nouns as *courtship* and *embrace*, along with *engagement* and *never-ending* love, and animal lovers love the playwright's language, from *puppy dog* to *watchdog*.

Some of Shakespeare's choice words have remained commonplace (*skim milk* and *critic*), while others remain in the dictionary though they are rarely used (*consanguineous* and *kickshaw*). Examine enough of the Bard's coinages, however, and certain patterns begin to appear. Few words, in fact, emerge from a vacuum (although some words, such as *puke,* must remain labeled "origin unknown"); the majority develop from a handful of word-making practices.

SHAKESPEARE'S WORD-MAKING PRACTICES

First and foremost is functional shift, as Shakespeare changes nouns into verbs (*film* and *champion*) or verbs into nouns (*dawn* and *scuffle*), verbs into adjectives (*hush*) or adjectives into nouns (*accused*). Another frequent practice is the adding of a prefix or a suffix to an existing word, from *eventful* to *remorseless*. Sometimes part of a word is subtracted by means of back-formation, leading to *impede* from *impediment*. Words derived from proper names proliferate, from the adjective *Promethean* to the noun *Xantippe* and the verb *pander,* derived from the name of Pandarus.

New meanings are given to old words. (To realize how meanings may change, note that *sharer* in Elizabethan times meant a stockholder in a theater company, and *housekeeper* was not a maid but a landlord of the theater building or "house.") Old words are also given new spellings by Shakespeare (*alligator*). Also frequent is compounding, the putting together of existing words, from the nouns *birthplace* and *eyeball* and the verb *undervalue,* to the adjectives *coldblooded* and *softhearted* and the adverb *downstairs*.

OTHERS' COINAGES AND REVISIONS

Since his death in 1616, Shakespeare himself has fallen subject to neologizing. In 1896, George Bernard Shaw introduced *Shakespeare* as a verb meaning "to act in a Shakespeare play." Excessive worship of Shakespeare was first dismissed in 1864 as *Shakespearolatry,* spawning *Shakespearolaters* eleven years later. In 1903, Shaw coined the simpler *Bardolaters,* based on the Middle English *Bard,* "poet," which was first popularized as a title for Shakespeare by the eighteenth-century actor David Garrick. Six years after the introduction of Shaw's word, Mark Twain attacked the *Stratfordolaters,* those who believe that Shakespeare was indeed the author of the works attributed to him. Such supporters of the Bard have also been dubbed *Shakespearites* and *Stratfordians* (as opposed to *Baconians* or *Oxfordians*), as well as Twain's dubious *Shakesperoids* for those who consider Shakespeare's words sacrosanct.

During the nineteenth century, Dr. Thomas Bowdler tried to rewrite those words. A "bowdlerized" edition, *The Family Shakespeare,* appeared in 1818, omitting "those words and expressions . . . which cannot with propriety be read aloud in the family." In this century [the twentieth], others have also rewritten the plays, ostensibly to simplify the words for modern understanding, although purists will argue that Hamlet's "Get thee to a nunnery" loses something in its translation to "Become a nun!"

Today the words of Shakespeare, coinages or not, have become fair game for advertisers and headline writers, who thrive on Shakespearean puns. As an affectionate tribute to the Bard, the cosmetics company Avon took its name from the river that flows through Stratford; less endearing is "Bubble, bubble, no toil or trouble" from a current commercial for a contact lens solution, echoing the Three Witches in *Macbeth.* Among recent headlines, "Now Is Winner of Our Disc Content" in *Variety* plays upon the opening line of *Richard III,* and "Most Unkindest Glut of All" in *The Chronicle of Higher Education* lightly twists Mark Antony's words from *Julius Caesar.*

A WORD OF CAUTION

Shakespeare's words, no matter how they may be reshaped, continue to move and to inspire. In using this dictionary of the Bard's originals, though, keep in mind one word of warning: it is extremely difficult to say with absolute certainty that a given individual invented a particular word. Coinages typically arise out of speech and are not documented for some time after they are actually introduced. The problem of identifying the precise origin of a word is magnified when dealing with manuscripts from the Renaissance period, when new words might not have been written down until long after they were coined and manuscripts often were not accurately dated. Nobody can say for certain that a word credited to Shakespeare will not be found someday in an older manuscript by another writer, but for the present, the Bard is the earliest known user of the words given here and can, for the time being at least, be considered their originator. . . .

A SELECTION OF SHAKESPEARE'S NEW WORDS AND PHRASES

BE-ALL AND END-ALL (noun) everything, the complete form or result

As soon as the title character of *Macbeth* contemplates assassinating King Duncan, he begins to fear the consequences of the murder. "That but this blow," Macbeth vainly wishes, "Might be the *be-all and the end-all.*"

Here is a noun phrase invented by Shakespeare and overworked in modern use to the point of cliché. . . .

Shakespeare never uses the phrase again after its first appearance. When a word or phrase occurs just one time in a writer's works, scholars refer to it as a *hapax legomenon,* a formal Greek term that means "something said only once." Shakespeare may well have felt that his own, singular use of this peculiar expression would be its *be-all and end-all,* but if that was his expectation, time has proved him very wrong. . . .

BUZZER (noun) one that makes a buzzing sound; gossiper or noisemaker

King Claudius in *Hamlet* tells his wife, Gertrude, that young Laertes has secretly returned from France after the killing of his father, Polonius, by Hamlet. Claudius fears that gossip will falsely label him the murderer, now that Laertes has "*buzzers* to infect his ear."

Buzz (like *bump*) is an onomatopoeic word, inspired by the sound of a bee or other winged insect. Earlier in *Hamlet,* Polonius informs the Prince of the arrival of the Players. Hamlet, irritated to hear news that he already knows, responds impatiently with "*buzz, buzz!*" Shakespeare uses *buzzer* to mean "gossiper," a sense that is now obsolete (though the noun *buzz* can still be used to mean "gossip," as in "the latest *buzz* from Hollywood"). In 1606, a contemporary of Shakespeare was the first to use *buzzer* more literally to indicate a noisy insect in "Swarms of busy *buzzers.*"

Buzzer was an uncommon word in any sense until relatively recently, when it developed what is now its usual meaning, "an electric signaling device that makes a buzzing sound." Nowadays the noun is most familiar in the sports world, where basketball players throw up last-second desperation shots "at the *buzzer*" (that is, just before the buzzer ending a period sounds), and on television game shows, in which contestants likewise race against time to "beat the *buzzer.*" In the nineteenth century, however, thieves had their own specialized use for the term; a pickpocket who stole from women was known as a "wire," while the pickpocket who sought out male victims was a *buzzer.* . . .

DICKENS (noun) devil; deuce

No, this coinage does not come from the name of Charles Dickens, the novelist who lived two centuries after Shakespeare. Instead, it appears first in *The Merry Wives of Windsor*, when Ford asks Mistress Page about Falstaff's servant, and she replies, "I cannot tell what the *dickens* his name is."

Exactly how *dickens* came to used this way isn't known. Perhaps the term comes from a familiar form of the name *Dick.* Another possibility is suggested in the *Oxford English Dictionary*, which points out that "*Dickens* as a surname was probably also already in existence."

What is clear is that Shakespeare is using *dickens* as a euphemism for *devil.* It appears only once in Shakespeare's work, but others have since emloyed it to soften their own cursing. Set phrases using this term have developed, including "The *dickens* take you!" and "Go to the *dickens!*" It can appear in compliments as well, as in "You cute little *dickens!*". . .

HINT (noun) occassion or oportunity; suggestion or clue

The noun *hint* appears first in *Othello*. Explaining to the Duke how he won Desdemona's love by telling her of his adventures, Othello says, "It was my *hint* to speak", meaning his opportunity. Later in the same speech, when Othello describes Desdemona's encouraging reaction to his life's story, the word denotes "suggestion or slight indication": "She thank'd me, / And bade me, if I had a friend that lov'd her, / I should but teach him how to tell my story, / And that would woo her. Upon this *hint* I spake."

Hint is thought to be derived from Middle English *hent*, "the act of grabbing or seizing," with the underlying connection that a *hint* provides or suggests an opportunity to be seized. *Hint* is used by Shakespeare eight times, but only as a noun, never as a verb. (The verb *hint* was not recorded until 1648.) In the 1900 novel *Lord Jim,* Joseph Conrad used the noun to celebrate "that faculty of beholding at a *hint* the face of his desire and the shape of his dream, without which the earth would know no lover and no adventurer." Nowadays "suggestion" has overtaken "opportunity" as the word's usual meaning, occurring in connection with everything from hair coloring ("a *hint* of gray") to politics ("a *hint* of scandal").

One of the most common constructions in which the noun is found, "take the *hint,*" appears first in *Antony and Cleopatra.* When the defeated Antony advises his attendants to leave him, he tells them to "take the *hint* / Which my despair proclaims." Robert Frost used the phrase repeatedly in a 1939 essay about poetry: "How many times it thundered before Franklin took the *hint!* How many apples fell on Newton's head before he took the *hint!*" Later in the same essay he added, "The greatest thing in family life is to take a *hint* when a *hint* is intended—and not to take a *hint* when a *hint* isn't intended.". . .

JADED (adjective) worn out; made dull or sated

About to be slain by a commoner, the Duke of Suffolk claims relation to the royal family in *2 Henry VI.* "King Henry's blood", the Duke says of himself, "The honorable blood of Lancaster, / Must not be shed by such a *jaded* groom." The passage echoes an earlier reference in the same scene to the *jades,* the dragons that pull the chariot of night across the sky. Shakespeare uses *jaded* as a word of contempt, but in modern use the adjective more strongly connotes exhaustion or world-weariness.

These uses are unrelated to the English word for a green gemstone. (That stone gets its name from a Spanish term meaning literally "loin stone," ultimately based on the Latin word for "flanks," from the belief that the gem cures renal disease.) Shakespeare's adjective *jaded* likely comes instead from a Middle English noun meaning "mare"—specifically a "hack" or worn-out horse—which later, by extension, came to denote a disreputable woman, a flirtatious girl, and even a dragon of the night's chariot.

Jaded is also the past participle of the verb *jade,* and Shakespeare uses this form of the word twice. Antony's friend Ventidius boasts in *Antony and Cleopatra* that the previously unbeaten Parthian army has been "*jaded* out o' th' field", or driven off like the inferior horses known as *jades*. The word can also mean "ridden or treated like a jade; made a fool of," as in *Henry VIII,* when the Earl of Surrey is infuriated by the arrogance of the red-robed Cardinal Wolsey and cannot bear "To be thus *jaded* by a piece of scarlet.". . .

PROMETHEAN (adjective) of or like Prometheus; daringly original or creative

From the proper name of the Titan Prometheus comes the adjectival form *Promethean,* which appears in English for the first time in Shakespeare's works. Its earliest appearance is in *Love's Labor's Lost,* in Berowne's tribute to women: "From women's eyes this doctrine I derive: / They are the ground, the books, the academes, / From whence doth spring the true *Promethean* fire." Perhaps more famous is its use in *Othello,* when the Moor hesitates to kill Desdemona because, he says, "I know not where is that *Promethean* heat / That can thy light relume."

Shakespeare's audience would presumably have recognized these allusions to Prometheus. According to Greek mythology, Prometheus created the human race out of clay and taught mankind how to use fire, which he had stolen from the gods. He was punished by Zeus by being chained to a rock and subjected to eternal torture.

Prometheus and its derivatives have had a long and varied career in English, denoting everything from a moth (*promethea*) to an element in the periodic table (*promethium*). The association of Prometheus with fire led to the use of *Promethean* in the nineteenth century to denote a type of match, employed by Charles Darwin to impress the natives during his voyage to South America: "I carried with me some *Promethean* matches, which I ignited by biting." The association of Prometheus, the mythical creator of mankind, with creativity has also made the word *Promethean* a favorite of poets. William Wordsworth wrote in an 1834 poem about a portrait of a woman, "Look at her, whoe'er / Thou be that . . . / Hast loved the painter's true *Promethean* craft."

PUKE (verb) to vomit

In *As You Like It,* Shakespeare chooses Jaques's memorable "All the world's a stage" monologue as the unlikely place to record the first use of the verb *puke*. According to Jaques, men and women play many parts in this life, and the first act or age is that of the infant "Mewling and *puking* in the nurse's arms."

This verb first attested in Shakespeare is of obscure origin; it could be related to the Old English *spiwan* ("to spew or spit") and to the modern German verb with the same meaning, *spucken.* The less common noun form did not appear until nearly a century and a half after Shakespeare's use of the verb. (Prince Hal's mention of "*puke*-stocking" in the second act of *1 Henry IV* refers to a dark sock; according to *A Shakespeare Glossary* by C.T. Onions, this attributive use of *puke* comes from a noun for a "superior kind of dark woollen cloth.")

Puke was a perfectly respectable word for the first two centuries of its use, and it can be found in the works of some preeminent English writers. Lord Byron used it in his comic masterpiece, *Don Juan:* "There's not a sea the passenger e'er *pukes* in, / Turns up more dangerous breakers than the Euxine." Modern writers and speakers, however, tend to avoid it in formal contexts, preferring *throw up* or the straightforward *vomit* when the subject is unavoidable. The more adventurous may choose from among dozens of slangy synonyms, from "toss your cookies" to "lose lunch." *Puke* lives on, though, and it continues to develop new senses. Tom Dalzell's *Flappers 2 Rappers* lists 1960s terms for newly arrived American soldiers in Vietnam, including "newby, *puke*, or turtle."

PUPPY DOG (noun) a young domestic canine; a lovable dog

In *King John*, the illegitimate Philip belittles a warrior's threat to fight as ineffectual words. He ridicules the fighter as one who "Talks as familiarly of roaring lions / As maids of thirteen do of *puppy-dogs!*" The compound also appears in *Henry V.* Again occurring in the context of war, the word is used by Fluellen to demean Captain Macmorris as one who "has no more directions in the true disciplines of the wars . . . than is a *puppy-dog.*"

Puppy in the sense "a small dog" was first recorded in the fifteenth century. It derives from Middle French *poupée*, "doll, toy," which in turn can be traced to Latin *pupa*, "girl, doll." Related English words include *pupil* and *puppet.* The earliest recorded use of *puppy* in its current sense, "a young dog," is in Shakespeare's *Two Gentlemen of Verona*, when the servant Launce ruefully speaks of his dog as "one that I brought up of a *puppy.*" Shakespeare also uses a related compound in *The Tempest*, when Trinculo meets Caliban and laughs "at this *puppy*-headed monster.". . .

SEAMY SIDE (noun) underside with stitches showing; degraded aspect or part; sordid side

Emilia, Iago's wife in *Othello,* uses a metaphor from sewing to help her berate the "scurvy fellow" she says must have turned Othello against Desdemona (unaware that the villain she describes is her husband). When Iago warns her about being overheard by the wrong people, she fires back with "O fie upon them! Some such squire he was / That turn'd your wit the *seamy side* without, / And made you to suspect me with the Moor." Literally "the underside of a garment," *seamy side* also connotes roughness, unpleasantness, or degradation.

The noun *seam* dates back to at least the twelfth century and is probably related to *siwian,* the Old English word for "sew." Shakespeare uses *seam* and related words only four times throughout his works. In addition to *seamy,* which appears for the first time in *Othello,* the noun *seam* occurs in *Pericles* and *sempster* (for *seamster*) in *The Two Noble Kinsmen.*

By the middle of the nineteenth century, the cliché "the *seamy* side of life" found its way into contemporary usage, as illustrated by the British writer Thomas Carlyle, who commented in 1865 on "the splendid and the sordid, the *seamy side* and the smooth, of Life at Cirrey." *Seamy* now serves as a synonym of *sordid* or *degraded;* its original connection to the *seams* of clothing is now largely forgotten.

Shakespeare Perfected Dramatic Blank Verse

George T. Wright

Shakespeare composed his plays in a combination of prose and poetry. While some of the poetic lines are rhymed, much of the poetry in the plays is blank verse, unrhymed iambic pentameter. (An iamb is a metrical foot in which an unstressed syllable is followed by a stressed syllable, like "ălóne." Iambic pentameter means there are five of these iambic feet per line: "Whăt oft wăs thoúght bŭt né'er sŏ wéll ĕxpréssed.") According to University of Minnesota professor George T. Wright, Shakespeare's mastery of blank verse is revealed in the variations he introduces to exemplify changing emotions, internal conflict, rivalry, rage, or reconciliation. Wright also considers the implications of Shakespeare's verse tactics, contending that regular meter suggests cosmic order and deviations from it reveal the troubling anxieties and presumptive willfulness of individual characters.

Wright has written *Hearing the Measures: Shakespearean and Other Inflections*, *The Poet in the Poem*, and several articles on Shakespeare's metrical practices including "The Play of Phrase and Line in Shakespeare's Iambic Pentameter" and "Shakespeare's Poetic Techniques."

The principle that Shakespeare mainly follows in his dramatic verse (and it holds for his poems, too) is that virtually every moment must be marked by some significant change in form, emotional temperature, point of view, or other stylistic or dramatic feature. The feet in a line must be varied; the lines themselves must differ from one another in syntactical structure, in force, in metrical patterning, in rhetorical character; scenes and parts of scenes must develop in

George T. Wright, *Shakespeare's Metrical Art*. Berkeley: University of California Press, 1988. Copyright © 1988 by The Regents of the University of California. Reproduced by permission.

different ways. As a consequence of this requirement, the emotional or imaginative heat of a passage or a scene is constantly changing. Characters in earlier plays, from *Gorboduc* to [Christopher] Marlowe, often carry on their blank verse discourse in an emotional monotone; their intensity may not vary a degree in five minutes; and all the characters onstage are likely to be equally hot or cold, though only one of them is talking. But Shakespeare, from the beginning of his career, relishes that root situation of drama—two persons in dispute—and uses it, not, as his predecessors did, to present long wooden debates between persons in official contention, but to dramatize the deep and sometimes sudden anger and animosity that harrow political and domestic life. . . .

THE RHYTHM OF RAGE

Some of the most memorable moments in his plays involve characters in sudden rages or recognitions:

> O thou dissembling cub: what wilt thou be
> When time hath sow'd a grizzle on thy case?
>
> *(Twelfth Night)*

> Why, *yet* he doth deny his prisoners
> *(I Henry IV,* italics added here and below)

What gives some such speeches, especially later ones, their notably furious sound is that much of the anger seems concentrated in single words. This is an important Shakespearean metrical technique: one extremely forceful syllable (or sometimes two) may come to dominate a whole line and destroy any appearance of stress-equality among its strong syllables:

> *Love?* His affections do not *that* way tend *(Hamlet)*

> What *beast* was't then
> That made you *break* this enterprise to me? *(Macbeth)*

Sometimes the strongly stressed syllables rise out of a long series of fairly strongly stressed ones, like suddenly dramatic peaks in a range of mountains:

> Villain, be sure thou *prove* my love a whore;
> Be sure of it. Give me the *ocular* proof,
> Or by the worth of mine eternal soul,
> Thou had'st been better have been born a *dog*
> Than answer my wak'd wrath! *(Othello)*

> Bloody, bawdy *villain!*
> Remorseless, treacherous, lecherous, kindless *villain!*
> *(Hamlet)*

The suddenness of Richard III's anger at Lord Hastings is a classic case:

> *Hastings.*   If they have done this deed, my noble lord—
> *Gloucester.*   *If?* thou protector of this damned strumpet,
>   Talk'st thou to me of *Ifs?* thou art a *traitor,*
>   *Off* with his *head*   *(Richard III)* . . .

Rage is not the only emotion that heats up the verse; fear, love, remorse, revenge, anguish, relief, or joy may have the same effect. Any emotion, discovery, perception, any change in understanding, may find voice in a quickened language. Certain characters—Hotspur, Capulet, Shylock, and Coriolanus, among others—are distinguished by their readiness to passion, by the rapidity with which they rouse when crossed. Certain plays—especially *Romeo and Juliet, Coriolanus,* and *King Lear*—are constructed in series of flare-ups. Indeed, Shakespeare's plays, in comparison with others of the period, are notable for the way they usually follow carefully managed arousals and diminutions of dramatic intensity. . . .

THE METRICAL LINE REFLECTS CHARACTER RELATIONSHIPS

Compared with his predecessors on the English stage, or even with nondramatic English poets, Shakespeare evidently had a more highly tuned sense of differences, of oppositions between classes, worlds, manners, and personalities. He must have felt more variously and profoundly the elemental dramatic situation: that two significantly different forces meet and contend on the stage, that the contending forces are not just disembodied voices or interests or titles (King, Queen, First Lord, Second Lord, and so on) but distinctive personalities with different views of the world. Shakespeare's scenes almost always (perhaps always) involve some sharp contrast between positions, genders, ages, or interests, and what Shakespeare is recognizing as he thrusts them on the stage is that life unfailingly pits opposites against each other, perpetually places us in relations of contrast (male-female, elder-junior, master-servant) with virtually all the other persons we meet (English against French, sons against fathers, friends against friends), and that we are always working out such relationships. Shakespeare carries these oppositions further and deeper than any other playwright, but he develops them with a feeling for nuances and subtleties that no mere dialectician could contrive. Most of his predecessors are simple and childlike in comparison; it is Shakespeare whose psychological penetration and layered plotting give a dense life-likeness to the bare dramatic principle of opposition.

Something similar goes on within the iambic pentameter line. And here again it is Shakespeare's feeling for variety and contrast that helps to make his lines smoother and more melodious than most others—and much more dramatic. First, the line can appear in many more forms than earlier, with almost infinite internal variation, and unpredictably enjambed or endstopped. The sentence and the line, like human personalities, may meet in inexhaustible combinations, never immediately repeating exactly the same rhythms or the same larger units. The line becomes a miniature of the infinitely various and variously polarized larger world. In meter, even the syllables compete, cannot avoid doing so, as two people in the world cannot avoid the necessity that requires them to parry and thrust, to be and act differently toward one another, even in love. No relation is static, without rivalry or differently based understanding. For all of this the relations of meter are emblematic, for well-made iambic pentameter lines satisfy our appetite for perpetual adjustment, that need of ours to dwell more on some stressed syllables than on others, more on some unstressed syllables than on others, just as in speech we single out, especially at moments of emotion, the words and syllables that seem in a stretch of words to carry the heart of our feeling, but do so only in patterned conjunction with the rest.

In effect, meter looks at least two ways: toward the sentence, which it both reflects and rivals, and toward the larger world of character and character, whose relations it mirrors—ultimately, to that world's structure of authority and resistance, and of inner selves and outer layers of reality (other person, family, party, state, cosmos). Of course, iambic pentameter is used also in nondramatic poetry, but it has a special relevance to drama which Shakespeare seems instinctively to have exploited.

The structure of oppositions that we find in meter is also a structure of linkages. The meter of Shakespeare's dramatic verse, though it looks looser than the iambic pentameter of traditional later poets, is only carrying further than they do the principle of linkage that is inherent in iambic (or, more broadly, in metrical) poetry, and it does so largely as an appropriate means of recognizing the linkages inherent in drama. If earlier Tudor poets had a sharpened sense of the foot as linking two syllables and of a line as linking five feet, Shakespeare's dramatic verse keeps stressing the way other elements of line, speech, scene, and play are shared. The straddling trochee links two phrases, the shared line links two voices speaking two phrases, syllables share feet, phrases share lines. On a larger scale, speeches share scenes, characters share the stage, audience and actors share the theater, play and reality share the world. The plays often make the point that power and love, splendid in themselves, result in disaster when they are too narrowly and selfishly pursued. An aesthetic and an ethic of mutual dependence and obligation are deeply inscribed in Shakespeare's drama. More intently than in most nondramatic verse, we hear the elements of Shakespeare's language exercising a force on each other, one element compelling another to respond. Actor and audience, text and reader, require each other. Syllable, foot, phrase, line, speech, scene, even play invites or challenges its companion, its cohort, its rival, its reader to supply its needed complement. Not that there is usually any obvious principle of pairing that one can follow through the verse. In this respect, as in others, Shakespeare's art eludes excessively symmetrical arrangement. . . .

REGULAR METER SUGGESTS ORDER

If Shakespeare's verse system stands generally but persistently for the principles of opposition and linkage which are felt everywhere in his work, it may also reflect and affirm more particularly the world order that underlies Shakespeare's writing. We have already noted that eighteenth-century prosodists came to identify strict observance of metrical propriety with moral probity; in effect, they saw iambic pentameter as a social institution in the contemporary social order. In Renaissance iambic pentameter, something of the same force is felt: meter appears to be identified, however, with cosmic rather than social order, and departures from it (Macbeth's extreme agitation is a useful example) represent efforts of energetic human individuality to burst out of the confining framework ("But let the frame of things disjoint"). In the plays, in the sonnets, in the metrical line, we can trace a powerful continuing struggle between authority and rebellion, between law and impulse, between divine order and the beauty of particular evasions of it. . . .

DEVIATIONS REVEAL ANXIETY

Meter stands (but not simply) for some such principle as order, truth, certainty, completeness—doom; deviation is energy, mischief, trouble—and beauty. Even when the character's perception of truth is clouded, the calmness of the
perceiving perhaps steadies the beat. But in the later plays at
least, from *Hamlet* on, hardly anyone is perfectly steady. As
the characters are flawed, so is the meter, which betrays
them, either by its genuine metrical deviations or by the con-
tinual divergence of line and phrase. As [critic Marina] Tar-
linskaja observes, heroic characters, or those who are trying
to appear so, are likely to speak in a more regular line. The
broken line testifies to anxiety, either immediate, in the present situation (Othello, Macbeth, Leontes), or ingrained in the
character (Iago, Coriolanus, the Queen in *Cymbeline*) or universal, in the nature of intense human experience (Isabella,
Lear, Prospero), or some strong combination of these. Not all
segmented lines express anxiety or distress, but the pervasive
use of them (in Shakespeare's manner) seems to, and the return to the full line at the end of a final scene (like the return
of the full court) marks the resumption of order. As [W.H.]
Auden puts it in the commentary on *The Tempest* which he
assigns a scrubbed-up Caliban to deliver: "the sounded note
is the restored relation". . . .

THE FATE OF IAMBIC PENTAMETER AFTER SHAKESPEARE

To put it all too blatantly: iambic pentameter in the Renaissance symbolizes a cosmic order that limits human aspiration; human experience can be heard in the counter-
rhythm; together, the two compose a system of creative
departures from metrical authority. That is, in any verse the
ground-rhythm is likely to represent whatever human experience is tested by—in Renaissance verse the divine order, in
eighteenth-century verse the social order. But in nineteenth-
century verse, as conceptions of human existence begin to
change, the old orders seem shaky, and what now appears
as the ground of reality—either the natural world, in which
we participate, or our perceptions and experiences of it—
can no longer be appropriately expressed by a traditional
line whose measure is neither one thing nor the other—
looser than the beat, tighter than the phrase.

As a consequence, Romantic poetry begins to move in the
two contrary directions indicated by its separating compo-

nents—toward the wholly accentual and toward the wholly phrasal. The beat of the former easily becomes identified with the physical rhythms of Nature—the sea, the moon's phases, the pulse—against which no intelligible countercurrent can contend. In free verse, on the other hand, the phrase achieves the apotheosis toward which the whole metrical development of Renaissance poetry had been carrying it. At first subservient to the line, then in late Shakespeare and late Milton becoming a powerful rival authority to the verse line, then dammed for a century at the line-ending by the couplet of Dryden and Pope, the phrase at last breaks free to *become* the line. The liberation is an exuberant one, but the price it pays is formidable: loss of tension, loss of inflection, loss of the power to represent symbolically in the verse itself the defining oppositions and linkages of life in English.

Yet even this is not the end of the story. Iambic pentameter survives in twentieth-century verse in a dwindling remnant of superb practitioners, most notably [W.B.] Yeats, [Wallace] Stevens, [T.S.] Eliot, [John] Berryman, [Robert] Lowell, [Philip] Larkin, [Richard] Wilbur, [Stuart] Merrill, [Anthony] Hecht, and [John] Hollander, for some of whom, as for the poets of the Renaissance, the regular meter once again seems a figure for normal life, departure from it a trope for individual eccentricity, manner, or mania. Rarely, however, does "normal life" mean anything so grand as "the cosmic order"; and departures from it usually have the effect, at best, of elegant pathos rather than high tragedy. The world has changed, and iambic pentameter, whose deepest connections must always be to contemporaneous world-views, has had to change with it. Verse at present, which always somewhat blindly choose its forms, has made other arrangements for mirroring the world, and iambic pentameter is no longer conspicuous on the program.

Shakespeare's Works Inspire Songs, Operas, and Orchestral Arrangements

Ellen T. Harris

University of Chicago professor Ellen T. Harris dis-
cusses in this selection the variety of composers who
have been inspired by Shakespeare's works. Actual
songs from Shakespeare's comedies have been set to
music with great success, but the sonnets pose technical difficulties which have made them less popular
as song-texts, Harris explains. Opera treatments of
entire plays, on the other hand, have proven exceptionally successful. Verdi's *Otello*, for example, is a
superb treatment of Shakespeare's *Othello*. Like most
opera treatments, Verdi's work concentrates on the
characters, their passions, and the central conflicts in
the play rather than on wordplay, philosophy, or societal background. Mendelssohn's Overture to *A Midsummer Night's Dream* is the archetypal orchestral
treatment of a Shakespeare play. It is developed on
the sonata principle, in which contrasting themes are
presented in opposing keys, developed, then recapitu-
lated. Musical treatments of Shakespeare's works offer both analysis and interpretation, Harris explains.

Harris is the author of *Handel and the Pastoral
Tradition*, *Handel As Orpheus: Voice and Desire in the
Chamber Cantatas*, and *Henry Purcell's Dido and
Aeneas*.

Composers have long been inspired by the beauty of Shakespeare's lyrics, by the strength of his drama, and by the richness of his characters. Shakespearean song settings abound,

Ellen T. Harris, "Shakespeare in Music," *William Shakespeare: His World, His Work, His
Influence*, volume III, edited by John F. Andrews. New York: Charles Scribner's Sons,
1985. Copyright © 1985 by Charles Scribner's Sons. Reproduced by permission.

operas proliferate, and instrumental music continues to be composed. . . .

SHAKESPEARE AND SONG

There are three sources of lyrics for Shakespearean songs: the songs from the plays, other verses from the plays, and the Sonnets. The words that composers have most often been drawn to set are the song lyrics. These texts were meant for musical settings, and by and large they are constructed according to the principles for sung text summarized by [poet] John Dryden in the preface to his libretto for the opera *Albion and Albanius* (1685). The lyrics are short; they use rhymes (sometimes double); they contain short verses (sometimes of different lengths); they use frequent stops; they often contain a refrain; and they emphasize open vowel sounds rather than "clogg'd consonants." The songs from *The Tempest,* for example, fit this description well. Ariel's song of freedom follows all of the stipulations:

> Where the bee sucks, there suck I;
> In a cowslip's bell I lie;
> There I couch when owls do cry.
> On the bat's back I do fly
> After summer merrily.
> Merrily, merrily shall I live now
> Under the blossom that hangs on the bough.

Note especially the lack of consonants at the ends of lines. In the song of Juno and Ceres, Shakespeare additionally employs double rhyme: plenty/empty, growing/bowing, and farthest/harvest. Ariel's two magical songs—"Come unto these yellow sands" and "Full fathom five"—also follow the pattern described by Dryden. The former especially contains irregular verse lengths; both songs have refrains. In fact, all of the most popular song texts follow the criteria later set down by Dryden; and these songs, not surprisingly, come predominantly from the comedies.

The Sonnets have never been as popular for song texts. Only Richard Simpson (d. 1876) set them all; his compositions, however, remain largely unpublished. Mario Castelnuovo-Tedesco set thirty-two (Op. 125, 1944–1945), all of which remain unpublished, and Dmitri Kabalevsky set ten (1953–1954); but Igor Stravinsky's setting of "Music to hear, why hear'st thou music sadly" (1953) is the only sonnet setting generally known. The reason for the relative paucity of musical settings of the Sonnets, as for the popularity of the lyrics from the plays, lies in their construction. They have long verses of even length (decasyllabic); the verses are often constructed with enjambment; and most importantly, the language is elevated. The fixed form combined with a consummate use of language creates a poem finished in itself with no need of music for completion. In this, the Sonnets and lyrics are diametrically opposed. Compare, for example, the following verses.

> Blow, blow, thou winter wind,
> Thou art not so unkind
> As man's ingratitude:
> Thy tooth is not so keen,
> Because thou art not seen,
> Although thy breath be rude.
> Heigh-ho, sing heigh-ho, unto the green holly.
> Most friendship is faining, most loving mere folly:
> Then heigh-ho, the holly.
> This life is most jolly.   *(As You Like It)*

> Then let not winter's ragged hand deface
> In thee thy summer ere thou be distilled.
> Make sweet some vial; treasure thou some place
> With beauty's treasure ere it be self-killed.   *(Sonnet 6)*

The first, one of the most popular song texts, contains simple images in short, uneven verses that can be molded without damage into different musical lengths and shapes. The second, which remains unset except by Simpson, contains difficult imagery in long sweeping lines that resist conformity to regular musical structures or metrical patterns.

Composers have occasionally chosen texts from outside the repertoire of the lyrics and Sonnets. For example, the first few verses of "I know a bank" from *A Midsummer Night's Dream*, with their vibrant depiction of a flower-covered shore, have been popular. Similarly, the lines from *The Merchant of Venice* beginning "How sweet the moonlight" have frequently been set; music is directly invoked in these lines: "Here we will sit and let the sounds of music / Creep in our ears." In other cases, passages have become well known as song texts because of the popularity of a single setting. For example, Ralph Vaughan Williams set Prospero's magnificent speech from *The Tempest*, "The cloud-capp'd tow'rs", and Joseph Haydn set Violet's lines beginning with "She never told her love" from *Twelfth Night*. All four of these excerpts are, like the Sonnets, in decasyllabic verse and also, like the Sonnets, are used rarely as song texts. . . .

OPERATIC TREATMENTS

Operatic composers are not drawn to Shakespeare's plays by the beauty of the language or the structure of the verse. What is primary is the emphasis on strong passions, characters, and conflict. . . .

Operatic treatment of Shakespeare began during the Restoration with the literary adaptations written by Sir William Davenant *(Macbeth)* and John Dryden *(The Tempest).* In these works, called "dramatic operas" or "semi-operas," the torso of a play was used to sustain a succession of musical interludes combining chorus, solo song, and dance. Often the texts for the musical sections did not derive from the original play but were newly written for the adaptation. For example, the music written by Henry Purcell for *The Fairy Queen* (1692), which is based on *A Midsummer Night's Dream,* occurs in discrete sections placed at the ends of the five acts. These are meant to serve as entertainments for Titania and are sung by her fairies. The main characters—the young lovers, Theseus, Hippolyta, Titania, and Oberon—do not sing, and Purcell never sets any of Shakespeare's own words.

In the middle of the eighteenth century, three all-sung Shakespearean operas were performed in London: Veracini's *Rosalind* (1744) . . . and two operas by John Christopher Smith, *The Fairies (A Midsummer Night's Dream,* 1755) and *The Tempest* (1756). All were heavily altered. In the late eighteenth century, however, the number of Shakespearean operas on the Continent exploded concurrently with the rise of realistic comic opera. In the era of *The Barber of Seville* and *The Marriage of Figaro,* it is no surprise to find *The Merry Wives of Windsor* suddenly an extremely popular libretto. At the same time, multiple settings of *Romeo and Juliet* heralded the romantic era. None of the late-eighteenth-century operatic versions of these two plays, however, is as important as the adaptations that followed in the nineteenth century: for example, Charles Gounod's *Roméo et Juliette* (1867), Otto Nicolai's *Die lustigen Weiber von Windsor* (1849), and Verdi's *Falstaff* (1893).

Shakespearean operas have continued to be written in the twentieth century. In addition, particularly fine adaptations have been created for the Broadway stage: Richard Rodgers' *The Boys from Syracuse* (*The Comedy of Errors,* 1938), Cole Porter's *Kiss Me Kate* (*The Taming of the Shrew,* 1948), and Leonard Bernstein's *West Side Story* (*Romeo and Juliet,* 1957).

All operatic adaptations follow similar principles in revising the original texts. Since words, because of the sustenance of sound and musical repetition, take much longer to sing than to speak, a play must be cut. This is done in a number of ways. First, subsidiary plots and characters are reduced or eliminated, allowing attention to be focused on the main story. Second, scenes based on punning or wordplay are omitted, as they lose most of their effectiveness when set to music. Third, long philosophical texts are also eliminated; lacking passion or drama, they are deemed inappropriate to musical setting. Fourth, the societal background is usually eliminated; the passion displayed is thus intended to be independent of both time and place. Finally, where it is not already the main focus, the love interest is increased. . . .

VERDI'S *OTELLO*

Perhaps no composer has ever succeeded in using music to illustrate dramatic change or conflict as well as Giuseppe Verdi. Verdi set three Shakespearean operas: *Macbeth* (1847), *Otello,* and *Falstaff (The Merry Wives of Windsor).* The last two were set to librettos by [Arrigo] Boito; the first had a libretto originally coauthored by Francesco Maria Piave and Andrea Maffei that was substantially revised by Piave for the Parisian performances in 1865. The first two of Verdi's Shakespearean operas illustrate many of this composer's techniques.

In his libretto for *Otello,* Boito omits the opening act in Venice and closes with Othello's death, cutting out Lodovico's final speech with its reference to Venice. . . . Thus, the societal frame is, as usual, eliminated. This also precludes our knowing the characters before their arrival on Cyprus. In Shakespeare's first act, for example, the audience hears negative reports of Othello from his enemies, sees him placing trust in an avowed foe, and witnesses the Moor's self-assurance and pride in the scene before the senate. Without this introduction, Othello becomes a less complex character. In the opera, Iago can no longer precipitate an action that is logical and natural, given the weaknesses of the other characters; rather, he becomes the sole cause of all the destruction. It is noteworthy that Boito described Othello and Desdemona in purely positive terms; he wrote not that Othello is destroyed by his own jealousy, but that he is "the supreme victim of the tragedy and of Iago."

In Shakespeare's play, then, Othello is much spoken about before he enters, and when he appears, he is on stage throughout the scene, speaking first with Iago and afterward with Brabantio. There follows the scene before the senate. In the second act, when Othello arrives safely on Cyprus, he has three speeches, exits, and reenters to signal the start of festivities. In the opera, on the other hand, the action begins with the storm raging and with Othello's ship foundering off the coast of Cyprus. We learn nothing of Othello. After his entrance, he sings three lines and then exits. His text is not only brief but uninformative:

Rejoice! The mussulman's pride is buried in the sea;
The glory is ours and heaven's!
First our arms, and then the storm defeated him.

In a spoken drama this would undoubtedly be insufficient as an introduction of character. In *Otello*, however, it becomes through the music an absolute depiction of Othello's character.

Just as Boito omitted the first act of the play, Verdi eschews the formal introduction or overture to the opera and—like Boito with the storm—begins musically in *medias res* with no sense of boundary, beginning, or shape. The opening music has no tonal stability, rhythmic coherence, or melodic continuation. Only when Othello enters does the turbulent music settle into a single tonality, bringing closure for the first time. Othello is thus depicted as hugely powerful, for it is he who brings cadence and coherence to the music. His style changes perceptibly, however, when he comes under Iago's spell.

In Act II, when Othello is first affected by Iago's scheming insinuations, he is angered and upset. He says goodbye to a "tranquil mind," "to fame," and "to glory" in music that is still firmly in one key, its rhythms martial; but more and more throughout the brief aria the chromaticism that Verdi uses to characterize Iago emerges in the accompaniment. By the end of the act, Othello as we have known him is indeed lost. In his duet with Iago it is hard at first to make out Othello's part, for so much of it is in monotone. Only when Iago enters do we understand, for it is he who has the melody—who literally is calling the tune. Othello's accompaniment is ultimately fitted to Iago's melody, illustrating clearly that he has lost control over the music and thus over himself and the situation.

By the third act Othello cannot regain his composure even

while alone. Just as in the first act his presence was felt musically even after his exit (by the sustenance of his key), Iago's presence is now musically apparent even in his absence. In "Dio! mi potevi scagliar!" [Oh God, my most powerful afflictor] (the speech beginning with IV. ii. 48 of Shakespeare), Othello cannot muster a tune but is reduced again to a monotone; he is accompanied, moreover, by Iago's chromatically descending lines, and, worst of all, he maintains no tonal stability.

The changes in Othello's character as depicted musically lead directly to the crisis of the last act. Boito omits the scenes in which Othello questions Emilia about Desdemona's conduct, Desdemona complains of Othello's behavior to Emilia and Iago, and Desdemona and Emilia talk about marriage before Desdemona goes to bed. They would have been overly long and tedious in musical settings, as well as unnecessary, for the use of economical musical gestures has been more than adequate to depict both Desdemona's constancy and Othello's change of character.

An actress performs in Macbeth.

In the play, Desdemona retires at the end of Act IV, and Act V begins with the scene in which Roderigo sets upon Cassio and is killed. Only then is a return made to Desdemona's bedchamber for Othello's entrance and his speech beginning "It is the cause, it is the cause, my soul." In the opera Desdemona retires at the beginning of the last act: she says her prayers—as added by Boito—and goes to bed. Immediately Othello enters. There has been no act break, no intermediary scene. In real time Desdemona could not possibly have fallen asleep. But in the opera Othello does not speak. His previous solos have illustrated his degradation, and this musical style would be wholly inappropriate to the text of his soliloquy. Thus, he remains mute. Verdi has the orchestra alone depict his thoughts, taking the drama up without any assistance from the sung word. This orchestral interlude also accounts for the elapsed time that would allow Desdemona to fall asleep. Here Verdi uses musical closure, not like Gounod to expand time, but to contract it; and the interlude takes less time than the various actions would take in reality.

In the play, Othello muses both on the necessity of killing Desdemona and on the method. He draws an analogy between putting out the light and quenching Desdemona's life spark. Drawn to her sleeping form, he kisses her. The relationship of this speech to Verdi's interlude can readily be noted in the specific stage directions in the score: "Othello appears at the threshold . . . he comes forward . . . he lays a scimitar on the table . . . he stands before the candle undecided whether to extinguish it or not . . . he looks at Desdemona . . . he extinguishes the candle . . . he goes to the bed," and so on. But more important, when Othello leans over to kiss Desdemona, Verdi recalls the music that accompanied the culmination of the love duet of the first act (added by Boito and fashioned out of text from Shakespeare's Act I), where the lovers also kiss. The repetition of this motive signifies not only their kiss, but also their great love, evoking the time when Othello was a different person.

This so-called kiss motive returns once more at the very end of the opera after Othello has stabbed himself. Before he dies, he leans over to kiss Desdemona. Although his last word—*bacio* (kiss)—is given in the libretto, Othello is not given a note for the last syllable, and its omission in the score is Verdi's final stroke of characterization. Othello's inability to complete the obvious cadence, to complete a gesture that had served to characterize him definitively upon his entrance, reveals that not even in death, not even for a moment, can he return to his former glory. . . .

ORCHESTRAL TREATMENTS

Nineteenth-century symphonic music tends to create dramatic effects through the use of strong conflict, usually followed by a resolution of some kind. The sonata principle, which underlies the majority of nineteenth-century orchestral works, relies on this concept: two contrasting themes in opposing key areas are presented (exposition); developed through expansion, fragmentation, juxtaposition, and other means (development); and then restated in the home key (recapitulation). The dramatic character of this form seems to have made composers consider it a perfect vehicle for representing a stage drama: the compositional structure follows dramatic form nicely (statement, crisis, denouement), but it also gives the composition an absolute form apart from any programmatic meaning. . . .

Felix Mendelssohn's Overture to *A Midsummer Night's Dream* (1826) is the locus classicus of the genre. It begins with four sustained chords in a cadential progression played by wind instruments. The pattern of closure makes an odd opening; Mendelssohn begins with an end. The restatement of these chords at the end of the overture, however, clarifies their meaning. They are the gateway in and out of fairyland; their cadential structure thus marks a boundary between two worlds. This effect is heightened by having the chords follow a harmonic progression typical of sacred music, which connotation, along with the soft dynamic, adds something of the supernatural, something *misterioso,* to the passage. Like [Benjamin] Britten in his later opera, Mendelssohn carefully closes off the fairy world from everyday life.

The fast, staccato, and sprightly first theme, played by the violins, introduces the fairies. Its forward motion is twice interrupted by single chords played by the winds, reminiscent of the opening chords. One has the sense of an intrusion through the gateway by humankind, and, in confirmation of this, the first theme group ends with the regal theme for full orchestra that can later be associated with Theseus and Hippolyta, whose actions precipitate the ensuing disturbance in the wood. (Their wedding is the cause of Titania and Oberon's presence near Athens and the rustics' decision to produce a play; moreover, Theseus' edict leads to the lovers' decisions to enter the wood.)

After a long transition, the second theme group represents the various mortals as they appear: first the lovers, then the rustics with a theme including an ass's bray, and finally Theseus and Hippolyta combined with the calls of their hunting horns. Needless to say, this compresses the action of the play into a very reduced time frame. The development section thus plays on the urgency of action by pitting the fairy theme against the horn calls, seemingly depicting

Puck's speech beginning "My fairy lord, this must be done with haste, / For night's swift dragons cut the clouds full fast, / And yonder shines Aurora's harbinger".

At the end of the development a downward scale passage is played four times. It is unrelated to any previous material, but the return of the lovers' theme immediately after this section connects it to them. . . .

The recapitulation begins with a repetition of the gateway chords. We must now be at the reawakening—first of Titania, and then, after a much shortened transition, of the lovers, and finally of Bottom. Only then is the listener transferred to Theseus' palace; the royal couple's theme is thus delayed until the end of the recapitulation. In the coda the fairies return; and just before the end, the theme of Theseus and Hippolyta returns as if from a great distance. The overture closes with the gateway chords.

The major themes in this overture all represent specific characters, and the drama of the music resides in the clarity of their conflicting natures. Not all Shakespearean plays, to be sure, contrast kings and clowns, fairies and mortals, but in *A Midsummer Night's Dream*, Mendelssohn is able to depict the action by manipulating his themes in traditional ways. For example, Theseus and Hippolyta do not appear in the development, during which the fairy magic is worked; but their hunting horns represent the impending dawn. In the recapitulation their theme is delayed until each of the characters affected by fairy magic awakens. It is rare to find an absolute musical form so successfully wedded to a specific dramatic program. . . .

From the setting of Shakespeare's words in songs, to the operatic reworkings of the dramas, to the wordless orchestral representations of the characters and themes, musical transformations of Shakespeare abound. In some cases composers have been drawn to the melody and rhythm of the verse itself; in other cases composers have been inspired by the dramatic conflict and passion of the plays. In all the most successful adaptations, the music is not mere accompaniment to Shakespeare, but analysis and interpretation; and listening to a good musical setting of Shakespeare enables us to learn something about the original.

Shakespeare's Works Influence Poets, Novelists, and Dramatists

John Gross

John Gross introduces his book *After Shakespeare* by reflecting on the number of writers who have been inspired by Shakespeare's works. Poets have responded to individual characters and to the author himself. Novelists have adapted his themes and appropriated his lines. Dramatists have interrogated his values while paying tribute to his power as an exemplary dramatic model. This selection from John Gross's book includes both his introductory remarks and several short works drawn from his anthology of literary responses to and uses of Shakespeare.

John Gross is a writer, reviewer, and theater critic. He was editor of the *Times Literary Supplement* from 1974 to 1981 and served on the staff of the *New York Times* from 1983 to 1988. He is the author of *The Rise and Fall of the Man of Letters* and *Shylock: A Legend and Its Legacy*, and he is editor of the Oxford books of *Aphorisms, Essays, Comic Verse*, and *The New Oxford Book of English Prose*.

No writer has served as such a powerful source of inspiration for other writers as Shakespeare. (Well, Homer perhaps, if there was a Homer.) No writer has attracted such widespread and varied comment. There is a Shakespeare literature which extends far beyond formal Shakespeare criticism or Shakespeare scholarship—a literature which the present anthology sets out to represent.

That his influence should have proved as fertilizing as it has is not just a gauge of his greatness. It also reflects the particular nature of that greatness, or some of its major aspects. He wrote for a popular medium. He created strong dramatic structures. Most of his characters, whatever their internal complexities, are readily grasped in outline. His plays have a mythic quality, and more than any other form of fiction myths lend themselves to borrowing and adaptation.

There are many works which can lay some claim to being Shakespearian by virtue of taking over Shakespearian plots or motifs. Sometimes the debt is unspoken though obvious: *West Side Story* is a celebrated example. Sometimes it advertises itself, as in [Ivan] Turgenev's *A Lear of the Steppes* or [Nikolai] Leskov's *Lady Macbeth of Mtsensk.* . . .

Influence, in principle, is something which flows, and influences which can be demonstrated in detail are usually (though not always) influences which haven't been properly digested. Conversely, the most profound influences are commonly the most diffuse. Countless writers have been roused or liberated by Shakespeare, among them some of the greatest—[Aleksandr] Pushkin, for example, or [Herman] Melville; and what they have mostly learned have been new ways of organizing their experience, of unlocking their full powers of expression, of relating public themes to the life of the individual. Such lessons are broad and general, and in the works which embody them Shakespeare tends to be everywhere and nowhere in particular.

In my choice of imaginative writing, then, I have confined myself to material which is specifically Shakespearian—which builds on individual characters and plays, or on the life and personality of Shakespeare himself. That still leaves a great deal to be getting on with.

POETS, NOVELISTS, AND DRAMATISTS RESPOND

First, the poets. Many of them have been moved to write poems about Shakespearian characters, from Herman Melville on Falstaff to Ted Hughes on Prospero and Sycorax. Sometimes they have extended the stories of such characters backwards or forwards in time; sometimes they have offered a different view of them from the one presented in the plays; sometimes they have used them to furnish dramatic parallels—[Heinrich] Heine on Jessica and Lorenzo—or as a vehicle for their own preoccupations. In this department, . . . *Hamlet* predominates to what many may feel is a disproportionate degree, in literary terms, but one which accurately

reflects the play's status as a cultural icon. Certainly the
Hamlet poems are impressive both for their quality and their
international range: [Boris] Pasternak and [Bertolt] Brecht
on the prince himself, [Arthur] Rimbaud and Marina Tsve-
tayeva on Ophelia, [Constantine] Cavafy on Claudius,
Miroslav Holub on Polonius, the Polish poet Zbigniew Her-
bert's 'Elegy of Fortinbras'.

There are also a few poems devoted to entire plays. Derek
Walcott packs a good deal of feeling about *Othello* into 'Goats
and Monkeys', and some of the finest verse ever inspired by
Shakespeare can be found in [W.H.] Auden's 'commentary
on *The Tempest*', *The Sea and the Mirror*. . . .

Nor are poems with an admixture of Shakespeare limited
to poems on Shakespearian themes. In the right context, a
single borrowed phrase or allusion can set up strong rever-
berations—Prufrock averring that he is not Prince Hamlet [in
T.S. Eliot's "The Love Song of J. Alfred Prufrock"], Seamus
Heaney quoting Captain MacMorris [in "Traditions"]; and although trying to write in 'Shakespearian' is an obvious dead
end, poets as far apart as [John] Milton and Emily Dickinson
have successfully integrated Shakespearian echoes into their
own work. Such echoes abound in prose, too; and the entries
in John Ruskin's extraordinary 'Brantwood Diary' show how
deeply they can become woven into an individual psyche.

From the eighteenth century onwards, novelists have
drawn on Shakespeare in a variety of ways. They have adapted
his themes, drawn parallels with him (one whole section of
[Feodor] Dostoevsky's *The Devils* is entitled 'Prince Hal'), used
him as a cultural reference-point (as in *Brave New World* [by
Aldous Huxley]), or for ironic contrast, or to create atmos-
phere (as in [Charles] Dickens—although Dickens's Shakespearian references often have a thematic point as well). *Hamlet* hovers on the edge of the first great self-reflexive novel,
Tristram Shandy [by Laurence Sterne], and provides one of
the central themes in the first great *Bildungsroman*, [Johann
Wolfgang von] Goethe's *Wilhelm Meister*. . . .

In the theatre, the most notable Shakespearian offshoots
have been largely negative, much more so than in poetry or
the novel. This apparent paradox is easily explained. As an
exemplar of dramatic art, a model of how things should be
done, Shakespeare's influence has been immense, especially
on foreign dramatists—on [Friedrich von] Schiller, on the
[Aleksandr] Pushkin of *Boris Godunov*, on Victor Hugo, on

[Henrik] Ibsen in his early historical plays, on scores of others. But to get too close to his actual subject-matter (or, for an anglophone playwright, his actual language) is to invite being scorched by the comparison. A few intrepid spirits have tried—the Georgian poet Gordon Bottomley in his verse-plays about King Lear's wife and the early life of Lady Macbeth, for instance—but almost the only neo-Shakespearian plays with any life in them are anti-Shakespearian in spirit, or at any rate (since they pay implicit tribute to his power) hostile to his values: *Ubu Roi* [by Alfred Jarry], [Bertolt] Brecht's *Coriolan*, Aimé Césaire's *Une tempête*, [Eugène] Ionesco's *Macbett*, the cynical revision of *King John* by Friedrich Dürrenmatt. Tom Stoppard's *Rosencrantz and Guildenstern are Dead* stands somewhat apart, however: it is a witty interrogation of *Hamlet* rather than an outright lampoon.

Perhaps the most striking feature of the imaginative writing which derives from Shakespeare is the amount of it devoted to Shakespeare himself. Beginning with Ben Jonson's tribute in the First Folio, he has inspired a number of notable poems. The most Shakespeare-saturated of great novels, *Ulysses* [by James Joyce], is preoccupied with the man rather than the work. Story-tellers as different as [Rudyard] Kipling and Anthony Burgess offer us equally plausible Shakespeares; and the fascination of the portraits they paint is a tribute not only to his greatness, but also to the fact that we know so much about him (since we have the plays) and so little, that he is forever just eluding our grasp. In the most effective modern play in which he figures, Peter Whelan's *The Herbal Bed*, he establishes a forceful presence by remaining out of sight: he is the man living next door of whom we almost catch a glimpse. . . .

Some of the most stirring written reactions to Shakespeare have come from artists in other fields who have adapted his work to their own medium—[Louis Hector] Berlioz, for example, or the Russian film director Grigor Kozintsev. Among other categories, I have been especially tempted to concentrate on rulers and politicians. Not only do they offer, between them, some rich contrasts. Their involvement with Shakespeare also underlines the extent to which, over the centuries, he has continued to play an active political role—recruited by warring parties, cited by rival ideologues, sometimes transcending social divisions, sometimes reinforcing them. He has been enlisted for propaganda purposes, and used as a refuge from propaganda; and he has a knack of showing up at fateful historical moments. At the end of the nineteenth century, he was being read on Devil's Island by Alfred Dreyfus. Seventy-five years later, he was being read on Robben Island by Nelson Mandela. . . .

I hope that my selection will at least give a fair idea of the extent to which Shakespeare has been, like Falstaff, the cause of wit in others—and not only wit, but poetry, creative fantasy, and searching reflection as well. . . .

MATTHEW ARNOLD'S "SHAKESPEARE"

> Others abide our question. Thou art free.
> We ask and ask—Thou smilest and art still,
> Out-topping knowledge. For the loftiest hill,
> Who to the stars uncrowns his majesty,
>
> Planting his steadfast footsteps in the sea,
> Making the heaven of heavens his dwelling-place,
> Spares but the cloudy border of his base
> To the foil'd searching of mortality;
>
> And thou, who didst the stars and sunbeams know,
> Self-school'd, self-scann'd, self-honour'd, self-secure,
> Didst tread on earth unguess'd at.—Better so!
>
> All pains the immortal spirit must endure,
> All weakness which impairs, all griefs which bow,
> Find their sole speech in that victorious brow.

• • •

CHARLES DICKENS'S *DAVID COPPERFIELD*

'Then it was that I began, if I may so Shakespearianly express myself, to dwindle, peak, and pine.[1] I found that my services were constantly called into requisition for the falsification of business, and the mystification of an individual whom I shall designate as Mr. W. . . . This was bad enough; but as the philosophic Dane observes, with that unusual applicability which distinguishes the illustrious ornament of the Elizabethan Era, worse remains behind!'[2]

Mr. Micawber was so very much struck by this happy rounding off with a quotation, that he indulged himself, and us, with a second reading of the sentence under pretense of having lost his place.

[1] "dwindle, peak, and pine" (*Macbeth* I. iii)

[2] "This bad begins, and worse remains behind" (*Hamlet*, III. iv)

• • •

JAMES JOYCE'S *FINNEGANS WAKE*

The main Shakespearian borrowings in *Finnegans Wake* are structural rather than ornamental. In particular, *Hamlet* is used to reinforce the family patterns in the book, the conflicts between parents, children and siblings. But there are also a multitude of secondary echoes. Virtually all Shakespeare's works have their titles transformed into Joyce's nocturnal dialect—Miss Somer's nice dream, All Swell That Aimswell, the Smirching of Venus, measures for messieurs, kingly leer . . . "The Rape of Lucrece" is elongated into a ripping rude rape in his lucreasious togery. And most of the works yield broken or distorted quotations. One passage conjures up a sense of desolation through its references to *Macbeth*, for instance:

. . . Yet's the time for being now, now, now.

For a burning would is come to dance inane. Glamours hath moidered's lieb and herefore Coldours must leap no more. Lack breath must leap no more.

Shakespeare himself frequently appears in the pages of the *Wake*, along with the legends surrounding him. His name—whether through the circumstances of the dream that is being narrated, or because Joyce saw him as a rival—is often given a derisory twist. He resurfaces as 'shaggspick', 'Shikespower', 'sheepskeer', 'Scheekspair' (a pair of buttocks), even as 'Shopkeeper' (with a glance, perhaps, at the nation of shopkeepers from which he sprang). But he is also, most memorably, the godlike, world-creating 'Shapesphere'—though even here Joyce can't resist citing him as a precedent for his own incessant wordplay: 'As Great Shapesphere puns it.'

Shakespeare's Works Invite Compelling Reworkings

Martha Tuck Rozett

Shakespeare reworked old stories in his plays, and a plethora of contemporary artists are reworking Shakespeare's plays to suit their own purposes, explains University of Albany professor Martha Tuck Rozett. In this selection from her book *Talking Back to Shakespeare*, Rozett comments on four writers whose works "talk back" to Shakespeare. Tom Stoppard's pivotal 1966 play *Rosencrantz and Guildenstern Are Dead* interrogates *Hamlet* by shifting the focus to three minor characters, Rosencrantz, Guildenstern, and the Player. Martiniquean writer Aimé Césaire transforms *The Tempest* into *A Tempest*, his 1969 drama depicting colonialist stalemate. Ann-Marie MacDonald's 1988 play *Goodnight Desdemona (Good Morning Juliet)* and Jane Smiley's 1991 novel *A Thousand Acres* are both feminist transformations which, in quite different ways, save female characters (Desdemona, Juliet, and King Lear's evil daughters Goneril and Regan) from their Shakespearean fates: premature death.

Rozett is also author of *The Doctrine of Election and the Emergence of Elizabethan Tragedy* as well as numerous articles and reviews on Shakespeare and related subjects which have appeared in *Shakespeare Quarterly, Renaissance Drama, Shakespeare Bulletin*, and other publications.

The prefix *re* has assumed a prominent place in contemporary Shakespeare criticism. The plays are represented, reproduced, and reinvented by legions of readers, actors, directors, writers and academics, who regularly find new ways of re-

Martha Tuck Rozett, *Talking Back to Shakespeare*. Urbana, IL: Associated University Presses, 1994. Copyright © 1994 by Associated University Presses. Reproduced by permission.

thinking the body of work we continue to refer to as "Shakespeare." This process is hardly new. F.E. Halliday's chapter headings in his 1957 book *The Cult of Shakespeare* provides a witty rundown on the fortunes of Shakespeare from the 1630s onward. "Shakespeare Eclipsed" gave way to "Shakespeare Reformed," and thence to "Shakespeare Refined," "Shakespeare Restored," "Shakespeare Celebrated," "Shakespeare Fabricated," "Shakespeare Eviscerated," "Shakespeare Incorporated," "Shakespeare Commemorated," "Shakespeare Disintegrated," and onward into the early twentieth century, culminating with "Shakespeare Reintegrated." Since the 1950s Shakespeare Reintegrated has become Shakespeare interrogated, psychoanalyzed, and politicized. . . .

The plays have also been transformed—some would say debased—through parodies, travesties, and burlesques, enough to fill hundreds of volumes, but many of them ephemeral and unpublished. The transformations that are of most interest to contemporary readers, however, are those that, in Alan Sinfield's words, "appropriate and confront the Shakespeare myth" in one way or another. . . .

TOM STOPPARD TALKS BACK TO SHAKESPEARE

Rosencrantz and Guildenstern Are Dead [by Tom Stoppard] is a brilliantly conceived synchronic transformation that turns Hamlet inside out, as the Player remarks: "We keep to our usual stuff, more or less, only inside out. We do on stage the things that are supposed to happen off. Which is a kind of integrity, if you look on every exit being an entrance somewhere else". Shakespeare's language is frequently consigned to the stage directions and to the periphery of scenes. Both Stoppard and [Charles] Marowitz were in effect objecting to the "centrality" of Hamlet the character. By literally moving him offstage, Stoppard was challenging the authority of standard readings of *Hamlet* and asking his audience why we have always considered Hamlet the play's most honest, intelligent, and interesting character (all problematic terms). Just as [Lillie] Wyman brought Gertrude to center stage and invented some new scenes for her, so Stoppard gives the so-called "minor characters," Rosencrantz and Guildenstern and the Player, the stage time, introspective monologues, and star turns that belong to the protagonist. . . .

The Hamlet of *Rosencrantz and Guildenstern Are Dead* seems remarkably uninteresting, perhaps because we know exactly what he is going to say, whereas Rosencrantz and Guildenstern and the Player are constantly surprising us with their meandering mock-philosophical speculations, their non sequiturs, and their witty wordplay. Hamlet, in contrast, seems humorless, intimidating, incomprehensible, a nuisance. When Claudius sends Rosencrantz and Guildenstern to seek out Hamlet after the closet scene they are understandably nervous, since from their perspective he is an unpredictable madman, who, as Rosencrantz cautions, "might be violent". And when Stoppard has them revert to their Shakespearean language in order to communicate with him or Claudius or Gertrude, we know they are playing roles, acting their parts in "a trying episode" that they don't pretend to understand. "What's he doing?" they keep asking one another, as they warily watch Hamlet go through the motions of his role in dumb show. For without Shakespeare's language, Hamlet is no longer the great tragic poet; he is merely "Walking" or "Talking to himself."

Stoppard's final act takes place on shipboard, playfully filling in the gaps left by this offstage scene in *Hamlet*. Rosencrantz and Guildenstern read the letter to the King of England and discover that they are taking Hamlet to England to be killed; thus, unlike their counterparts in *Hamlet*, they have an opportunity to examine the ethical implications of their position. But they are players, their parts are "written" and cannot be changed:

> *Guil* (*broken*): We've travelled too far, and our momentum has taken over; we move idly towards eternity, without possibility of reprieve or hope of explanation.

Moments later, they read the second letter, the one that substitutes their names for Hamlet's. Now they know they are going to die, but instead of rising to the occasion like tragic figures, they are paralyzed, resentful, puzzled:

> *Ros:* Who'd have thought that we were so important?

> *Guil:* But why? Was it all for this? Who are we that so much should converge on our little deaths? (*In anguish to the* PLAYER:) Who are we?

This, Stoppard suggests, is the secular modern alternative to Hamlet's serene knowledge that "the readiness is all." It remains for the Player, ever the authoritative voice, to respond "You are Rosencrantz and Guildenstern. That's enough". But it isn't, at least not for Guildenstern, who finally asserts himself and turns on the Player, in an effective variation on the "To be or not to be" speech.

> I'm talking about death—and you've never experienced that. And you cannot act it. You die a thousand casual deaths—with none of that intensity which squeezes out life . . . and no blood runs cold anywhere. Because even as you die you know that you will come back in a different hat. But no one gets up after death—there is no applause—there is only silence and some second-hand clothes, and that's death—

The players play at death, enacting the deaths of Rosencrantz and Guildenstern in England; the Player dies *"tragically; romantically."* Whereas Rosencrantz enjoys and applauds the show, Guildenstern continues to struggle with language that is unequal to the reality it attempts to grasp:

> No . . . no . . . not for us, not like that. Dying is not romantic, and death is not a game which will soon be over. . . . Death is not anything . . . death is not. . . . It's the absence of presence, nothing more . . . the endless time of never coming back . . . a gap you can't see, and when the wind blows through it, it makes no sound. . . .

For Rosencrantz, death is a relief; his last words, before he disappears, are "I don't care. I've had enough." Guildenstern, however, is still wondering about causality in life: "There must have been a moment, at the beginning, where we could have said—no. But somehow we missed it." Then he, too, is gone, with a philosophical, "Well, we'll know better next time," and the play reverts to Shakespeare's language, with the Ambassador announcing that Rosencrantz and Guildenstern are dead. The last lines are Horatio's speech offering to explain "how these things came about". But Stoppard's talking back has all along questioned the assumption that events can be explained, have meanings, make sense. From the mysterious suspension of the laws of probability in the coin-flipping sequence to the arbitrariness of Rosencrantz and Guildenstern's deaths, he has challenged the "special providence" that explains and somehow justifies the fall of a sparrow in Hamlet. Hamlet died confident that Horatio could report him and his cause aright. Stoppard's Rosencrantz and Guildenstern inhabit a world that renders such reports impossible. . . .

AIMÉ CÉSAIRE'S *A TEMPEST*

A Tempest [by Aimé Césaire] follows the sequence of scenes in Shakespeare's play more closely than any of the other transformations of the sixties. . . .

The only new scene—that is, a scene without a counterpart in Shakespeare's play—is a dialectical encounter between Caliban, "a black slave," according to the cast list, and Ariel, "a mulatto slave." This occurs at the beginning of act 2, right after a scene that corresponds to act 1, scene 2, in which the dialogue between Caliban and Prospero has been expanded significantly. Caliban rejects "the name given me by hatred" and chooses to be called X instead (following a Black Muslim practice), to draw attention to the way his name "has been stolen". His first word in the text, repeated throughout, is "Uhuru!" (Swahili for independence), a word that Prospero does not understand. When Caliban and the obedient servant Ariel are alone together, Ariel tells his "brother" that "we both want our freedom—only our methods are different." He has come "on my own" to warn Caliban that Prospero "is planning horrible acts of revenge" and to convince him that "you aren't the stronger, you'll never be the stronger". Caliban's contempt for what he calls Ariel's "Uncle Tom patience" is transparent; Ariel responds that he does not believe in violence, which meets with more scorn. Césaire used Ariel to represent an optimistic belief that the oppressor can and will change and "acquire a conscience" through the power of patience, love, will power, and dreams. Caliban, by contrast, says he would choose death over humiliation and injustice. . . .

Césaire's reworking of the final scene of *The Tempest* explicitly questions the psychological validity of Shakespeare's comic resolutions in which characters leave the "green world" behind and return to "civilization" to resume their former lives. Ignoring Gonzalo's warning that Caliban is "a hardened criminal," Prospero says expansively, "Draw near, Caliban. What say you in your own defense? Take advantage of my good humor. Today, I feel in a forgiving mood". Caliban angrily rejects his overture, but Prospero persists: "In spite of everything I'm fond of you, Caliban. Come, let's make peace. We've lived together for ten years and worked side by side. . . . We've ended up by becoming compatriots!" Caliban understands his master better than Prospero understands himself: he predicts that Prospero won't go back to Europe because, "You're just an old colonial addict, that's what you are!" Prospero experiences a characteristically Shakespearean moment of recognition: "For it is you who have made me doubt myself for the first time." He turns to the nobles and tells them that he will remain on the island: "My fate is here: I shall not run from it." When everyone else has left the stage he turns to Caliban and says

> And now Caliban, it's you and me!
> What I have to tell you will be brief:
> Ten times, a hundred times, I've tried to save you,
> above all from yourself.
> But you have always answered me with wrath and venom,
> like the opossum that pulls itself up by its own tail
> the better to bite the hand that tears it from the darkness.
> Well, my boy, I shall set aside my indulgent nature
> and henceforth I will answer your violence
> with violence!
> *(Time passes, symbolized by the curtain's being lowered halfway and reraised. In semi-darkness Prospero appears, aged and weary. His gestures are jerky and automatic, his speech weak, toneless.)*
> PROSPERO: Odd, but for some time now we seem to be over-run with opossums. Peccarys, wild boar, all of the unpleasant animals! But mainly opossums. With those eyes! And the vile grin they have! It's as though the jungle was laying siege to the cave. . . . But I shall stand firm . . . I shall not let my work perish! *(Shouting.)* I shall protect civilization! *(He fires in all directions.)* They're done for! Now, this way I'll be able to have some peace and calm for a while. But it's cold. Odd how the climate's changed. Cold on this island . . . Have to think about making a fire . . . Well, Caliban, old fellow, it's just us two now, here on the island . . . only you and me. You-me . . . me-you! What in the hell is he up to? *(Shouting.)* Caliban! *(In the distance, above the sound of the surf and the chirping of birds, we hear snatches of Caliban's song.)* FREEDOM HI-DAY, FREEDOM HI-DAY!!

And on this note Césaire's *A Tempest* ends, its Caliban unvanquished and still aspiring to freedom, its Prospero locked in a self-destructive embrace with an other who has become part of himself. It is not at all clear that Caliban has triumphed; nor, however, has he been defeated. The colonialist stalemate persists. . . .

ANN-MARIE MACDONALD REINVENTS SHAKESPEARE

More recently, Shakespeare's tragic women have also invited revisions that challenge the rules of genre. Ann-Marie MacDonald's *Goodnight Desdemona (Good Morning Juliet)* and Jane Smiley's *A Thousand Acres*, two . . . recent transformations, raise the question "What unhappy endings?" that is the logical corollary to "What happy endings?" Who says that Juliet, Desdemona, Cordelia, Goneril, and Regan have to die—and die in these particularly violent ways—at the ends of their respective plays? How might we begin to reinvent the lives of women characters who are so much a part of our literary (and popular) culture according to less rigid notions about tragic causality and closure? . . .

Goodnight Desdemona (Good Morning Juliet) tackles these issues head-on, from an explicitly feminist perspective. First produced in Toronto in 1988, it was subsequently revised and won Canada's Governor General's Award for Drama in 1990. This Shakespeare offshoot is a time-travel fantasy that pokes fun at the foibles of academia. Its protagonist is Constance Ledbelly, a pathetically unself-confident university lecturer laboring over a thesis entitled "*Romeo and Juliet* and *Othello*: The Seeds of Corruption and Comedy." Constance is not alone in her inclination to see *Romeo and Juliet* as "comedy gone awry, when a host of comic devices is pressed into the blood-soaked service of tragic ends." Like the students quoted in Chapter 1 (albeit in more florid language), she finds herself exclaiming "O Othello, O Tragic Man, stop your ears against the false yapping of that cur, Iago". As Constance sits in her office, reading aloud from her thesis, an ingenious academic argument emerges:

> what if a Fool were to enter the world of both "Othello" and "Romeo and Juliet"? Would he be akin to the Wise Fool in "King Lear"?: a Fool who can comfort and comment . . . the Fool is conspicuous by his very absence, for these two tragedies turn on flimsy mistakes—a lost hanky, a delayed wedding announcement—mistakes too easily concocted and corrected by a Wise Fool.

In a preposterous parody of textual scholarship, Constance announces:

> I postulate that the Gustav Manuscript, when finally decoded, will prove the prior existence of two comedies by an unknown author; comedies that Shakespeare plundered and made over into ersatz tragedies!

Suddenly a "Warp" effect pulls her into her office wastebasket, Alice-in-Wonderland style, and into the *Othello* world; this is MacDonald's adaptation of the time-travel strategy of introducing a traveler from the present into the closed system of a complete text. Unlike the other transformations I have been discussing, *Goodnight* calls attention to and enacts its own interventions, by having as its protagonist the author, or unwitting agent, of change, rather than one of

Shakespeare's characters. Thus, when Constance finds herself in the middle of *Othello*, she impulsively interrupts the dialogue and "*plucks the handkerchief from IAGO's hose and hands it to OTHELLO.*" As Othello "*proceeds to bind and threaten IAGO*" she realizes with horror: "I've wrecked a masterpiece. I've ruined the play, / I've turned Shakespeare's 'Othello' to a farce".

When Desdemona enters, it becomes immediately clear that her character has undergone a change. . . . She proves herself to be just as gullible and violent as her husband, once Iago succeeds in convincing Desdemona that Constance is that most transgressive of female knowledge-seekers, a witch, and a seductress, besides.

In the final burst of swordplay and confusion with which the scene ends, Constance narrowly escapes being skewered by Desdemona as the "Warp" effect transports her to Verona. The Constance of act 3, scene 1 has somehow lost her skirt and enters wearing "*long johns, boots and tweed jacket*" as the duel between Tybalt and Mercutio is getting under way. Constance "*tackles*" Romeo just as he "*is about to fatally intervene in the sword fight,*" and together they knock Tybalt and Mercutio apart. She thus transforms *Romeo and Juliet* by preventing the action from veering off into tragedy. Predictably, she is mistaken for a "boy"; thinking fast, she rechristens herself Constantine. In a burst of assertive speech-making Constantine does what many readers long to do: she announces that "young Juliet and Romeo have wed . . . and so you fellows should shake hands." Amazingly, they do. In an ironic re-vision of Shakespeare's quintessential love story, Juliet and Romeo have tired of one another after "one hot swift night," and Romeo goes off "to find the lovely Greek boy Constantine" to whom he has taken a fancy. Juliet, meanwhile, confesses to her nurse that she's ready to "die of tedium" and prays to the god Hymen to "Make me a maid again!" Comic gender-confusion follows at the Capulets' masked ball (now Romeo and Juliet's wedding party); Juliet, like her husband, is attracted to Constantine, and in a private colloquy with "him" she reveals her conviction that love is inherently tragic: "the readiness to die doth crown true love". Juliet's passion for death, evidently, is her comic obsession, an obsession from which Constance will try to free her.

The play degenerates into silliness and confusion from

this point on, and though it would be tempting to see this as MacDonald's comment on the improbable complications and mistaken identities of *Othello* and *Romeo and Juliet*, parody for its own sake threatens to overwhelm the play's feminist agenda. MacDonald regains control of the action at the very end, when Constance finally asserts herself, and delivers a long scolding oration to both Juliet and Desdemona:

> I've had it with all the tragic tunnel vision around here. You have no idea what—life is a hell of a lot more complicated than you think! Life—real life—is a big mess . . . Desdemona, I thought you were different: I thought you were my friend, I worshipped you. But you're just like Othello—gullible and violent. Juliet, if you really loved me, you wouldn't want me to die. But you were more in love with death, 'cause death is easier to love. . . .

Because Constance has emerged from the crucible of experience a stronger, more self-confident woman and scholar, she is able to empower Juliet and Desdemona to rewrite their fates, to open up and renegotiate their endings. . . .

JANE SMILEY'S *A THOUSAND ACRES*

Set in Iowa farm country in 1979, the novel [*A Thousand Acres*] reenacts Shakespeare's *King Lear*, as narrated by Ginny, the oldest of landowner Larry Cook's three daughters. In translating the *King Lear* story to another time and place, Smiley rewrites our experience of the play and its cultural accretions by inventing a past for her Goneril, Regan, and Cordelia to provide the kinds of explanations for their personalities and behavior that contemporary liberal social theory would endorse. Ginny (Goneril) and Rose (Regan) inhabit a patriarchal culture that permits fathers to abuse their daughters and then channels these young women into early marriages where their success as wives derives from their fertility. In Smiley's transformation of *King Lear*, the perspective of the sympathetically and realistically portrayed older sisters frames and defines the readers' encounters with Larry [(Lear)] Caroline (Cordelia), Harold Clark (Gloucester), Jess Clark (Edmund), Pete (Cornwall), and Tyler (Albany). Smiley adds characters, like Rose's teenage daughters Linda and Pammy, in order to draw attention to Ginny's childlessness and to increase the female population of this women-centered novel about families and family secrets. . . .

Generations of audiences have been profoundly moved by Lear's speech [cursing Goneril with sterility]

Hear, Nature, hear, dear goddess, hear!
Suspend thy purpose, if thou didst intend
To make this creature fruitful.
Into her womb convey sterility,
Dry up in her the organs of increase,
And from her derogate body never spring
A babe to honor her!

Smiley weaves a thematic pattern around this curse, by making the hard-won and highly prized farmland, with its network of drainage wells, a source of the cancer-producing toxins that curse the lives of so many of its inhabitants. Ginny, enlightened by Jess, comes to a bitter realization that the fertilizer run-off in the farm's well water is responsible for her several miscarriages. The miscarriages, in turn, give rise to the jealousy that poisons her devotion to Rose and make her marriage barren and unsatisfying, which, in turn, makes her susceptible to Jess's manipulative charm. The water is also responsible for the cancer that killed both Larry's and Harold Clark's wives and required Rose to undergo a mastectomy three months before the events of the novel began. When Smiley attempts to follow Shakespeare closely—by writing the storm scene into her book or paraphrasing Lear's curse ("You'll learn what it means to treat your father like this. I curse you! You'll never have children, Ginny, you haven't got a hope."), she is less convincing that when she uses her own fiction-writing strategies to embark on a large-scale exploration of contemporary topical issues. These include infertility, the relative inattention to breast cancer among medical researchers, and the destruction of the environment in the name of progress. The verbal curses in this novel are far less important than their counterparts in *King Lear;* the real curse is a distinctively male commitment to progress and productivity that poisons the water and ultimately drives the farm families into bankruptcy and early death. . . .

At the end of *King Lear*, all three sisters are dead; at the end of *A Thousand Acres*, Ginny has begun a new life on her own as she and Caroline, now utterly estranged, pay off the last of the farm's debts. Rose has died from a recurrence of breast cancer. As readers we knew from the beginning, of course, that the narrator would live to tell the tale, so we are not surprised that Ginny has moved on in her life to the point where she can look back, assess, and reconstruct the past. This is not exactly a comic ending, but it is, in some respects, an affirmative one. Ginny has freed herself from her repressed existence on the farm and from the shadow cast over her life by her father, her husband, and the patriarchal culture that created them. Smiley is talking back not only to Shakespeare, but more tellingly, to the comic conventions he so invariably adhered to in his fifth acts, even when they seemed uncomfortably inconsistent with the characters he had created. Rather than ending with a marriage and implied promise of future domesticity, *A Thousand Acres* leaves its readers with the unhappy wife's fantasy, 1990s style. Ginny is taking psychology classes at the University of Minnesota, with Pammy and Linda as her "family," in an all-female household where everyone helps with the housework, and Ginny can experience motherhood without the guilt and hostilities that so often accompany it.

CHAPTER 4

SHAKESPEARE
PERMEATES
POPULAR
CULTURE

PEOPLE
WHO MADE
HISTORY

WILLIAM SHAKESPEARE

Franco Zeffirelli Popularizes Shakespeare in Film

Robert Hapgood

Robert Hapgood, Professor Emeritus of English at the University of New Hampshire, is author of *Shakespeare the Theatre Poet* and numerous articles on Shakespeare in performance, including studies of Orson Welles's *Chimes at Midnight* (based on *Henry IV, parts I and II*) and Japanese director Akira Kurosawa's Shakespeare films, *Throne of Blood* (based on *Macbeth*) and *Ran* (based on *King Lear*).

In this selection Hapgood focuses on the Shakespeare films directed by Italian filmmaker Franco Zeffirelli: *Taming of the Shrew* (1966), *Romeo and Juliet* (1968), and *Hamlet* (1990). According to Hapgood, Zeffirelli was determined to make Shakespeare accessible to ordinary people and succeeded by choosing popular stars, appealing particularly to a younger audience, cutting scenes that did not contribute to the core ideas of the play or that slowed the action, and using visual images to parallel the richness of Shakespeare's language. In Hapgood's opinion, Zeffirelli's *Taming of the Shrew* and *Romeo and Juliet* have not become dated, and his *Hamlet*, starring Mel Gibson, remains a compelling version of Hamlet as an action hero.

"I have always been a popularizer," Franco Zeffirelli declares in the self-portrait that concludes his *Autobiography*. He is speaking of his work in staging and filming opera, but his words apply equally well to his Shakespeare films: *The Taming of the Shrew* (1966), *Romeo and Juliet* (1968), and *Hamlet* (1990). As he once explained to an interviewer: "I have always felt sure I could break the myth that Shakespeare on stage and screen is only an exercise for the intellectual. I want his plays to be enjoyed by ordinary people.". . .

RAPPORT WITH THE AUDIENCE IS CENTRAL

From the fact that during his student days Shakespeare's plays reached him in Italian, Zeffirelli draws confidence that they apply "to every human being on earth, no matter what cultural background". By the same token he, even though Italian, can serve as their intermediary to others: "If we really believe in the great values, we communicate one way or another, despite the difference in language, civilization, background, and age". Essentialist and universalist as can be, Zeffirelli here sums up in a sentence the extravagantly all-inclusive faith of a popularizer.

As a go-between, Zeffirelli is wary of "parting company with the audience and asking them to contribute the kind of attention which comes through the brain". Instead he has sought to provide "something they could really identify with", "to make the audience be there with their guts and heart". And their imaginations: he seeks "to make the fantasy of the audience come to life and run together with the actors". The search for this kind of compelling rapport drives all his work: "to make the thing really happen for the audience of today—to make the audience understand that the classics are living flesh".

At the same time Zeffirelli seeks also to be faithful to Shakespeare's work and to hold tenaciously true to what he sees as its core. In *Romeo and Juliet* this core idea was Zeffirelli's decision to take literally Shakespeare's indication that Juliet was about fourteen and that, in that time of boy actresses, "he wanted a young kid to play the part". From that everything else followed: "In every scene I said, 'Don't forget she is fourteen. She's fourteen, and that holds the structure of the play together.'" Given that fidelity to what he sees as Shakespeare's central intention, Zeffirelli is unrepentantly prepared for the sake of audience rapport to make necessary "sacrifices and compromises" where non-essentials are concerned. The apothecary had to go because the episode raises questions in the audience's mind that impede the wave of emotion that makes Romeo's suicide acceptable. The killing of Paris was shot but finally cut because if Romeo "was a murderer—'ugly boy, ugly boy!' It wouldn't have worked". At times, as with his inventive handling of Mercutio's sword-fight with Tybalt and death, he is prepared to grant himself some poetic license: "it is not quite what Shakespeare meant, but I think he would have liked it".

In Zeffirelli's view, alterations may also be justified because of the centuries that stand between Shakespeare and ourselves. It is the popularizer's responsibility to bridge this gap to the classics and imagine that the author had been able "to write that play today for us". So Romeo and Juliet's love-making in the film was appropriately more physical than Shakespeare's circumstances permitted.

A movie-maker who seeks a popular audience must also mediate boldly between the original theatrical medium and film: "cinema creates a different chemistry with the audience, a different taste, and the attention of the audience moves so fast . . . fantasy gallops in the audience in movies . . . your mind flashes-flashes-flashes". Hence Zeffirelli felt justified in cutting the parts of the original that slowed this rapidity—the pestilence Mantua, the clowns, the friar's speech at the end: "sometimes it is better to do without certain things than jeopardize rapport". . . .

STARS WHO APPEAL TO YOUNG AUDIENCES

Some of Zeffirelli's success at the box office has come from frankly commercial calculations, although their crassness has typically been redeemed by a touch of imagination. His first feature film, *Taming of the Shrew*, was conceived as a remake of the Douglas Fairbanks/Mary Pickford version. With Elizabeth Taylor and Richard Burton for *Taming of the Shrew*, as with Mel Gibson and Glenn Close for *Hamlet*, he chose hugely popular stars. Of course, it is a fact of Hollywood life that bankable stars are virtually essential to funding feature films. Indeed, Taylor and Burton themselves put up most of the money for *Taming of the Shrew*. Yet Zeffirelli's casting has also consistently had an element of discovery and risk about it. Neither Taylor nor Gibson were thought of as Shakespearians, and until they proved otherwise serious doubts were expressed about their ability to perform their roles. Such risks could also prove an opportunity. "Cinema is a day-by-day discovery, and fresh is best," he has observed. For example, he found it more satisfying to direct Taylor than Burton because certain of his acting patterns were stale . . . whereas with Taylor: "she was fresh like me. She was new [to Shakespearian acting] and very insecure, and so we worked on a lot of new ideas, and she burst out in a much more unexpected way than her husband". In *Romeo and Juliet* he pushed this element of discovery to an extreme, choosing then unknowns for the leading roles—only to find that at first no major company would finance it.

What finally made Zeffirelli's *Romeo and Juliet* possible was another way of attracting financial backing for a film project: that it promised to draw young audiences. Consistently, he has sought to be timely and especially to address the young. For the opening carnival in *Taming of the Shrew* he had hired young extras. In his approach to *Romeo and Juliet*, as we have seen, his characteristic accent on youth was of the essence. For his Old Vic production of the play he chose unusually young principals and cast. While rehearsing the play he is said to have frequented *West Side Story*, then playing in London. Certainly his film draws on similar youth-culture, generation-gap appeals. As he recounts in his *Autobiography*, the fact that a Hollywood producer's teenage son was moved by what he saw of the film in progress was crucial in the producer's decision to fund its completion. In its first year, Paramount's one and a half million dollar investment returned forty-eight million dollars at the box office. . . .

PERIOD DRESS AND SETTINGS

Aspiration toward timeliness, although it helps to attract paying customers, need not lead to a cheapening of the original. Zeffirelli has not, for example, succumbed to the too-easy updating that can come with modern dress; all of his Shakespeare films have had period mountings. "You can't take the Fifth Symphony and play it as jazz," he has observed. There was much more to the power of his *Romeo and Juliet* than an appeal to the latest teenage fad. In my own experience the film, overnight, made the play teachable to college students, who had hitherto rejected it as celebrating the high school puppy love they were trying to put behind them. What they found in the film is illustrated by the testimony of Michael Cole and Helen Keyssar, who have looked back as adult teachers on their student experiences of the play and the film. Both were put off by the play when they read it; both were caught up by the film's immediacy. Cole "was captured first by the fight among the boys", and as the precise "tragic possibilities of all-consuming passion" came home to him, he "wanted to reach out and say, No! Stop!

Don't do it." Keyssar also wanted to say "Stop," but—carried away by "their fervor of reckless abandon"—she "also wanted neither of them to stop because to stop was to arrest their passion as well as mine". The film's "unabashed eroticism" was thus one of its attractions for her, but with it came a tragic "sense of irretrievable loss": "the film made me feel what death was all about: It was about absence, and I recognized that absence because the human beings on the screen had been made so present to me".

Zeffirelli's concern with youth and contemporaneity goes deeper than a desire for dollars. What he writes about renovating his house applies equally well to his adaptation of classics: "my real pleasure is to make whatever I have added look as if it has always been there . . . this notion of belonging both to the past and the future pleases me so much. When I succeed, I feel I have defeated time. . . ." Through his ongoing work in cinema, he has said with a sigh, "I want to keep young for my work for the future". In turn his work has appealed to the young because it is itself young at heart. . . .

Zeffirelli revels in the audience-involving visual opportunities that motion pictures afford. The wonderful richness of Shakespeare's words, their Renaissance copiousness and plenitude, has its cinematic parallel in the profusion of Zeffirelli's images. Although the fertility of his invention seems effortless, it is also based on hard work, inspired by the "passionate attention to detail" he learned as a stage designer for his mentor Visconti:

> Everything was always researched to a point far beyond the needs of the actual scene. You immersed yourself in the period, the place, its culture, so that even though the audience might not take in every detail they would be absolutely convinced of its essential "rightness".

A Florentine, Zeffirelli was already thoroughly at home in Renaissance Italy. A master-stroke of his *Taming of the Shrew* and *Romeo and Juliet* was to capitalize on his birthright and take literally the Italian-ness of their Shakespearean settings in Padua and Verona. Both are very much "Made in Italy," being shot there and with largely Italian designers and technicians. . . .

DYNAMIC ENERGY CHARACTERIZES THE FILMS

Above all is the kinetic appeal of these two films, intensified in well-chosen places by explosions of violence. They are very much "movies," and Zeffirelli makes the most of the charge of vitality that they can give his viewers. Not only are his principals active and energetic (no one stands still to deliver a speech) and their stories dynamically told, but on the sidelines numerous little stories are sketched, suggesting the flow of ongoing community life. Not for nothing did Zeffirelli as a director of opera learn to individualize his La Scala choruses. This is especially true of *Taming of the Shrew*. For one example among dozens, through reaction shots at the wedding, we can follow Bianca's anxiety that the marriage will not happen (with its impact on her own marriage prospects) and her joy when it does occur. Even the props are given stories, as when Michael Hordern's Baptista—hunched over with paternal cupidity—is amusingly careful to retrieve the family silver Petruchio has been fondling. In *Romeo and Juliet* Capulet's ball is similarly treated. The first meeting of the lovers takes place amid round-dances so dizzying that even the camera is caught up in the whirl. On the sidelines, a domestic triangle is sketched between Tybalt and Lord and Lady Capulet. But elsewhere in this film Zeffirelli gives most attention to working out fewer stories at greater length and depth.

Taken together these various elements in Zeffirelli's filmmaking comprise a composite art of story-telling, by which he claims and rewards the attention of his viewers while ensuring that, without too much effort, they will be alerted to everything they should know. Again, his methods are instructively overt in *Taming of the Shrew*, where indeed the neophyte film director seems intent on displaying everything he can do at once. So he is busy cross-cutting between the wooings of Kate and Bianca, exaggerating (hilariously but to scale) the slap-stick part of Kate's first wit-combat with Petruchio, ramifying the chase motif, underlining the dialogue by repeating key phrases, visually undercutting Petruchio's line "I will not sleep till I see her" by having him immediately drop off to sleep, musically mocking his bombastic speeches by a march on the soundtrack. Such textured interworking of parts extends to all aspects of the film.

Romeo and Juliet is no less integrated, but in it the director's hand is less obtrusive. As before he allows his inventiveness several virtuoso displays—the opening brawl, the ball, the duels—all of them handled in his characteristically supercharged, richly textured style. These come in the first part of the film. As in *Taming of the Shrew*, Zeffirelli then changes emotional gears in mid-course, as he delineates the problems that confront the two marriages. But in *Romeo and Juliet* this change is reflected much more graphically, in the subdued style of the interiors. And for the most part Zeffirelli seems to let the story tell itself, pausing in places to admire the beauty of the lovers' faces and bodies, but in a compelling away entering into the story's own pace, rhythm, and points of climax, which he emphasizes by lavish use of background music.

The style of *Romeo and Juliet* is thus much more mature than that of *Taming of the Shrew*. Yet looking back over the features the two films share, one can see that they all help to enhance the intense rapport that Zeffirelli seeks with a popular audience.

THE CHALLENGE OF *HAMLET*

After a farce and an early tragedy, *Hamlet* presented much more of a challenge to Zeffirelli's skills as a popularizer. In telling its long and complex story, he takes his usual approach. He focuses sharply on the core of family tragedy; politics scarcely figure, Fortinbras is gone without a trace, as is the opening appearance of the Ghost. The pace is rapid (this is an "action film"). Of Hamlet's soliloquies, only "to be or not to be" emerges entire; "how all occasions" is cut entirely and the others are severely reduced. The characterization of the Prince accords with this approach. Virile, dynamic, violent, wild, Gibson's Hamlet is not a more than usually thoughtful man. Zeffirelli in fact goes to elaborate pains to provide external occasions for his reflections, even in soliloquy. This Hamlet, as Gibson says, is "a man of action".

To readers conscious of what is omitted from the original, the film may seem choppy. But if we take the film-script on its own terms we can see that Zeffirelli finds a number of ways to enhance its flow for moviegoers who may not know the play. He frequently divides Shakespeare's scenes into shorter segments. So the second scene opens as in the original with Claudius's statement from the throne about his marriage, but what follows is broken into a series of fast-moving, private exchanges. Unlike Shakespeare's hero, who must make intuitive leaps in order to understand the forces against him, Zeffirelli's Hamlet, thanks to extensive eavesdropping, is never taken by surprise. We are always therefore carried forward by the clear logic of what he does.

Many of Zeffirelli's alterations of the original are resourceful. Simply by having Polonius observe Hamlet's silent visit to Ophelia sewing, he is able to move directly to the scene where Polonius expounds to the king and queen the causes of Hamlet's lunacy. He efficiently accomplishes some exposition by substituting King Hamlet's funeral for the Ghost's first appearance. But this time the commercial compromise Zeffirelli made to obtain funding (holding the running time to two and a quarter hours) cramped everyone's style, especially his own. This is most evident in his handling of Hamlet's aborted voyage to England, where the story-telling is almost as jerky as in a silent film: first comes a short shot of Hamlet's boat at sea; then—between Ophelia's mad-scenes—a short sequence in which the Prince exchanges the fatal packets and Rosencrantz and Guildenstern are summarily beheaded; finally, Hamlet is back in Elsinore, with no indication of how he got there. How much more adroitly Zeffirelli abbreviates the delayed delivery of Friar Laurence's message to banished Romeo! He simply shows the messenger riding his donkey on the road to Mantua and being overtaken by Romeo's servant on horseback; he then points the irony by having the two of them unknowingly pass the messenger on their way back to Verona. . . .

Whatever the stylistic shortcomings of his Shakespeare films, Zeffirelli never loses sight in them of the human drama at the heart of the originals. This is the most important source of his success as a popularizer. "Squeeze Shakespeare's characters to the utmost," he told an interviewer, "and you still find poetry." His focus therefore is on "this poetry of the human relationships . . ."

BRANAGH FOLLOWS ZEFFIRELLI AS A POPULARIZER

Kenneth Branagh is often compared with [Laurence] Olivier, and as an actor his delivery of his lines does show a comparable sensitivity to Shakespeare's language, whether grand or subtle. Yet where popularizing Shakespeare on film is concerned he is—as screenwriter and director of *Henry V* (1989) and *Much Ado About Nothing* (1993)—as much in the tradition of Zeffirelli. His shooting *Much Ado About Nothing* in Italy with a mixed cast of American and British performers certainly recalls Zeffirelli's practices, and the parallels, whether conscious or not, go further. Always careful to label his scripts as "adaptations" of the original, Branagh is almost as free as Zeffirelli in cutting and interpolating to suit his filming needs. Both clearly love film and delight in the opportunities it offers, occasionally permitting themselves fantasias that extrapolate on Shakespearean moments—as when Mercutio clowns in his fountain or Benedict capers in his. Yet their work is still recognizably based on Shakespeare: as with Zeffirelli much of the appeal of Branagh's films comes from his ability to revitalize qualities that originally made the plays popular. Except for *Hamlet*, both have sidestepped the most challenging of Shakespeare's works (for the most part they are probably best left to stage productions and art-films); instead they have chosen relatively early ones, plays whose dialogue could be cut without great loss and whose characterization was tolerant of the simplifications endemic to popular culture. Branagh is as bold as Zeffirelli in seeking rapport with the audience and makes the same kind of extensive use of mood-music. Audiences find their films of Shakespearean comedies genuinely funny; like the first meeting of Kate and Petruchio, the eavesdropping scene of *Much Ado About Nothing* evokes spontaneous laughter, a rare distinction. Neither is shy about laying claim to compelling reasons for audience identification with their leading characters: even more than Zeffirelli, Branagh's films have been about young people; he is himself young. And no less than Zeffirelli he plays on our sympathies by enhancing the vulnerability of his leading characters—his Henry V sheds more tears in the exercise of his royal office than does Shakespeare's and his Beatrice, like Zeffirelli's Kate, is warmer and softer than in the original.

In all these ways, whether from instinct or observation, Branagh seems already to have learned and applied the lessons in popularization that have emerged from this analysis of Zeffirelli's Shakespeare films. As I write [in 1997] he is about to release his four-and-a-half-hour version of *Hamlet*. There is thus every reason to hope that Branagh will continue to carry on where Zeffirelli has left off.

Shakespeare Goes Hollywood in the 1990s

Lynda E. Boose and Richard Burt

A plethora of Shakespeare films appeared in the
1990s and numerous other films of the decade contained Shakespearean subtexts, explain professors
Lynda E. Boose and Richard Burt. Although the
young, to whom these films are directed, may not
read Shakespeare's plays, they are well-acquainted
with such movies as Zeffirelli's *Hamlet,* starring Mel
Gibson, *Renaissance Man,* starring Danny DeVito,
Gus Van Sant's *My Own Private Idaho,* and Baz
Luhrmann's *William Shakespeare's Romeo and Juliet.*
These popular teen movies, and avant-garde adaptations like Peter Greenaway's *Prospero's Books,* Jean-
Luc Godard's *Lear,* and Ian McKellen's *Richard III*
convince Boose and Burt that the author, Shakespeare, is being displaced in popular culture by the
film director. These films, in addition to CD-ROM
editions of the plays, animated movies, and sophisticated comic-book versions of the plays guarantee
Shakespeare's accessibility, but, according to Boose
and Burt, they also contribute to an increasingly
fragmented image of the plays among teenagers.

Lynda E. Boose, professor of English at Dartmouth
College, is coeditor of *Fathers and Daughters* and author of numerous articles on Shakespeare and Renaissance drama. University of Massachusetts at
Amherst professor Richard Burt is author of *Licensed
by Authority: Ben Jonson and the Discourse of Censorship* and coeditor of *Enclosure Acts: Sexuality,
Property and Culture in Early Modern England.*

A short sequence in the 1995 summer film comedy *Clueless*
(dir. Amy Heckerling) offers what might be considered a
mini-allegory of Shakespeare's circulation within the popu-

Lynda E. Boose and Richard Burt, "Totally Clueless? Shakespeare Goes Hollywood in
the 1990s," *Shakespeare, the Movie,* edited by Lynda E. Boose and Richard Burt. New
York: Routledge, 1997. Copyright © 1997 by Lynda E. Boose and Richard Burt. Reproduced by permission of the publisher.

lar culture of the 1990s. Based on Jane Austen's *Emma*, the film narrates the coming of age of "Cher," a Beverly Hills high school ingenue and media-savvy teen queen who reformulates the pleasures of discourse into side-by-side telephone conversations conducted on mobile telephones. In the manipulation of cultural capital as a means for asserting status, Cher (Alicia Silverstone) clinches her superiority inside of a contest that defines itself through Shakespeare. When her stepbrother's excessively Harvard girlfriend misattributes "to thine own self be true" to Hamlet and Cher corrects her, the girlfriend then rejects Cher's substitution of "that Polonius guy" and slams home her apparent victory with the smugly dismissive line, "I think I remember *Hamlet* accurately." But Cher beats her, point, set, and match, with the rejoinder that while she, by comparison, may not know her *Hamlet*, she most certainly does know her Mel Gibson! . . .

1990s Action Hero Hamlets

Cher's recoding of *Hamlet* could be located in a wider range of 1990s *Hamlet*(s). The *Hamlet* created by the 1990s wasn't big just among the literati—he was so big that he was making guest appearances in all sorts of unexpected places, with different implications of its gendered reception. In 1991, Oliver Stone cast the Kennedy assassination through the lens of *Hamlet* in *JFK*. In 1994, Danny DeVito and the US Army found *Hamlet* to be the perfect force for transforming wimps and misfit soldiers into the STRAK army company that concludes *Renaissance Man* (dir. Penny Marshall) reaffirming the male bond in "Sound Off" lyrics that inventively substitute "Hamlet's mother, she's the Queen" for the usual female object of cadenced derision. Similarly, Disney's 1994 *The Lion King* (dir. Roger Allers and Ron Minkoff), reworked *Hamlet* for a younger generation. In 1995, Kenneth Branagh released his *A Midwinter's Tale*, a film about a provincial English production of *Hamlet*, and then in 1996 and 1997 his own full-length and abridged versions of *Hamlet*.

Ultimately, however, it was Arnold Schwarzenegger's 1992 film, *The Last Action Hero* (dir. John McTiernan), that most clearly allegorized the transformation of Hamlet from melancholy man into an image that could be valued by the young male consumers to whom the newly technologized violence of the 1990s was being played. In a displacement explicitly fictionalized as the direct product of a young male viewer's contemporary fantasies of masculinity, on screen the image of Olivier hesitating to kill the praying Claudius literally dissolves into a Schwarzenegger Hamlet who is actively engaged in "taking out the trash" of the something-rotten Denmark into which he is thrust. And in a clever bit of metatheatricality, the substitution of Schwarzenegger, America's highest paid actor of the early 1990s, is situated as the ultimate insurance that movie houses will stay open and movies will keep on playing. Kids like the film's ardent young filmviewer will keep right on getting sucked into the action-packed worlds of heroically imagined male violence that is both promulgated by American film and simultaneously guarantees the industry its seemingly unassailable hegemony. Though ironic, it is nonetheless true that the *Hamlet*(s) of the 1990s construct a world even more obsessively masculine than did the *Hamlet*(s) that preexisted any articulated feminist critique of popular culture. Mel Gibson as Hamlet means *Hamlet* as *Lethal Weapon Four.* But Mel also means Hamlet as Hollywood Hunk, an object of desire who, like Glenn Close's Gertrude, projects an image implicitly accessible to female and male viewers alike. [Franco] Zeffirelli's film may well be *Lethal Weapon Four;* but Hamlet-as-Mel suggests Shakespeare's prince as a 1990s model of unrestrictedly appropriatable desire, and it was through an appropriation of Mel-as-Hamlet that Cher triumphs over her truly clueless adversary, eventually winning a college guy (read: Harvard Law) boyfriend at the film's close. . . .

FILM DIRECTORS DISPLACE SHAKESPEARE THE AUTHOR

In some ways, the present historical moment only clarifies the way Shakespeare has always already disappeared when transferred onto film. Taken on their own terms, films like [Peter] Greenaway's *Prospero's Books,* Derek Jarman's *Tempest,* and [Jean-Luc] Godard's *Lear* involve not merely the deconstruction of Shakespeare as author but his radical displacement by the film director; and the interest in any of these films could legitimately be said to lie less in its relation to Shakespeare's play than in its relation to the director's own previous *oeuvre.* Even films which adapt the Shakespeare script as faithfully as does Branagh's *Much Ado About Nothing* speak within a metacinematic discourse of self-reference in which, through film quotation, they situate themselves in reference as much to other films as to a Shakespeare tradition.

Yet judging from the commentary and the advertising matrix surrounding the release of the most recent Shakespeare adaptations, the fact that Shakespeare is the author seems to be becoming not only increasingly beside the point but even a marketing liability—an inference that *Los Angeles Times* movie critic David Gritten quite clearly picks up from the voices of both the director and producer of Ian McKellen's 1995 *Richard III:*

> Here on the set of *Richard III,* a film adaptation of one of the world's best known plays starring a bunch of distinguished classical actors, it comes as a surprise that everyone is trying to play down the S-word. The S-word? That stands for "Shakespeare." He's the guy who wrote *Richard III* some four hundred years ago, in case you weren't quite sure. In truth, the people behind this *Richard III . . .* are hoping to attract those very people who aren't quite sure of the film's provenance. "I'm encouraging everyone working on this film not to think of it as Shakespeare," says director Richard Loncraine. "It's a terrific story, and who wrote it is irrelevant. We're trying to make the most accessible Shakespeare film ever made," says producer Lisa Katselas Pare.

The similar trend that Don Hedrick points out in an essay in this collection—that any mention of Shakespeare is exactly what was under avoidance in the marketing of Branagh's *Henry V*—is a truism equally applicable to Zeffirelli's *Hamlet.* Likewise, Gus Van Sant notes about the making of *My Own Private Idaho* that while the foreign producers wanted to put in as much Shakespeare as possible the American producers wanted to cut out as much as possible. Yet just when we might assume that the Bard's name was truly a marketing liability or that veneration of Shakespeare had come to be regarded in popular contexts as uncool, the notably cool film director Baz Luhrmann put out a new *Romeo and Juliet* that is unquestionably situated in the pop culture, made-for-teens film market and is called *William Shakespeare's Romeo and Juliet.*

The popularization of Shakespeare on film, video, and television—which began inside the stalwartly liberal tradition of noblesse oblige attempting to bring culture to the masses—now finds itself, in America at least, in a strictly market-responsive milieu in which literary knowledge is in general a decidedly low capital, frequently mockable commodity, caught within the peculiarly American ambivalence about intellectualism, and therefore to be eschewed at all

Shakespeare for CEOs

University of New Hampshire professor Douglas M. Lanier finds Shakespeare corporate-management manuals a pop-culture phenomenon, which provides a useful context for understanding the 1990s Shakespeare film boom.

The final years of the twentieth century have seen a curious and, to my mind, telling phenomenon in the realm of Shakespeare and pop culture, one that provides an illuminating context for certain elements of the much-ballyhooed Shakespeare film boom of the '90s. It is the emergence of a distinct subgenre in business publishing, the Shakespeare corporate-management manual. With titles such as *Shakespeare in Charge, Power Plays,* and *Shakespeare on Management,* these volumes take as their premise the notion that Shakespeare portrays the intricacies of a universally shared human nature and direct that notion toward providing lessons in corporate motivation, leadership, personnel management, and decision-making: "Business involves people," we are told [by Norman Augustine and Kenneth Adelman], "and people—fundamentally—don't change. The essence of business is thus remarkably constant." And so, for example, *The Taming of the Shrew* offers us a portrait of a successful merger between two strong-willed, independent organizations; *Hamlet*'s Claudius becomes a case study in flawed crisis management; Portia provides an ideal model for "the art and danger of risk-taking . . . in the only Shakespearean play named after a businessman" [according to Augustine and Adelman]; and Richard II, Lear, and Antony depict managers who fail because they forget that their power and authority cannot be [in the words of Augustine and Adelman] "personalized and abstracted from the organization." Not surprisingly, [as Augustine and Adelman suggest] Henry V emerges as the undisputed hero of all of these manuals, a corporate motivator who, "new on the throne and forced to prove himself, . . . uses time-tested leadership techniques to succeed most royally." Paul Corrigan [author of *Shakespeare on Management*] sets Henry's rise to power alongside that of Jack Welch, CEO of General Electric, who moved from being a brutal corporate axman in the '80s to a paragon of dynamic corporate management in the '90s, all because he began to "listen to his 'subjects' and learn from the people who really knew GE's various businesses at their grass-roots," allowing him to "[harvest] good ideas from the workforce" and dramatically boost productivity. The message is clear: like E.F. Hutton, when Shakespeare talks, people listen.

Douglas M. Lanier, "Shakescorp *Noir,*" *Shakespeare Quarterly,* vol. 53., no. 2, 2002.

costs. When Gus Van Sant imports the various Hal and Falstaff scenes from the *Henry IV* and *Henry V* plays and sticks
them into *My Own Private Idaho*'s world of contemporary
Portland gay hustlers and street dwellers, neither the film
nor the characters speaking the lines register any acknowledgment that they are drawing upon Shakespeare. If this
film is a Shakespeare spin-off, no one has to admit knowing
it. But as a market screening device, the omission must have
worked, since only those people who had read the Henriad
or read commentary on the film in specifically "intellectual"
magazine and review venues seemed conscious of any
Shakespeare connection. The same might be said of *L.A.
Story.* While many members of the audience may have
picked up the allusions to *Hamlet* and other Shakespeare
plays, only a Shakespearean would have read the movie as a
rewriting of the play. . . .

AMERICAN POP CULTURE FRAMES BRANAGH'S FILMS

To be sure, the late 1980s saw the English tradition of Shakespeare film refurbished by Kenneth Branagh into an enter-
prise comparable in energy to that of the 1940s when Sir
Laurence Olivier was making *Richard III, Henry V, Hamlet,*
and, in 1955, starring in Stuart Burges's *Othello.* But what
Branagh has done is infuse the filming of Shakespeare with
a marketeer's sense of popular culture. In his productions,
high and low culture meet in moments where Shakespeare's
scripts get subtly reframed inside of references to Hollywood
pop culture: Branagh's adaptation actually rewrites *Henry V*
as Clint Eastwood's "dirty Harry," and his *Much Ado About
Nothing* opens with a witty visual evocation of *The Magnificent Seven.*

The sudden contemporary renaissance in filmed Shakespeare is British-led, but by 1995 even British casting practices had changed to reflect the exigencies of market capi-
talism. Following in the direction that Zeffirelli had been the
first to seize upon, the new British productions were now
promoting their global commerciality through a mixture of
what has been derisively referred to as a cast made up of
"British actors" and "American stars." Branagh's 1989 *Henry
V* had been filmed with a British cast. But by the time of
Much Ado About Nothing, the British principals were sur-
rounded by American pop film stars that made brothers out
of America's most popular black actor (Denzel Washington)

and America's most popular teen heart-throb (Keanu Reeves). . . . By 1995 Branagh, too, had gone American: Hollywood's Lawrence Fishburne played the Noble Moor to Branagh's Iago; and in 1996 Branagh's *Hamlet* included such box office draws as Billy Crystal (first gravedigger), Robin Williams (Osric), Charlton Heston (the Player King), and Jack Lemmon (Marcellus). Yielding to the implicit logic of such casting, Baz Luhrmann simply invited the stars of his *Romeo and Juliet* "to speak the famous lines in their own American accent.". . .

Branagh having shown Hollywood that there was a market, production money seemed suddenly to be flowing; Branagh released his complete, uncut *Hamlet* (1996); Trevor Nunn—having demonstrated his entitlement on stage by directing big bucks productions of *Les Miserables* and *Cats*—directed a new *Twelfth Night* that debuted at Telluride (1996); another *Romeo and Juliet* in addition to Baz Luhrmann's 1996 production was on its way out; the Loncraine/McKellen *Richard III* (1994) had broken new ground in terms of reframing Shakespeare inside of pop-culture strategies; and, using an inventive new format for producing a Shakespeare film, Al Pacino had allegorized his own experience of playing *Richard III* in a documentary called *Looking for Richard* (1996). . . .

LEARNED TRADITION GIVES WAY TO YOUTH CULTURE

Of all the films of the 1990s, some of the most innovative come from an avant-garde tradition whose energies are infused both by popular culture and an international mode of film production. Through avant-garde filmmaker Peter Greenaway's very attempt to unpack the place that intellectual and aesthetic elitism has played in Western culture, *Prospero's Books* (1990), forms in many ways an important investigation of the idea of "the popular." A meditation on *The Tempest*, the film reproduces Shakespeare's play as caviar to the general and grants few if any concessions to the popular; Greenaway's revision of *The Tempest* relocates Prospero in the image of the elite filmmaker bidding farewell to a tradition that he himself, as technological magus, participates in destroying. In a science fiction bound together by a technologically produced iconography of western culture stretching from the pages of Renaissance humanism to computer-generated models of virtual reality, the revels seen as ending in this latest rendition of Shakespeare's final play are played out as a kind of intellectualized, nostalgic farewell to even the existence of a culture that might be called learned or elite. The book disintegrates, and before us we see a virtual meltdown of all that symbolizes the learned tradition, even the word itself. Yet in a kind of acknowledgment—indeed, almost an allegory—of the end of the twentieth century's new culture and its new possessors, it is Caliban, its implied inheritor, who reaches into the flood and saves the First Folio from the literary armageddon on screen before us. Meanwhile, at the margin, orchestrating the deluge, stands the figure of the maker—the Gielgud who is Prospero who is Shakespeare who is Peter Greenaway—mournfully bidding culture—at least as he and we have hitherto imagined it—into oblivion. Elite reproductions, whether avant-garde or devoted to the "classics," as well as popular productions, then, meet in the disappearing of Shakespeare.

Dealing with specifically filmic reproductions or appropriations of Shakespeare means that "the popular" must be thought through not only the media and institutions in which Shakespeare is now reproduced—mass culture, Hollywood, celebrity, tabloid—but above all, youth culture. For as Shakespeare becomes part of pop culture and Shakespearean criticism (especially film criticism) follows suit, both move into an arena increasingly driven by a specifically youth culture, and Hollywood has clearly picked up on that fact. The animated versions already released for more than a dozen of the plays and scheduled for additional releases are only the most literal version of this development. Clearly playing to the potent consumerism of what is recognized as a notoriously visual subculture, all four of the so-called "big" tragedies have recently been reproduced in sophisticated comic-book form, appropriate for college students. . . .

CONSEQUENCES OF POPULARIZING SHAKESPEARE

Given that popularization is linked to youth culture, the crucial question for cultural critics rests, finally, with the pedagogical implications of Shakespeare's popularization on film, TV, and video. Popularization has meant the proliferation of representations, on the one hand, and thus an enlargement of what can be legitimately studied as part of the Shakespeare canon. But it has also meant the disappearance of (what was always the illusion of) a single, unified Shake-speare whose works could be covered. Students in today's av-erage, college-level Shakespeare course are now more often shown select scenes from two or more versions of a given play than they are a single production in its entirety.... CD-Rom editions of the plays necessarily further this frag-mentation. With film and/or digital image as the version through which Shakespeare is primarily known, Shake-speare's accessibility is guaranteed, but along with this move to film comes a perhaps inevitable new sense of Shake-speare's reproduction, one which offers certain challenges to cultural criticism of Shakespeare as it is now practiced.

Consider, once again, the scene of Shakespeare pedagogy as narrated in *The Last Action Hero*. In this film, the kid who plays hookey in order to see action films starring Schwar-zenegger grudgingly returns to class in time to hear his teacher regaling the students with the pleasures of *Hamlet*. The scene offers a bit of caviar to the theater-going elite in the private knowledge that the teacher is being played by Joan Plowright, Olivier's wife of many years and herself a renowned Shakespearean actress. The in-joke is included, but it is at the same time made purely extraneous to the pleasures of *The Last Action Hero*, where pleasure is dis-tinctly located in the smash-bang thrills of pop culture. As the truant takes his seat and the teacher informs the stu-dents that they may recognize the actor, Sir Laurence Olivier, from his work in a television commercial or from playing Zeus in *Clash of the Titans* (dir. Desmond Davis, 1981), the relevance of Shakespeare seems most vividly rep-resented by the comically outmoded 16mm projector through which the old Olivier film is being shown. The old-fashioned, dated feel of Olivier's film may be accounted for, at least in part, by the way the scene in *The Last Action Hero* marks a new relation between the plays and their audience, one in which the aura that pervaded the filmed Shakespeare "classics" is gone, and, with it, the sense of embodied inti-macy between the audience and Shakespeare himself. The displacement of Olivier by Arnold Schwarzenegger marks the disappearance of an older sense of the actor as someone who actually knew Shakespeare, who communed with him, understood his mind, and perhaps at times even thought that he himself was Shakespeare.

Nonetheless, this film marks neither the unequivocal triumph of a new American cultural imperialism nor the displacement of a Shakespeare understood to be English by one who has become brashly American. As much as the film would seem to dismiss Shakespeare, it may also be understood as playing out one more version of the way that America, through the aesthetic medium that is as peculiarly American as the stage is English, tries to come to terms with its own, unregenerate fascination with the Bard of Avon. As apparently irrelevant as *The Last Action Hero* would seem to make Shakespeare, in this and all such recent filmic moments in which the Bard is suddenly invoked, William Shakespeare is still somehow a necessary signifier. He is that which must be posited and the debt that must be acknowledged before—and in order for—popular culture to declare itself so unindebted to the S-guy that it may get on with the production of itself and its own narratives.

Shakespeare: The Animated Tales

James R. Andreas

In this selection Clemson University professor James R. Andreas examines several of the thirty-minute films which compose *Shakespeare: The Animated Tales*. First presented on HBO in 1992–1993, the *Tales* were designed for children aged ten to fifteen. Andreas focuses on which plays were selected for the series and how they were cut, and on their handling of moral and political questions, violence, and sex; he also considers the portrayal of outsiders like Othello and Caliban. Andreas concludes that the selection reflects standard middle and high school curricula. Subplots and potentially offensive bawdy language are consistently cut, as one would expect, but plenty of blood, violence, and glamorized nudity are presented visually in the *Tales*. Andreas finds the portrayal of outsiders uneven. He considers the animated *Othello* a courageous presentation of interracial jealousy and rivalry; on the other hand, Caliban is portrayed as a "cartoon monster" in the animated *Tempest*.

Andreas has also written numerous articles on Chaucer and on Shakespeare, including "'Wordes betwene': The Rhetoric of the *Canterbury Tales*," "Remythologizing the Knight's Tale: *A Midsummer Night's Dream* and *Two Noble Kinsmen*," "Othello's African American Progeny," "Signifyin' on *The Tempest* in Gloria Naylor's *Mama Day*," and "Teaching Shakespeare's Bawdy: Orality, Literacy, and Censorship in *Romeo and Juliet*."

While there has certainly been no grand bureaucratic conspiracy to sanitize the classics for children, there has been a gentle translation of Shakespeare's tough play texts into tales

James R. Andreas, "The Canning of a Classic: *Shakespeare: The Animated Tales*," *Shakespeare and the Visual Arts*, edited by Holger Klein and James L. Harner. Lewiston, NY: The Edwin Mellen Press, 2000. Copyright © 2000 by The Edwin Mellen Press. Reproduced by permission.

meant for children, driven in part by market forces but largely by what has been labeled the 'community standards' of decency stringently applied by school boards in the selection of literary textbooks. . . .

As an example of the 'classicizing' process, I will examine eight of the twelve films released in the project known as *Shakespeare: The Animated Tales* that were produced (1992–93) by Shakespeare Animated Films Ltd and Random House: *The Taming of the Shrew, A Midsummer Night's Dream, Twelfth Night, Romeo and Juliet, Macbeth, Hamlet, Othello,* and *The Tempest.* The tales represent the best traditions of collaborative film-making: the animation was produced in Russia and Wales, the editing in England, and distribution was initiated in the United States. Advisors for the project included Professor Stanley Wells, a distinguished editor of the plays, and Rex Gibson, who edits the Cambridge School Shakespeare. Martin Lamb and Penelope Middelboe served as editors for the series, and Leon Garfield produced the scripts for the individual tales. The first series included *Macbeth, Romeo and Juliet, A Midsummer Night's Dream, Twelfth Night, The Tempest,* and *Hamlet.* Due to the commercial success generated by the first release, a second series followed rapidly and included *Julius Caesar, Richard III, A Winter's Tale, The Taming of the Shrew, As You Like It,* and *Othello.* The second series, however, has proved difficult to purchase for reasons that will be self-evident from this paper: its films are not listed in any of the current video distribution catalogs. *The Animated Tales* were first presented on the HBO cable network with clever, irreverent introductions by Robin Williams in various spoofs on the Bard. I want to consider a number of questions relevant to these versions, or rather con-versions, of Shakespeare's dramatic vehicles into visualized narratives designed for children: (1) why were these particular plays chosen for reproduction or reprocessing, and which are still available for distribution? (2) what plots and subplots are sacrificed in the necessary compression these texts undergo, and how is Shakespeare's verbal artistry, particularly narrative moments in the plays, translated into visual, animated imagery? (3) how are touchy subjects which raise moral, religious, and political questions in the plays dealt with in the tales? (4) what violent scenes from the texts are retained and how is violence rendered visually in the films? (5) how is Shakespeare's notorious bawdry handled in the tales, both comic and tragic bawdry? (6) and finally, what is made of the portrayal of Shakespeare's famous aliens—Othello and Caliban—in the animated versions? . . .

THE SELECTIONS

The selections of plays for adaptation in animation was fairly predictable from a curricular point of view. As most teachers of Shakespeare know, for the last thirty years and more the standard, unchallenged curriculum in the schools has been exclusively tragic, highly violent, and often heavily expurgated: *Romeo and Juliet, Julius Caesar, Macbeth,* and *Hamlet.* Three of the standard tragedies are included in the first series of tales, and the fourth, *Julius Caesar* heads the second series. The initial exclusion of *Julius Caesar* is probably due not so much to its ambiguous and controversial political content as it is to the fact that this play has proven the most difficult to make interesting to school children, unrelieved, as it is, by the comedy and foolery that make the other tragic selections enticing, even in expurgated texts. Besides, now that *Othello* has been openly accepted as a highly controversial text about race, the play has emerged as a new favorite in the classroom and was, accordingly, the fifth tragedy to be filmed in the animated series, although it has not been re-released and is virtually impossible to order from video distribution catalogs at the present time. Shakespeare's major tragedies are to be celebrated as the closest thing to a core curriculum in the humanities that we are ever likely to get in this country, but one puzzles over the exclusive focus on what [Spanish philosopher and poet] Miguel de Unamuno [1864–1936] called "the tragic sense of life", so it is refreshing to see that four comedies, two 'romances', and a history play have been included in the *Animated Tales.* The two series include several comedies: *Twelfth Night* which, along with *Much Ado About Nothing,* is rapidly gaining acceptance as one of the comedies of Shakespeare worth producing for general audiences; *A Midsummer Night's Dream* which has proven to be the play in the canon most often produced in the twentieth century and was the introductory play in high schools around the country for baby boomers; *Taming of the Shrew,* popularized in the sixties by Franco Zeffirelli's colorful film rendition (1966) and revived in the nineties as a potboiler for contemporary teens under the title *Ten Things I Hate Most About You;* and *The*

Tempest, identified as the first of the comedies in the First Folio edition of Shakespeare's plays.

THE TAMING OF THE SHREW IS THE BEST

The best of the animated comedies, the best offering, in fact, of the eight tales under discussion here is *The Taming of the Shrew* because of its determination to reconstruct the conditions of actual dramatic performance. The hilarious and dramatically effective induction of the play, which is so often sacrificed in live production, frames the entire animation. In the HBO introduction to the film, Robin Williams appears as Christopher Sly, drunk in the tavern with two loaves of bread at the front of the table looking like breasts, or "buns" as he identifies them. The animated tale itself begins with Christopher Sly being thrown out of the tavern, falling into a drunken sleep, and transported to the Lord's mansion. When he awakens, he is informed that he has been asleep for fifteen years and that, as a lord himself, a play is to be performed in honor of his recovery. From that point on, a dwarf—Biondello or Grumio, perhaps—narrates the play with a conspicuous on-stage presence, drawing a curtain from scene to scene and sometimes raising the set itself as if it were a curtain. In several scenes the theatre itself is represented as a room in the Lord's castle, with a proscenium stage to be sure but a dramatic platform nevertheless.

The success of the animated production of *Shrew* is also predicated on the clever use of the puppet medium. Puppets are also used in the productions of *Twelfth Night* and *The Tempest,* in other words, in the comedies. We can probably thank the Welsh-Russian collaboration for the insight of drawing on a tradition of dramatic reproduction far older than the Elizabethan stage itself. One of Shakespeare's popular sources for *The Taming of the Shrew* is the *commedia dell'arte* and the tradition of puppeteering from which it might well have sprung. The most effective puppet in the animated production is, as it should be, Kate, who is given uncontrollable red hair arranged—or rather disarranged—in Gorgon-like strands that jump out and about like snakes when she is angry. In the final scene, where Kate finally "submits" to her "lord", "king", and "governor", the snakelike strands are subdued. In terms of our theme, the raucous exchange between Kate and Petruchio is vigorously exercised from time to time but tamed a bit itself. For instance, when the couple first meets, the witty repartee is delivered substantially intact, but the final line of the famous "sting in the tail" bit is cut. Petruchio asks if he should depart as ordered with his "tongue" in Kate's "tail", and protests, "Good Kate; I am a gentleman". Kate does manage to fire a chamber pot out the window at Petruchio's head early on, reminiscent of Xantippe's indignant treatment of her philosopher husband, Socrates, but alas, the pot is empty. Most surprising, perhaps, is the decision to cut the wedding ceremony, which is narrated by Biondello in the text, but fully represented in the funniest scene in Franco Zeffirelli's staging of the nuptials for Elizabeth Taylor and Richard Burton as Kate and Petruchio in his celebrated film version of the play. Opportunities, however, to represent Petruchio quaffing the communion wine or knocking the officiating priest about are avoided, thus toning down the scandal of Shakespeare's play and Zeffirelli's film. Also cut, to accommodate the brevity of the cartoons, are the subplots involving the courtships of Lucentio and Bianca and Gremio [Hortensio] and the Widow. These characters are introduced by the dwarf, however, in anticipation of the final banquet scene and Petruchio's wager about whose wife is most obedient to her husband. Actually, in terms of feminist reinterpretations of the play, the ending of the animated tale is rather bland. The cartoon Kate, dutiful by the tale's end, has been systematically tamed throughout her ordeal, deprived of food but apparently not sex (pillows are thrown mysteriously out the bedroom door in Petruchio's castle on the wedding night), has her tailored dress ripped to shreds, her hat taken from her, and subscribes to Petruchio's recalcitrant readings of the time on their journey back to Padua. The animated *Shrew* concludes by returning to the story of Christopher Sly. In the original, of course, the induction plot is dropped as the play begins. The animated Sly, however, impressed with the taming of Kate he has watched—"I now know how to tame a shrew", he exclaims—returns to the tavern and scolds his own wife as a shrew, only to be summarily kicked out the door by her.

SUBPLOTS AND BAWDY LANGUAGE ARE ELIMINATED

The plays are simplified in these films by eliminating the complications of subplots rather than sacrificing detail in the main plot or 'tale'. The near on-stage chaos that characterizes most Shakespearean productions, that sense of overripe rhetorical abundance and dramatic contrivance, is shaved down to its essentials in these 'cartoons'—taken in the original sense of the term as sketch—which are reduced ultimately to those unities of time and space privileged by neoclassic aesthetics. While the "rude mechanicals" do appear and rehearse once in *A Midsummer Night's Dream,* the Pyramus and Thisbe play is cut completely. What a loss to children and students! Shakespeare rigs his play so that the "hempen homespuns" steal the show, transforming the potentially tragic tale of the young predecessors of Romeo and Juliet—if we are to believe the sequence of the plays according to Stanley Wells and Gary Taylor—into a "lamentable comedy." The focus in the film is on the fairies and especially the lovers. Most of the grotesque comedy of class-mixing in the forest— gods quarreling over children, elite lovers cavorting and exchanging mates, and menial laborers arguing about dramatic theory—is discarded in favor of a romantic focus without distraction. *Hamlet* is pared down as well. Much of the bawdy exchange between, say, Hamlet and his old buddies-turned-toadies, Rosencrantz and Guildenstern, is eliminated because their parts are cut in the film. The complications to the standard revenge plot Shakespeare cooks up for us in *Hamlet* are also eliminated. For instance, Hamlet, who in the play is looking for ways to avoid his destiny as murderer, is never shown sparing Claudius in the film because in killing the king at prayer he might "this same villain send / To heaven". The animated *Hamlet,* in short, reconverts the play into the simple revenge plot Shakespeare inherited from Thomas Kyd and which he obviously intended to subvert and compromise in his own tale of vengeance forestalled. . . .

VIOLENCE IN THE *TALES*

It may be generalized that the animated tales are short on bawdy, if not sexual glamor, but they are long on violence with even flashes of what might be called 'gratuitous' violence. The bawdy exchange of Samson, Gregory, and the Montagues in 1.1 of *Romeo and Juliet,* which actually fends off the violence between the clans, is removed as it is in almost every film version of the play, but the violent dueling is retained. Actually, the animated *Romeo and Juliet* is the least violent of the three tragedies, somewhat surprising in the wake of Baz Luhrmann's bloody rehashing of the play in

his film version. The animated tale eliminates the murder of
Paris by Romeo in the tomb and scales down the violence of
the duels between Mercutio and Tybalt and the killing of Tybalt by Romeo. The animated *Hamlet* is relatively gentle, too,
but draws out the sword fight of its hero and Laertes which
Hamlet pursues in sport until he discovers the plot of
Claudius. Then there is plenty of blood, but the actual execution of Claudius by Hamlet is, for some reason, left out.

Where the animated *Romeo and Juliet* and *Hamlet* take us
gently, almost reluctantly, into the night of tragic violence
and death, the animated *Macbeth* virtually revels in the
blood and guts spilled on every occasion in the play. The animators of this segment of the tales obviously took Roman
Polanski's frightening film version of the play to heart. The
film opens with battle scenes not even included in the text
since Macbeth is returning from this war as the play begins.
Soldiers are hacked to death and one is decapitated complete with all the visual trimmings—the head flies, blood
spurts everywhere, and the soldier cries out in torment. The
witches are omnipresent, haggish, and spectral. A jester
wearing a mask of a skull beats a drum consumed in flames
to punctuate each new violent initiative of the Macbeths.
The murder of Duncan itself is performed off-screen, as it is
in the play but not the Polanski film. In preparation for the
banquet actually celebrating the murder of Banquo, which is
shown in flashback in the tale, a fish, bird, and a deer looking like Bambi are decapitated with a butcher's knife, once
again with blood spurting out of severed veins and arteries.
"Blood will have blood", Macbeth remarks about this point
in the tale just before Banquo appears flooding the table
with the stuff. His mutilated face appears to Macbeth in the
blood-red wine he is drinking as well. We are spared the violent murder of Lady Macduff and her "pretty little chick-
ens", but see it recreated in flashbacks when Macbeth is dis-
patched by Macduff. Interesting enough, almost all the
scenes where Macduff laments the loss of "all my pretty
children and their dam in one fell swoop" are retained in the
animated tale. The animators have been sensitive to the consequences of violence here. Macbeth reviews the murders
he has committed visually during the "tomorrow, tomorrow,
and tomorrow" soliloquy, particularly the execution of Lady
Macduff and her children. Another bloody battle scene follows focusing on the duel of Macbeth and Macduff, who in

vanquishing his rival, hoists the bloody, grimacing head of Macbeth up on a pike. . . .

NUDITY IN THE *TALES*

There is sexually explicit material in the animated films aplenty, mostly nudity, gratuitous nudity, in fact. Why Shakespeare's plays inspire nudity in modern productions like Peter Brook's *A Midsummer Night's Dream,* Roman Polanski's *Macbeth,* and Peter Greenaway's *Prospero's Books* is a mystery awaiting explanation, but they do. Instead of the verbal references to "nipples" in, say, *Romeo and Juliet,* we get 'virtual', visual nipples in the animated *Dream,* the nipples of Helena and Hermia protruding through diaphanous dresses. The costumes are Greek, so it is all right, one guesses. The nude scene between the lovers in Zeffirelli's *Romeo and Juliet*—scandalous for the teachers who use the film in middle school classrooms—is, surprisingly enough, retained in the animated tale of the play. With voice-overs filling us in on various twists and turn of the plot, an image of the nude lovers floats in the upper half of the screen: Juliet's bare back and breasts are revealed, minus nipples, however. And finally, in the animated *Macbeth* there is a diminutive cherub with a crown who represents the future kings descended from Banquo. As he delivers his political prophecies he rotates. The baby is nude with his infant genitals exposed, offensive enough in some conservative school districts in South Carolina to eliminate its uses in middle school. All in all, it is a curious phenomenon that violence and nudity are licit in these films presumably made for children, but the sexual details of the various tragic plots cannot be delivered as *speech* by the characters. It is the words that offend, not the images. Language, not visual content or even behavior, is the crux for the censors. Language must be contained and controlled. Offensive terminology cannot be glamorized; it represents a verbal freedom that cannot be contained. "Nipples", "dugs", "pricks" are certain to evoke offense and censure for school children. Visual nudity, on the other hand, can be and is glamorized through the technique known as air-brushing in the visual arts and in these animated versions of the plays. . . .

THE ANIMATED *OTHELLO*

In the plays Shakespeare provides us with a stunning range of aliens, mysterious "strangers", as [literary critic] Leslie

Fiedler called them years ago, characters dancing on the margin of European society in an age which witnessed the triangular collision of the New and Old Worlds and Africa—Aaron the Moor, the Prince of Morocco, Shylock the Jew, Othello, the Moor of Venice, and Caliban—to name the most conspicuous of the lot. So, in this age when teachers are mandated to expose students to the complicated interrelationships of the 'global village', how are Shakespeare's aliens represented in the animated tales marketed for such students? Most are left out, but two of the most conspicuous and tragic are portrayed: Othello and Caliban, the former with a real measure of African dignity, the latter, like a cartoon monster. There are no other Blacks or Jews in any of the animated tales, no instances of what we might call non-traditional casting, and no experimentation with gender-switching which is invited throughout the Shakespearean canon. I did note one character who is suspiciously dark, Prospero, but there is an explanation for that. As Peter Erickson has shown, there is a tradition of the black magus or wise man in the visual art of the Renaissance, magic being associated with 'blackness' and Africa, as Othello intimates in his discourse on the origin of his mysterious handkerchief.

The visual element is more crucial in *Othello*, perhaps, than in any other play of Shakespeare, and the animated rendition takes full advantage of this fact. After all, its hero demands the "ocular proof" of the handkerchief—in other words, "evidence" from and for the eyes—to corroborate his suspicion that his wife, Desdemona, has been "topped" by Cassio. More importantly, the play has in the last twenty years come to be understood as it must have been in its own time, as an exposure of the growing racial tensions that the institution of slavery was provoking between Europe and Africa. The "mark" of slavery in mid-millennial Europe was visual: skin color. The opening scene of the play is a veritable cornucopia of racist imagery: "what a full fortune does the thick-lips owe"; "an old black ram / Is tupping your white ewe"; "you'll have your daughter cover'd with a Barbary horse".

Miscegenation—and the interracial jealousy and rivalry that inspire it—is the scandal Iago whips up, and it drives this play as clearly as regicide drives *Macbeth* and revenge does *Hamlet*. The animated tale consequently opens with a passionate kiss between a very black Othello and a very white, indeed a pasty-faced Desdemona who remains dressed in various shades of pale throughout the film. Even her eyes are white with a tint of gray. After the kiss we jump forward in the play at the outset (filmmakers love to re-arrange and tinker with Shakespeare's explosive beginnings) to Desdemona playfully wrapping Othello's head with the handkerchief which "did an Egyptian to my mother give"— the visual motif linked clearly with Othello's African her-itage. Unlike most film versions of the play, including the productions of Orson Welles (1952) and Oliver Parker (1995), the animated tale courageously retains an abbreviated open-ing scene with most of its outrageously racial epithets in tact. Othello's *apologia* designed to show just how he wooed Des-demona, "charming" her only by "the dangers [he] had passed", is narrated in a series of visual tableaux that vividly illustrate his African past. That past is touched on again in the visual depiction of his mother, looking very Egyptian, who bequeathed him the notorious handkerchief. Braban-tio's strange reversal in his opinion of Othello, totally predi-cated on the racist reaction that it was one thing to have a dis-tinguished 'blackamoor' as a house-guest and quite another to have him as a son-in-law, is also retained. In reaction to Desdemona's "treason of the blood", Brabantio warns Othello—reaffirming the visual theme in the play, "Look to her Moor, if thou hast eyes to see; / She has deceiv'd her fa-ther, and may thee". The visual motif extends to the color choreography of the film. Iago gives his speech about the ravages of the "green-ey'd monster which doth mock / The meat it feeds of" in a vernal forest, and the colors of the faces of Othello and Desdemona modulate depending on the situ-ation: Othello's from brown to ashen gray to "black as pitch", Desdemona's from pale to a "whiter shade of pale" to "al-abaster", depending on the passion of the encounter. When that passion is sexual, the colors blaze at opposite ends of the spectrum. Finally, in keeping with the tendency of the series to visualize narrative moments in the plays, Desdemona's story of "Barbary", who loved a man that "prov'd mad / And did forsake her" is dramatically depicted with a suicide by drowning reminiscent of the death of Ophelia. . . .

CALIBAN

The other alien who is dramatically represented in the ani-mated tales is Caliban, the slave of Prospero in *The Tempest*.

In the tale, as in the play, Prospero introduces Caliban by expressing his gratitude that the slave "does make our fire, / Fetch in our wood, and serves in offices / That profit" him and Miranda on the island. The appearance of Caliban is always a spectacle, because one rarely has an idea what version of the character will materialize on stage: the black slave, the noble savage, the Neanderthal, or the fish-like "monster of the isle with four legs", as Trinculo calls him. The clamation puppet representing Caliban in the tale is a freak of nature with amphibious feet, feathers instead of hair, scaly sides and flanks, and reptilian spikes down his back. He squats and hops about like a toad. Most contemporary productions of the play, like the recent production at the Shakespeare Theatre in Washington, D.C. (1998), and most current scholarly interpretations insist on a human and often a black Caliban to underscore the rise of European and American slavery which was contemporaneous with the original production of the play. The Caliban who appears on stage often represents the reification of the textual character in terms of racist, imperialistic language. To depict Caliban as literally amphibious could be likened to a portrayal of Othello as a leering ram with "big lips" and the body of a Barbary horse, for that is how the Moor is characterized by Iago and Roderigo in the opening scene of the play.

The Caliban in the animated tale makes no claim on the island, which in the text is his by Sycorax, a witch from "Argiers", in other words Africa. No mention is made of the other African motif in the play either, the marriage of Alonso's daughter Claribel to Tunis, also an African. Although the attempted rape of Miranda by Caliban is not discussed in the tale, one of the slave's first lines is, "If thou did not prevent me, I'd have peopled this isle with Calibans", a comment expressing the dangerous fecundity of the alien, his tendency to threaten and populate European territory. Nothing remains of the link of servitude between Ariel and Caliban that Shakespeare implies throughout the play. Ariel, like Puck in the animated *Dream*, is the dependable little stooge who never complains about his servitude, and who is never threatened, as Caliban is, with horrific corporal punishments for disobedience. Caliban is also never allowed to express his celebration of the island which was given to him by Sycorax before the arrival of Prospero. The islanders, represented in Peter Greenaway's *Prospero's Books* (1991) by a cast of thousands of European nudes, are merely grotesques in the tale—skeletal presences, inhuman. Nor does Gonzalo get to deliver his tribute to aborigines of the "plantation isle" in the tale, celebrating in the text their innocence, *naiveté*, and freedom from the greed and vengeance that [French philosopher Michel de] Montaigne, for one, portrayed as characteristically European. Finally, after acknowledging that "this thing of darkness" is his in the animated tale, Prospero surrenders the island to Caliban who runs around its perimeter frantically, obviously at a loss about what to do with the territory he has claimed as his from the outset. The animated *Tempest* is predictably Old World Shakespeare in its assumptions about the inferiority of Africans, aborigines, and women.

To sum up my point here, more Shakespeare is better, particularly on the popular level where the plays were initially generated. I appreciate and celebrate the enormous effort that went into the production of these eight animated tales, some of which are, as Stanley Wells effused, "not just educational aids that will introduce children to Shakespeare painlessly, but independent works of art which, like many of the operas, ballets, and paintings based on Shakespeare, transmute their raw material into something rich and strange in its own right". . . . [However,] the animated films, lovingly produced as they are, knock the stuffing out of Shakespeare, that is the comic farce that revels in the bawdry, tolerates the eccentric, and celebrates difference. The language of the plays often proves to be too hot to handle, too provocative, too scandalous for almost all modern renditions, even in the rock-and-roll idiom. Strategic editing of the verbal sort seems geared more to omitting transgressive text, or translating it into visual sentimentality, than letting it stand for the passionate pleasure and eventual analysis that it will certainly inspire.

Shakespeare for Everyone

Graham Holderness

As British scholar Graham Holderness considers the
giant 1994 Shakespeare Festival in Stratford and reflects on England's fascination with its national hero,
he contemplates the ways in which Shakespeare has
been claimed by everyone. At times Shakespeare is
read narcissistically, as a reflection of one's own
wishes and desires, Holderness explains; at other
times Shakespeare becomes the site of cultural conflict and competition, as happens in the ongoing authorship controversy. The media storm surrounding
a primary-school head teacher's decision not to take
her children to a performance of Prokofiev's ballet
Romeo and Juliet became another example of cultural conflict in 1994. In a context of narcissistic interpretations, nationalist presumption, and contending ideological factions, however, Holderness still
finds in Shakespeare's poetry a strangely transformative power. He concludes that Shakespeare remains a seemingly inexhaustible source of new
meanings.

Among Holderness's other publications are *The
Shakespeare Myth, Shakespeare: The Play of History,
Selections* (essays on Shakespeare), and *Shake-
speare's History.*

1994 can now rank with 1769 as the year of another 'Great
Shakespeare Jubilee', indeed as the year that witnessed [in
the words of the program for the international festival] 'the
first event of its kind in this country and probably the world:
an international multi-disciplined celebration of the work
and influence of Shakespeare'. This grand Bardfest took the
form of a massive two-month Shakespeare extravaganza,

Graham Holderness, *Cultural Shakespeare: Essays in the Shakespeare Myth.* Hatfield,
UK: University of Hertfordshire Press, 2001. Copyright © 2001 by Graham Holderness.
Reproduced by permission.

mobilised by the Royal Shakespeare Company, and focused on a major theatre season, with an associated series of events and exhibitions at the Barbican Centre. In order that no one should escape this Shakespearean saturation, there was also a wall-to-wall television Shakespeare season, broadcast on BBC2, and entitled 'Bard on the Box'. The latter provided innumerable ten-minute interludes of curious and interesting trivia about Elizabethan culture—from cooking cod-pieces to wearing them—and a number of full length feature programmes on issues such as the development of Shakespeare's reputation as the 'national poet'. One programme, entitled 'The Battle of Wills', addressed the long-running controversy over identity which takes the form of contending claims on the authorship of Shakespeare's plays.

SOMETHING FOR EVERYONE

The governing title of the festival was 'Everybody's Shakespeare'. There is something for everyone, the title suggests, in this broad-ranging and diversified, international and multi-cultural, celebration. Whatever your cultural background and personal preferences, you were bound to find here something of interest. In one sense the title was individualising, speaking to the number and multiplicity of persons. In another sense it was universalising, since the common ground on which this infinitely diversified constituency can meet, the global totality that contains all these individuals, was the one and only 'Shakespeare'. Thus 'Everybody's Shakespeare' was also 'the greatest ever celebration of the genius of Shakespeare'. What enables us collectively to inhabit 'Shakespeare' is not that which particularises and differentiates us, but that which universalises him. This immediate and contemporary availability of Shakespeare can be recognised as yet another manifestation of that universal genius proclaimed by Ben Jonson: 'He was not for an age, but for all time' and still echoed and embodied in the Department for Education's *National Curriculum for English* which sees Shakespeare's plays as so rich that in every age they can produce fresh meanings.

Shakespeare is everybody's. But the syntax allows for another reading: 'Everybody *is* Shakespeare'. This alternative interpretation remains sub-textual in the words but was foregrounded in the festival's publicity leaflet which exhibited a politically correct rent-a-crowd: black, white, yellow;

male and female; young and old. Each face peeped cheerfully out from behind the mask of Shakespeare's face in its most familiar representation, the Droeshout engraving from *Mr William Shakespeares Comedies, Histories, & Tragedies* of 1623. Everybody then can become Shakespeare, or at least personify Shakespeare; for the mask is also, of course, the standard symbol of drama, the theatrical prototype for assuming a role, playing a part. We can all play Shakespeare, or play at being Shakespeare, by participation in the proffered ritual of celebration. The Droeshout engraving is particularly appropriate to make this point since (as viewers of the TV programme 'The Battle of Wills' were informed) it has been suspected, by those concerned to question Shakespeare's true identity, that the face of the portrait is actually a mask. 'No human being could possibly look like that' affirmed one witness, plugging the claims of Christopher Marlowe. Setting aside the improbability of Marlowe's sitting behind a mask while the artist engraved its likeness, we can readily accept that the face *is* notoriously separable from its physical context, since it has become, through continuous familiar usage, an immediately recognisable cultural icon. That which is universal is also anonymous. Why *should* Shakespeare look like any other human being, if he is, by virtue of his 'genius', so essentially *different* from every other human being? 'Looke', Ben Jonson says, 'not on his Picture, but his Booke'. The author had already, by 1623, been subsumed into the work, the 'genius', present in the writing, quite invisible in the face. Anthony Burgess, in the conclusion of his fanciful 'biography' of Shakespeare, plays with this idea and formulates clearly the impossible paradox of genius and universality:

> Martin Droeshout's engraving, . . . has never been greatly liked . . . The face is that of a commercial traveller growing bald in the service of an ungrateful firm.

> We need not repine at the lack of a satisfactory Shakespeare portrait. To see his face, we need only look in a mirror. He is ourselves, ordinary suffering humanity, fired by moderate ambitions, concerned with money, the victim of desire, all too mortal. To his back, like a hump, was strapped a miraculous but somehow irrelevant talent . . . We are all Will. Shakespeare is the name of one of our redeemers.

Everybody is Shakespeare, then, minus the hump. Shakespeare is simply one of us, with the hump. The presence or absence of that hump, however, that 'talent' or 'genius', can (we are told) make all the difference between an ordinary mortal and a 'redeemer', a man and a god. . . .

SOME READ SHAKESPEARE NARCISSISTICALLY

'Shall I compare thee to a summer's day?' asks Shakespeare's *Sonnet XVIII.* No, is the answer, because the world of nature presents an image of change and extremity; while the beauty of the 'fair friend' to whom the sonnet is addressed is, by contrast, immutable and eternal:

> But thy eternall Sommer shall not fade,
> Nor loose possession of that faire thou ow'st,
> Nor shall death brag thou wandr'st in his shade,
> When in eternall lines to time thou grow'st,
> > So long as men can breath or eyes can see,
> > So long liues this, and this giues life to thee.

If the immortality of the lover is guaranteed by the durability of these celebratory 'lines' of poetry, then that immortality is conditional on their survival. In turn, the poetry only survives so long as it is spoken and read; uttered by the breath of men, seen by living eyes. Men, however, cease to breathe, eyes lose their vision and poetry can be forgotten. This beauty is immortal only in so far as it is embodied in poetry; on condition that the poetry is read and subject to the availability of living readers.

There could be no better illustration of this truth than the subsequent fate of that poem, as it was recently deployed in a contemporary advertisement for women's clothes. In this representation, as in innumerable other vernacular quotations and lay readings, the poem delivered a modern heterosexual ideal of erotic escapism: the freedom of an open beach, occupied by a stereotype of feminine beauty: tall, blonde, barefoot but incongruously sheathed in a tight black cocktail dress. The image of desire produced by the original sonnet was, of course, quite different, since its object was not a feminine but a masculine beauty. The poem celebrated the beauty of a young man, described in *'Sonnet XX'* as bearing 'a woman's face, by Nature's own hand painted'; created as a woman by Nature who then 'fell a-doting', equipped him with that 'one thing' that could make him an object of female desire ('prick'd out for women's pleasure') and thereby denied the poet his own proper erotic satisfaction. The 'desire' embodied in the poem is utterly unlike the 'desire' elicited by its modern appropriation. In the mirror of the poem's language, the modern reader is invited to discern a perfect reflection of his own desire. Meanwhile the poet, the young man, the painful and complex eroticism of those homosexual sonnets, are left to sink into the well without trace, dead indeed.

Now it is also true, of course, that another modern critic who might read the poem as a 'gay lyric', a celebration of homosexual love, is also finding in the poem's reflective surface a mirror-image of his own desire. . . .

THE AUTHORSHIP CONTROVERSY REVEALS COMPETING VISIONS OF BRITISH NATIONAL IDENTITY

Shakespeare's life is another territory of intense cultural conflict and competition. The long-running controversy over Shakespeare's identity provides another example of the need for almost everyone to claim and possess their own Shakespeare. These controversies are hardly at the centre of academic work on Shakespeare but certainly exercise some fascination over the public imagination: an entire BBC programme in the 'Bard on the Box' series was devoted to the competing claims of various candidates on authorship of the Shakespeare canon. The kind of personal appropriation represented by the 'Everybody is Shakespeare' slogan features very strongly here, in that rival claimants either are (or claim to be) descended from their preferred candidate. An American woman named Delia Bacon, who claimed direct descent from the former Lord Chancellor, initially established the Baconian hypothesis. The leading protagonist for the claim of Edward de Vere, Earl of Oxford, is the present holder of that name and title.

The curious thing about these controversies does not reside in the claims themselves but in the peculiar intensity of their focus on this particular writer. What does it matter, if the value lies in the writing, who actually penned it? The answer in fact has everything to do with the pre-eminent status accorded to Shakespeare, from the eighteenth century onwards, as the British national poet. If a writer is held to represent a nation, then people will expect him to perform that function effectively in their eyes. If there are within the nation radically different views of how the nation should be represented, it is likely that any one writer will be seen as a partial, inadequate or distorting image. Most of the rival claims on Shakespearean authorship were at the outset based simply on social class. It has been a matter of resentment that this great corpus of British national writing appears to have been produced by a man who had no university education and so a graduate alternative is found in Christopher Marlowe. It has been regarded as scandalous that the national poet should have been a product of the lower middle class and so aristocratic alternatives are sought in the Earl of Oxford or Frances Bacon, courtier, intellectual and statesman. It seems a national humiliation that Shakespeare not only emerged from relatively obscure and humble beginnings in a small Midlands market town but even retired back to them after completing the great Shakespearean *oeuvre*: so candidates of greater eminence and public visibility have been advanced, right up to Queen Elizabeth herself. . . .

A Teacher Who Said "No" to Shakespeare

In January of 1994 a media storm broke out around the headteacher of a Hackney primary school, who allegedly declined an opportunity for her children to receive discounted tickets for a performance of Prokofiev's ballet *Romeo and Juliet* at Covent Garden. Jane Brown was a much-respected professional, enjoying very strong parental support for her educational policies, and responsible for saving the school from a hit-list of 'problem' institutions. Her work in this context had been specifically praised by the Office for Standards in Education. The decision she made was the sort of administrative decision headteachers make every day: whether or not the school could invest the money, time and effort involved in taking the children on an organised trip.

The controversy however crystallised around the particular reason she is alleged to have given for not taking up this offer: that '*Romeo and Juliet* was a story almost entirely about heterosexual love'. The tabloid press predictably sounded their alarm bells around 'political correctness' and its pernicious effects on education. The Prime Minister jumped in feet first, declaring in the Commons that 'political correctness is widely unpopular among parents who want their children to be taught in schools the basics of the English language and English history'. (It is not entirely clear how these aims could be furthered by means of a Russian ballet, based on an English version of an Italian story, with all the words taken out).

Mʀ. WILLIAM

SHAKESPEARES

COMEDIES,
HISTORIES, &
TRAGEDIES.

Publiſhed according to the True Originall Copies.

LONDON
Printed by Iſaac Iaggard, and Ed. Blount. 1623.

Shakespeare's works continue to be relevant and meaningful to people of all ages and cultural backgrounds.

The media then unleashed what many described as a 'witch-hunt' against Jane Brown, who was forcibly 'outed' as a lesbian, and characterised by the tabloids as one whose imputed sexual 'deviance' had issued in the cultural deviance of objecting to Shakespeare. As the controversy got nastier, there were further allegations of corrupt and unethical professional conduct. The moral outrage co-ordinated by the press had its counterparts on the streets of Hackney, as Jane Brown began to receive death threats from some of her 'neighbours'.

The fundamental assumption in all this was that no one has the right to refuse Shakespeare. Here the idea of universal entitlement embodied in the National Curriculum appears in its coercive form: you will take your dose of 'everybody's Shakespeare', whether you like it or not. Shakespeare, like Guinness [beer], is good for you; so to prevent children from gaining access to the Bard is, in this ideology, to deny them the healthy and life-giving cultural sustenance of their universal birthright. So on the one hand in this controversy we have Shakespeare, the national culture, the literary heritage, and normalcy; on the other, political correctness, loony-left educational policies, studying [the TV show] *Neighbours,* and deviancy.

The reality of this situation in practice hardly fitted the standard ideological model. To start with, was it actually 'Shakespeare'? In one sense Shakespeare was required, since the violent clamour of media protest against the teacher could only have been mobilised around the national Bard. Would the same outrage have arisen over ballet, very much a minority cultural interest? Or over Prokofiev, not by any means everybody's glass of vodka, rather than Shakespeare? Headlines such as 'Lesbian Teacher opposed to Ballet', or 'Pupils prevented from Partaking of Prokofiev' would not have carried the same weight.

Despite [Prime Minister] John Major's appeal to the silent majority, the parents of the school's children were 100 per cent supportive of their headteacher. To them the issue of the trip seemed less important than the teacher's record on educational standards, cultural integration and social harmony in a school environment of severe poverty and deprivation, racial tension, crime and violence. A Turkish father described Jane Brown as a teacher who 'cares': 'my boy doesn't get beaten up in the playground any more'. An African parent told reporters that Jane Brown had taken a real interest in her children, and created a school 'safe and nice with lots of learning'. In this community of intense social problems and powerful social solidarity, the Tory government's policy of 'parent-power' seriously backfired.

Even the teacher's particular judgement on the suitability of that show for her children deserves more serious consideration. Can we be so sure that the action of *Romeo and Juliet* would automatically function as an innocuous aesthetic experience or as the vehicle of sound moral values for primary school children? A 15-year-old girl defies her parents to marry a man she chooses. What price family values? A young couple contracts a secret marriage, of doubtful legality, in clear transgression of parental authority and social convention. Aren't there enough teenage pregnancies in Hackney already?

More seriously, much of the action of *Romeo and Juliet* concerns urban violence and gang warfare, what would today be called organised bullying and systematic intimidation. Given that playground violence was the number one problem identified by *primary* Head Teachers in a survey published at the time of the Jane Brown controversy, doesn't Shakespeare at least have a case to answer? As one journalist put it, 'Jane Brown was worried that a ballet about family feuding, violence and death could upset some pupils. Away from Hackney that seems an implausible explanation; there it has a more authentic ring'.

Lastly, as we recall the complex sexuality of Shakespeare it seems perverse to use his name as the big stick of sexual normalcy with which to beat lesbians. Certainly when Jane Brown began to receive death threats from the cultural vigilantes of Hackney, possibly for the first time in history objection to Shakespeare came to be regarded as a capital crime. . . .

A CHANCE ENCOUNTER WITH SHAKESPEARE'S POETRY PROVES INSPIRATIONAL

Full fathom five thy father lies;
Of his bones are coral made;
Those are pearls that were his eyes
Nothing of him that doth fade,
But doth suffer a sea-change
Into something rich and strange.

I recently read these lines, from Ariel's song in *The Tempest*, not at my desk or in a library, but travelling on the London underground's Northern Line, full-fathom five beneath Leicester Square. The poem appeared as one of London Transport's series of posters *Poems on the Underground*. There I was, on what travellers know as the 'Misery Line',

my body impacted with the suffering flesh of a thousand
fellow-passengers. I looked up, read the poster, and for a
moment the Misery Line suffered a sea change. In that mysterious depth, a miraculous transformation took place. All
that was perishable and corruptible mutated into the glow-
ing phosphorescence of pearl and coral; all that was imper-
manent and decaying took on the immortality, the strange
fragile beauty of living mineral. The dirt, the physical dis-
comfort, the mental squalor of the Northern Line, embell-
ished by the words of Shakespeare, underwent a transformation into something rich and strange.

The train stopped at my station; I alighted; nothing had
changed. The Northern Line was still the Misery line. 'Poetry' wrote W.H. Auden, 'makes nothing happen' But also, 'it
survives in the valley of its making'. I could easily have felt
cheated and deceived but I found it more difficult to creep
up on this poem and surprise it by revealing it as a cheap
trick. Recalling [critic] Stephen Greenblatt's assertion that
the self-conscious fictionality of poetry can 'anticipate and
compensate for' the 'disappearance of the life that empowered it,' I remembered that this poem knows it is a fiction.
After all, Ferdinand's father is not dead at all; not drowned
and rotten, but alive and well and living in that magic island
subsequently identified as Bermuda. Ariel's song, compelling and beautiful as it is, is a pack of lies.

But still, I heard the music, whether it was true or false,
i'the earth or i'the air. My understanding of it may have
changed. Knowing that poetry 'makes nothing happen' I yet
find myself admitting the strange tenacity with which it survives, 'in the valley of its making', to disclose new meanings
from the seemingly inexhaustible phenomenon of Shakespeare.

APPENDIX OF DOCUMENTS

DOCUMENT 1: SHAKESPEARE DEDICATES *VENUS AND ADONIS* TO THE EARL OF SOUTHAMPTON

Shakespeare's long narrative poem, Venus and Adonis, *was published in 1593 and appears to have been carefully prepared for printing. Dedicated to a young patron of literature, Henry Wriothesley, Earl of Southampton, it was very popular and was reprinted nine times during Shakespeare's life. The dedication is one of the surviving letters that Shakespeare wrote.*

RIGHT HONORABLE,

I know not how I shall offend in dedicating my unpolished lines to your lordship, nor how the world will censure me for choosing so strong a prop to support so weak a burden; only if your honor seem but pleased, I account myself highly praised, and vow to take advantage of all idle hours, till I have honored you with some graver labor. But if the first heir of my invention[1] prove deformed, I shall be sorry it had so noble a godfather, and never after ear so barren a land, for fear it yield me still so bad a harvest. I leave it to your honorable survey, and your honor to your heart's content, which I wish may always answer your own wish and the world's hopeful expectation.

Your honor's in all duty,
William Shakespeare.

1. Possibly meaning Shakespeare's first printed work or his first non-theatrical work.

William Shakespeare, Dedication to *Venus and Adonis.*

DOCUMENT 2: SHAKESPEARE'S "WILL" SONNETS

Among Shakespeare's sonnets addressed to the speaker's mistress, the "Dark Lady," are several which play with the multiple connotations of the word "will" and the name "Will." Sonnets 135 and 136 are two of the "will" sonnets, and they are sometimes used as evidence that the poet is Will Shakespeare not Edward de Vere.

135
Whoever hath her wish, thou hast thy Will,
And Will to boot, and Will in overplus;

More than enough am I that vex thee still,
To thy sweet will making addition thus.
Wilt thou, whose will is large and spacious,
Not once vouchsafe to hide my will in thine?
Shall will in others seem right gracious,
And in my will no fair acceptance shine?
The sea, all water, yet receives rain still
And in abundance addeth to his store;
So thou, being rich in Will, add to thy
Will One will of mine, to make thy large Will more.
    Let no unkind no fair beseechers kill;
    Think all but one, and me in that one Will.

136

If thy soul check thee that I come so near,
Swear to thy blind soul that I was thy Will,
And will, thy soul knows, is admitted there;
Thus far for love my love suit, sweet, fulfill.
Will will fulfill the treasure of thy love,
Ay, fill it full with wills, and my will one.
In things of great receipt with ease we prove
Among a number one is reckoned none.
Then in the number let me pass untold,
Though in thy store's account I one must be;
For nothing hold me, so it please thee hold
That nothing me, a something, sweet, to thee.
    Make but my name thy love, and love that still,
    And then thou lovest me for my name is Will.

William Shakespeare, "Sonnet 135" and "Sonnet 136."

DOCUMENT 5: A BATTLE OF WITS IN *THE TAMING OF THE SHREW*

*Petruchio is determined to woo, win, and marry Kate for the dowry
her father has promised, but when he meets her he discovers that she
is his equal in verbal repartee. This selection from* The Taming of the
Shrew *reveals Shakespeare's creative use of the blank verse line.*

PETRUCHIO
    Good morrow, Kate, for that's your name, I hear.
KATHARINA
    Well have you heard, but something hard of hearing.
    They call me Katharine that do talk of me.
PETRUCHIO
    You lie, in faith, for you are called plain Kate,
    And bonny Kate, and sometimes Kate the curst;
    But Kate, the prettiest Kate in Christendom,
    Kate of Kate Hall, my superdainty Kate,
    For dainties are all Kates, and therefore, Kate,
    Take this of me, Kate of my consolation:

Hearing thy mildness praised in every town,
Thy virtues spoke of, and thy beauty sounded,
Yet not so deeply as to thee belongs,
Myself am moved to woo thee for my wife.

KATHARINA
Moved? In good time! Let him that moved you hither
Remove you hence. I knew you at the first
You were a movable.

PETRUCHIO   Why, what's a movable?

KATHARINA
A joint stool.

PETRUCHIO   Thou hast hit it. Come, sit on me.

KATHARINA
Asses are made to bear, and so are you.

PETRUCHIO
Women are made to bear, and so are you.

KATHARINA
No such jade as you, if me you mean.

PETRUCHIO
Alas, good Kate, I will not burden thee,
For knowing thee to be but young and light.

KATHARINA
Too light for such a swain as you to catch,
And yet as heavy as my weight should be.

PETRUCHIO
Should be? Should—buzz!

KATHARINA   Well ta'en, and like a buzzard.

PETRUCHIO
O slow-winged turtle, shall a buzzard take thee?

KATHARINA
Ay, for a turtle, as he takes a buzzard.

PETRUCHIO
Come, come, you wasp, i' faith you are too angry.

KATHARINA
If I be waspish, best beware my sting.

PETRUCHIO
My remedy is then to pluck it out.

KATHARINA
Ay, if the fool could find it where it lies.

PETRUCHIO
Who knows not where a wasp does wear his sting? In his tail.

KATHARINA   In his tongue.

PETRUCHIO   Whose tongue?

KATHARINA
Yours, if you talk of tales, and so farewell.

PETRUCHIO
What, with my tongue in your tail? Nay, come again.
Good Kate, I am a gentleman—
KATHARINA   That I'll try. *She strikes him.*

William Shakespeare, *The Taming of the Shrew* (act 2, scene 1, lines 182–220).

DOCUMENT 4: ROMEO AND JULIET SHARE A SONNET

When Romeo and Juliet meet at the Capulet's ball, their first words to one another form a sonnet. Romeo speaks the first quatrain (four lines), Juliet the second quatrain, and they share both the third quatrain and the closing couplet (two lines) just as they share a kiss at the end of the sonnet.

ROMEO [*to Juliet*]
If I profane with my unworthiest hand
    This holy shrine, the gentle sin is this:
My lips, two blushing pilgrims, ready stand
    To smooth that rough touch with a tender kiss.
JULIET
Good pilgrim, you do wrong your hand too much,
    Which mannerly devotion shows in this;
For saints have hands that pilgrims' hands do touch,
    And palm to palm is holy palmers' kiss.
ROMEO
Have not saints lips, and holy palmers too?
JULIET
Ay, pilgrim, lips that they must use in prayer.
ROMEO
O, then, dear saint, let lips do what hands do.
    They pray; grant thou, lest faith turn to despair.
JULIET
Saints do not move, though grant for prayers' sake.
ROMEO
Then move not, while my prayer's effect I take.

[*He kisses her.*]

William Shakespeare, *Romeo and Juliet* (act 1, scene 5, lines 94–107).

DOCUMENT 5: SHYLOCK EXPLAINS WHY HE WANTS A POUND OF FLESH

In The Merchant of Venice *the Christian merchant, Antonio, has borrowed money from the Jewish moneylender, Shylock, to finance young Bassanio's courtship of the noble Portia. If Antonio cannot repay the money he has borrowed, he, by written bond, has agreed to forfeit to Shylock a pound of his flesh. Just after Shylock learns that his daughter has eloped with a Christian, he explains to his friend Salerio why he would exact the mortal penalty of a pound of flesh from Antonio.*

. . . But tell us, do you hear whether Antonio have had any loss at sea or no?

SHYLOCK   There I have another bad match! A bankrupt, a prodigal, who dare scarce show his head on the Rialto; a beggar, that was used to come so smug upon the mart! Let him look to his bond. He was wont to call me usurer. Let him look to his bond. He was wont to lend money for a Christian courtesy. Let him look to his bond.

SALERIO   Why, I am sure, if he forfeit, thou wilt not take his flesh. What's that good for?

SHYLOCK   To bait fish withal. If it will feed nothing else, it will feed my revenge. He hath disgraced me, and hindered me half a million, laughed at my losses, mocked at my gains, scorned my nation, thwarted my bargains, cooled my friends, heated mine enemies; and what's his reason? I am a Jew. Hath not a Jew eyes? Hath not a Jew hands, organs, dimensions, senses, affections, passions? Fed with the same food, hurt with the same weapons, subject to the same diseases, healed by the same means, warmed and cooled by the same winter and summer, as a Christian is? If you prick us, do we not bleed? If you tickle us, do we not laugh? If you poison us, do we not die? And if you wrong us, shall we not revenge? If we are like you in the rest, we will resemble you in that. If a Jew wrong a Christian, what is his humility? Revenge. If a Christian wrong a Jew, what should his sufferance be by Christian example? Why, revenge. The villainy you teach me I will execute, and it shall go hard but I will better the instruction.

William Shakespeare, *The Merchant of Venice* (act 3, scene 1, lines 39–69).

DOCUMENT 6: FALSTAFF SPEAKS ON HONOR

In Henry IV, *Shakespeare reveals that Prince Hal's thieving friend and surrogate father, the fat old knight Falstaff, is free of the cant that leads other men, like the noble soldier Hotspur, to live and die for honor.*

FALSTAFF   Hal, if thou see me down in the battle and bestride me, so; 'tis a point of friendship.

PRINCE   Nothing but a colossus can do thee that friendship. Say thy prayers, and farewell.

FALSTAFF   I would 'twere bedtime, Hal, and all well.

PRINCE   Why, thou owest God a death. [*Exit.*]

FALSTAFF   'Tis not due yet; I would be loath to pay him before his day. What need I be so forward with him that calls not on me? Well, 'tis no matter; honor pricks me on. Yea, but how if honor prick me off when I come on? How then? Can honor set to a leg? No. Or an arm? No. Or take away the grief of a wound? No. Honor hath no skill in surgery, then? No. What is honor? A word. What is in that word "honor"? What is that "honor"? Air. A trim reckoning! Who hath it? He that died o' Wednesday. Doth he feel it? No. Doth he hear it? No. 'Tis insensible, then? Yea, to the dead. But will it not live with the living? No. Why? Detraction will not suffer it. Therefore I'll none of it. Honor is a mere scutcheon. And so ends my catechism.

William Shakespeare, *Henry IV* (part one, act 5, scene 1, lines 121–140).

DOCUMENT 7: "ALL THE WORLD'S A STAGE"

Using the stage as a metaphor, the melancholy Jaques explains the many parts one man plays in his lifetime. From infancy to old age, Jaques outlines the seven acts of a man's life. Jaques's speech from As You Like It *is one of the most well known from Shakespeare's plays.*

JAQUES   All the world's a stage,
And all the men and women merely players.
They have their exits and their entrances,
And one man in his time plays many parts,
His acts being seven ages. At first the infant,
Mewling and puking in the nurse's arms.
Then the whining schoolboy, with his satchel
And shining morning face, creeping like snail
Unwillingly to school. And then the lover,
Sighing like furnace, with a woeful ballad
Made to his mistress' eyebrow. Then a soldier,
Full of strange oaths and bearded like the pard,
Jealous in honor, sudden, and quick in quarrel,
Seeking the bubble reputation
Even in the cannon's mouth. And then the justice,
In fair round belly with good capon lined,
With eyes severe and beard of formal cut,
Full of wise saws and modern instances;
And so he plays his part. The sixth age shifts
Into the lean and slippered pantaloon,
With spectacles on nose and pouch on side,
His youthful hose, well saved, a world too wide
For his shrunk shank; and his big manly voice,
Turning again toward childish treble, pipes
And whistles in his sound. Last scene of all,
That ends this strange, eventful history,
Is second childishness and mere oblivion,
Sans teeth, sans eyes, sans taste, sans everything.

William Shakespeare, *As You Like It* (act 2, scene 7, lines 138–165).

DOCUMENT 8: HAMLET WRESTLES WITH "TO BE OR NOT TO BE"

In his most famous soliloquy, Hamlet ponders the relative nobility of passively suffering or actively battling his troubles. From Laurence Olivier to Mel Gibson, twentieth-century actors have considered this speech central to interpreting the character of the Danish prince in Shakespeare's play.

HAMLET

    To be, or not to be, that is the question:
    Whether 'tis nobler in the mind to suffer
    The slings and arrows of outrageous fortune,
    Or to take arms against a sea of troubles
    And by opposing end them. To die, to sleep—
    No more—and by a sleep to say we end
    The heartache and the thousand natural shocks
    That flesh is heir to. 'Tis a consummation
    Devoutly to be wished. To die, to sleep;
    To sleep, perchance to dream. Ay, there's the rub,
    For in that sleep of death what dreams may come,
    When we have shuffled off this mortal coil,
    Must give us pause. There's the respect
    That makes calamity of so long life.
    For who would bear the whips and scorns of time,
    Th' oppressor's wrong, the proud man's contumely,
    The pangs of disprized love, the law's delay,
    The insolence of office, and the spurns
    That patient merit of th' unworthy takes,
    When he himself might his quietus make
    With a bare bodkin? Who would fardels bear,
    To grunt and sweat under a weary life,
    But that the dread of something after death,
    The undiscovered country from whose bourn
    No traveler returns, puzzles the will,
    And makes us rather bear those ills we have
    Than fly to others that we know not of?
    Thus conscience does make cowards of us all;
    And thus the native hue of resolution
    Is sicklied o'er with the pale cast of thought,
    And enterprises of great pitch and moment
    With this regard their currents turn awry
    And lose the name of action.—Soft you now,
    The fair Ophelia. Nymph, in thy orisons
    Be all my sins remembered.

William Shakespeare, *Hamlet* (act 3, scene 1, lines 57–91).

DOCUMENT 9: MARK TWAIN PARODIES HAMLET'S SOLILOQUY

In Mark Twain's 1884 novel, Adventures of Huckleberry Finn, *two con artists, the duke and the king, who are freeloading on Huck's raft, practice for the Shakespearean Revival they plan to perform in "Bricksville, Arkansas." While the duke teaches Hamlet's "To Be or Not To Be" soliloquy to the king, Huck learns it. Of course, the duke's memory is faulty and the soliloquy as he recites it borrows images and phrases from other Shakespearean plays, such as references to Duncan and Birnam Wood from* Macbeth.

"Hamlet's soliloquy, you know; the most celebrated thing in Shake-speare. Ah, it's sublime, sublime! Always fetches the house. I haven't got it in the book—I've only got one volume—but I reckon I can piece it out from memory. I'll just walk up and down a minute, and see if I can call it back from recollection's vaults."

So he went to marching up and down, thinking, and frowning horrible every now and then; then he would hoist up his eye-brows; next he would squeeze his hand on his forehead and stagger back and kind of moan; next he would sigh, and next he'd let on to drop a tear. It was beautiful to see him. By and by he got it. He told us to give attention. Then he strikes a most noble attitude, with one leg shoved forwards, and his arms stretched away up, and his head tilted back, looking up at the sky; and then he begins to rip and rave and grit his teeth; and after that, all through his speech he howled, and spread around, and swelled up his chest, and just knocked the spots out of any acting ever *I* see before. This is the speech—I learned it, easy enough, while he was learning it to the king:

> To be, or not to be; that is the bare bodkin
> That makes calamity of so long life;
> For who would fardels bear, till Birnam Wood do come to
>   Dunsinane,
> But that the fear of something after death
> Murders the innocent sleep,
> Great nature's second course,
> And makes us rather sling the arrows of outrageous fortune
> Than fly to others that we know not of.
> There's the respect must give us pause:
> Wake Duncan with thy knocking! I would thou couldst;
> For who would bear the whips and scorns of time,
> The oppressor's wrong, the proud man's contumely,
> The law's delay, and the quietus which his pangs might take,
> In the dead waste and middle of the night, when churchyards
>   yawn
> In customary suits of solemn black,
> But that the undiscovered country from whose bourne no
>   traveler returns,
> Breathes forth contagion on the world,
> And thus the native hue of resolution, like the poor cat i' the
>   adage,
> Is sicklied o'er with care,
> And all the clouds that lowered o'er our housetops,
> With this regard their currents turn awry,
> And lose the name of action.
> 'Tis a consummation devoutly to be wished. But soft you, the
>   fair Ophelia:
> Ope not thy ponderous and marble jaws,
> But get thee to a nunnery—go!

Well, the old man he liked that speech, and he mighty soon got it so he could do it first rate. It seemed like he was just born for it; and when he had his hand in and was excited, it was perfectly lovely the way he would rip and tear and rair up behind when he was getting it off.

Mark Twain, *Adventures of Huckleberry Finn*, Norton Critical Edition. New York: W.W. Norton & Company, 1999.

DOCUMENT 10: KING JAMES ISSUES A ROYAL LICENSE FOR THE KING'S MEN

University of North Carolina professor Russ McDonald introduces the 1603 document licensing Shakespeare's theater company as the King's Men. Shakespeare is listed as one of the members of the theater troupe.

From its formation in 1594 until 1603, Shakespeare's company was known as the Lord Chamberlain's Men. King James assumed patronage of the troupe in a document dated May 19, 1603, from which this passage is taken. The new title, the King's Men, was retained until the closing of the theaters in 1642.

We . . . do license and authorize these our Servants Lawrence Fletcher, William Shakespeare, Richard Burbage, Augustine Phillips, John Heminges, Henry Condell, William Sly, Robert Armin, Richard Cowley, and the rest of their associates freely to use and exercise the art and faculty of playing comedies, tragedies, histories, interludes, morals, pastorals, stageplays, and such others like as they have already studied or hereafter shall use or study as well for the recreation of our loving subjects as for our solace and pleasure when we shall think good to see them during our pleasure.

Russ McDonald. *The Bedford Companion to Shakespeare.* Boston and New York: Bedford Books of St Martin's Press, 1996.

DOCUMENT 11: OTHELLO AGONIZES OVER HIS DECISION

Convinced by the dishonest Iago that Desdemona has slept with his friend Cassio, Othello attempts to persuade himself to execute Desdemona for adultery. He agonizes over the decision because he loves her and recognizes the consequences of his decision.

Enter Othello [with a light], and Desdemona in her bed.

OTHELLO
    It is the cause,[1] it is the cause, my soul.
    Let me not name it to you, you chaste stars!
    It is the cause. Yet I'll not shed her blood,
    Nor scar that whiter skin of hers than snow,
    And smooth as monumental alabaster.
    Yet she must die, else she'll betray more men.
    Put out the light, and then put out the light.

If I quench thee, thou flaming minister,
I can again thy former light restore,
Should I repent me; but once put out thy light,
Thou cunning'st pattern of excelling nature,
I know not where is that Promethean heat
That can thy light relume. When I have plucked thy rose,
I cannot give it vital growth again;
It needs must wither. I'll smell thee on the tree.

[*He kisses her.*]

O balmy breath, that dost almost persuade
Justice to break her sword! One more, one more.
Be thus when thou art dead, and I will kill thee,
And love thee after. One more, and that's the last.

[*He kisses her.*]

So sweet was ne'er so fatal. I must weep,
But they are cruel tears. This sorrow's heavenly;
It strikes where it doth love. She wakes.

1. Of justice; Othello believes he is carrying out justice.

William Shakespeare, *Othello* (act 5, scene 2, lines 1–22).

DOCUMENT 12: DR. SAMUEL JOHNSON'S REACTION TO THE END OF KING LEAR

Eighteenth-century writer, scholar, and editor of Shakespeare's plays, Samuel Johnson found the closing scene of King Lear *so shocking that he preferred Nahum Tate's radical adaptation of the play. Shakespeare's play ends soon after Cordelia is executed by Lear's enemy, the bastard son of the Earl of Gloucester; in Tate's adaptation Cordelia lives and marries the Earl of Gloucester's legitimate son, Edgar.*

Shakespeare has suffered the virtue of *Cordelia* to perish in a just cause, contrary to the natural ideas of justice, to the hope of the reader, and, what is yet more strange, to the faith of chronicles. . . . A play in which the wicked prosper, and the virtuous miscarry, may doubtless be good, because it is a just representation of the common events of human life: but since all reasonable beings naturally love justice, I cannot easily be persuaded, that the observation of justice makes a play worse; or, that if other excellencies are equal, the audience will not always rise better pleased from the final triumph of persecuted virtue.

In the present case the publick has decided. *Cordelia*, from the time of [Nahum] *Tate* [who radically revised Shakespeare's play in his 1681 play, *History of King Lear*], has always retired with victory and felicity. And, if my sensations could add any thing to the general suffrage, I might relate, that I was many years ago so shocked by *Cordelia*'s death, that I know not whether I ever endured to read again the last scenes of the play till I undertook to revise them as an editor.

Samuel Johnson, *Notes to Shakespeare* (1765). In R.D. Stock, ed., *Samuel Johnson's Literary Criticism*. Lincoln: University of Nebraska Press, 1974.

DOCUMENT 13: THE ALLURE OF CLEOPATRA

University of California professor Norrie Epstein explains why Cleopatra has become the model of female beauty and the ideal of male fantasy. The passages quoted are from Shakespeare's tragedy, Antony and Cleopatra.

Cleopatra is a male fantasy, both terrifying and glorious, engulfing men yet unattainable. She's every man's ideal, because she never lapses into domestic predictability: "Age cannot wither her, nor custom stale / Her infinite variety." She always keeps Antony guessing: look at the following passage between Charmian, Cleopatra's handmaid, and Cleopatra, as the two women debate the best way to keep a man. With few alterations in vocabulary, it could easily be a debate excerpted from a story in a modern woman's magazine.

CLEOPATRA. (*to Alexas*)
    See where he is, who's with him, what he does.
I did not send you. If you find him sad,
Say I am dancing; if in mirth, report
That I am sudden sick. Quick, and return.
CHARMIAN. Madam, methinks, if you did love him dearly,
You do not hold the method to enforce
The like from him.
CLEOPATRA. What should I do I do not?
CHARMIAN. In each thing give him way. Cross him in nothing.
CLEOPATRA. Thou teachest like a fool: the way to lose him.
                                                    (I.3.2–10)

As Antony's right-hand man, Enobarbus is a stolid, brisk, and practical soldier whose wry observations serve as a counterpoint to Antony and Cleopatra's rhetorical excess. As Antony throws himself into life with abandon, Enobarbus, his foil, cynically observes. Despite his disapproval of Antony's behavior, he remains loyal almost to the end. His is a minor tragedy that mirrors that of his superior's; in abandoning Antony, he forsakes his own ideals, losing his honor, and himself.

Act IV, scene 3, is very brief and unearthly. As the music of hautboys (an Elizabethan oboe) rises from the earth, Hercules, Antony's tutelary god, at last abandons his favorite son. The uncanny airs emanating from another world reveal that there is a realm of godlike beauty beyond this mortal one.

In Act II, scene 2, Shakespeare brilliantly puts one of the most famous descriptions of female beauty in all Western literature into the mouth of the unromantic Enobarbus, thereby making Cleopatra's allure all the more convincing. If she can inspire *him* to poetic heights, then she must be spectacular. The matter-of-fact opening, "I will tell you," does little to prepare us for the sumptuous description that follows:

> The barge she sat in, like a burnished throne,
> Burned on the water. The poop was beaten gold;
> Purple the sails, and so perfumèd that
> The winds were lovesick with them. The oars were silver,
> Which to the tune of the flutes kept stroke and made
> The water which they beat to follow faster,
> As amorous of their strokes. For her own person,
> It beggared all description. She did lie
> In her pavilion, cloth-of-gold of tissue,
> O'erpicturing that Venus where we see
> The fancy outwork nature. On each side her
> Stood pretty dimpled boys, like smiling cupids,
> With divers-coloured fans, whose wind did seem
> To glow the delicate cheeks which they did cool,
> And what they undid did.

(196–210)

Norrie Epstein, *The Friendly Shakespeare.* New York: Viking Penguin, 1993.

Document 14: Caliban Claims the Island in *The Tempest*

Often read today as a disenfranchised member of a colonial nation, Caliban, in The Tempest, *claims that the unnamed island, on which the play is set, is his. He calls the island's current ruler, Prospero, a usurper and he curses both Prospero and his daughter Miranda, who have taught Caliban their language.*

CALIBAN
> As wicked dew as e'er my mother brushed
> With raven's feather from unwholesome fen
> Drop on you both! A southwest blow on ye
> And blister you all o'er!

PROSPERO
> For this, be sure, tonight thou shalt have cramps,
> Side-stitches that shall pen thy breath up.
> Urchins Shall forth at vast of night that they may work
> All exercise on thee. Thou shalt be pinched
> As thick as honeycomb, each pinch more stinging
> Than bees that made 'em.

CALIBAN   I must eat my dinner.
> This island's mine, by Sycorax my mother,
> Which thou tak'st from me. When thou cam'st first,
> Thou strok'st me and made much of me, wouldst give me
> Water with berries in 't, and teach me how
> To name the bigger light, and how the less,

That burn by day and night. And then I loved thee
And showed thee all the qualities o' th' isle,
The fresh springs, brine pits, barren place and fertile.
Cursed be I that did so! All the charms
Of Sycorax, toads, beetles, bats, light on you!
For I am all the subjects that you have,
Which first was mine own king; and here you sty me
In this hard rock, whiles you do keep from me
The rest o' th' island.

PROSPERO   Thou most lying slave,
Whom stripes may move, not kindness! I have used thee,
Filth as thou art, with humane care, and lodged thee
In mine own cell, till thou didst seek to violate
The honor of my child.

CALIBAN
Oho, Oho! Would 't had been done!
Thou didst prevent me; I had peopled else
This isle with Calibans.

MIRANDA   Abhorrèd slave,
Which any print of goodness wilt not take,
Being capable of all ill! I pitied thee,
Took pains to make thee speak, taught thee each hour
One thing or other. When thou didst not, savage,
Know thine own meaning, but wouldst gabble like
A thing most brutish, I endowed thy purposes
With words that made them known. But thy vile race,
Though thou didst learn, had that in 't which good natures
Could not abide to be with; therefore wast thou
Deservedly confined into this rock,
Who hadst deserved more than a prison.

CALIBAN
You taught me language, and my profit on 't
Is I know how to curse. The red plague rid you
For learning me your language!

William Shakespeare, *The Tempest* (act 1, scene 2, lines 324–368).

DOCUMENT 15: PROSPERO ENDS THE REVELS

*Sometimes read as Shakespeare's personal farewell to the stage, Pros-
pero's "our revels now are ended" speech comes early in act four of*
The Tempest. *Literally Prospero ends the marriage masque that he
has asked his sprite Ariel to create to warn Ferdinand and Miranda
against premarital sex. He ends this pageant abruptly when he re-
members the foul conspiracy of Caliban and his cohorts who are
planning to murder him.*

Our revels now are ended. These our actors,
As I foretold you, were all spirits and
Are melted into air, into thin air;

And, like the baseless fabric of this vision,
The cloud-capped towers, the gorgeous palaces,
The solemn temples, the great globe itself,
Yea, all which it inherit, shall dissolve,
And, like this insubstantial pageant faded,
Leave not a rack behind. We are such stuff
As dreams are made on, and our little life
Is rounded with a sleep. Sir, I am vexed.
Bear with my weakness. My old brain is troubled.
Be not disturbed with my infirmity.
If you be pleased, retire into my cell
And there repose. A turn or two I'll walk
To still my beating mind.

FERDINAND, MIRANDA   We wish your peace.
                              Exeunt [Ferdinand and Miranda].

William Shakespeare, *The Tempest* (act 4, scene 1, lines 148–163).

DOCUMENT 16: BEN JONSON COMMEMORATES SHAKESPEARE

The following poem was written by Shakespeare's friend and rival, Ben Jonson. It was prefixed to the First Folio (1623), the earliest published collection of Shakespeare's plays.

TO THE MEMORY OF MY BELOVED,
THE AUTHOR
MR. WILLIAM SHAKESPEARE:
AND
WHAT HE HATH LEFT US

TO draw no envy (*Shakespeare*) on thy name,
    Am I thus ample to thy Booke, and Fame:
While I confesse thy writings to be such,
    As neither *Man*, nor *Muse*, can praise too much.
'Tis true, and all mens suffrage. But these wayes
    Were not the paths I meant unto thy praise:
For seeliest Ignorance on these may light,
    Which, when it sounds at best, but eccho's right;
Or blinde Affection, which doth ne're advance
    The truth, but gropes, and urgeth all by chance;
Or crafty Malice, might pretend this praise,
    And thinke to ruine, where it seem'd to raise.
These are, as some infamous Baud, or Whore,
    Should praise a Matron. What could hurt her more?
But thou art proofe against them, and indeed
    Above th'ill fortune of them, or the need.
I, therefore will begin. Soule of the Age!
    The applause! delight! the wonder of our Stage!
My *Shakespeare*, rise; I will not lodge thee by
    Chaucer, or *Spenser*, or bid *Beaumont* lye

A little further, to make thee a roome:
  Thou art a Moniment, without a tombe,
And art alive still, while thy Booke doth live,
  And we have wits to read, and praise to give.
That I not mixe thee so, my braine excuses;
  I meane with great, but disproportion'd *Muses:*
For, if I thought my judgement were of yeeres,
  I should commit thee surely with thy peeres,
And tell, how farre thou didst our *Lily* out-shine,
  Or sporting *Kid*, or *Marlowes* mighty line.
And though thou hadst small *Latine*, and lesse *Greeke*,
  From thence to honour thee, I would not seeke
For names; but call forth thund'ring *Æschilus*,
  Euripides, and *Sophocles* to us,
Paccuvius, Accius, him of *Cordova* dead,
  To life againe, to heare thy Buskin tread,
And shake a Stage: Or, when thy Sockes were on,
  Leave thee alone, for the comparison
Of all, that insolent *Greece*, or haughtie *Rome*
  sent forth, or since did from their ashes come.
Triúmph, my *Britaine*, thou hast one to showe,
  To whom all Scenes of *Europe* homage owe.
He was not of an age, but for all time!
  And all the *Muses* still were in their prime,
When like *Apollo* he came forth to warme
  Our eares, or like a *Mercury* to charme!
Nature her selfe was proud of his designes,
  And joy'd to weare the dressing of his lines!
Which were so richly spun, and woven so fit,
  As, since, she will vouchsafe no other Wit.
The merry *Greeke*, tart *Aristophanes*,
  Neat *Terence*, witty *Plautus*, now not please;
But antiquated, and deserted lye
  As they were not of Natures family.
Yet must I not give Nature all: Thy Art,
  My gentle *Shakespeare*, must enjoy a part.
For though the *Poets* matter, Nature be,
  His Art doth give the fashion. And, that he,
Who casts to write a living line, must sweat,
  (such as thine are) and strike the second heat
Upon the *Muses* anvile: turne the same,
  (And himselfe with it) that he thinkes to frame;
Or for the lawrell, he may gaine a scorne,
  For a good *Poet's* made, as well as borne.
And such wert thou. Looke how the fathers face
  Lives in his issue, even so, the race
Of *Shakespeares* minde, and manners brightly shines
  In his well torned, and true-filed lines:

In each of which, he seemes to shake a Lance,
  As brandish't at the eyes of Ignorance.
Sweet Swan of *Avon!* what a sight it were
  To see thee in our waters yet appeare,
And make those flights upon the bankes of *Thames,*
  That so did take *Eliza,* and our *James!*
But stay, I see thee in the *Hemisphere*
  Advanc'd, and made a Constellation there!
Shine forth, thou Starre of *Poets,* and with rage,
  Or influence, chide, or cheere the drooping Stage;
Which, since thy flight from hence, hath mourn'd like night,
  And despaires day, but for thy Volumes light.

Ben Jonson, "To the Memory of My Beloved, the Author Mr. William Shakespeare: And What He Hath Left Us," 1623.

DOCUMENT 17: SELECTIONS FROM SHAKESPEARE'S WILL

Shakespeare's last will and testament, dated March 25, 1616, has contributed to the controversy about his authorship of the plays because it does not specifically bequeath any literary property to his family or friends; however, it does mention three of his fellows in the acting company, the Lord Chamberlain's Men (later the King's Men). The following version is the editor's modernized transcription of selections from the will which appears in full in Russ McDonald's The Bedford Companion to Shakespeare.

In the name of God, Amen. I, William Shackspeare of Stratford upon Avon, in the county of Warwick, gentleman, in perfect health and memory, God be praised, do make and ordain this my last will and testament in manner and form following. That is to say, first I commend my soul into the hands of God my Creator, hoping and assuredly believing through the only merits of Jesus Christ my Saviour, to be made partaker of life everlasting; and my body to the earth whereof it is made. Item. I give and bequeath unto my daughter Judith one hundred and fifty pounds of lawful English money. . . .

Item. I give and bequeath unto my said daughter Judith one hundred and fifty pounds more if she or any issue of her body be living at the end of three years. . . .

Item. I give and bequeath unto my said sister Joan [Hart] twenty pounds and all my wearing apparel, to be paid and delivered within one year after my death. And I do will and devise unto her the house with the appurtenances [minor properties] in Stratford, wherein she dwells, for her natural life, under the yearly rent of twelve pence. Item. I give and bequeath unto her three sons, William Hart, [Thomas] Hart, and Michael Hart, five pounds apiece to be paid within one year after my death. . . .

Item. I give and bequeath unto the said Elizabeth Hall [Shakespeare's niece] all my plate (except my broad silver-gilt bowl) that I now have at the date of this my will. Item. I give and bequeath unto the poor of Stratford aforesaid, ten pounds. To Mr. Thomas Combe, my sword, to Thomas Russell, Esquire, five pounds, and to Francis Collins of the borough of Warwick in the county of Warwick, gentleman, thirteen pounds, six shillings, and eight pence to be paid within one year after my death. Item. I give and bequeath to Hamnet Sadler twenty-six shillings, eight pence to buy him a ring, to William Reynolds, gentleman, twenty-six shillings, eight pence to buy him a ring, to my godson, William Walker, twenty shillings in gold, to Anthony Nash, gentleman, twenty-six shillings, eight pence, and to Mr. John Nash, twenty-six shillings, eight pence in gold, and to my fellows John Hemings, Richard Burbage, and Henry Condell, twenty-six shillings, eight pence a piece to buy them rings. Item. I give, will, bequeath, and devise unto my daughter Susanna Hall (for better enabling of her to perform this my will and towards the performance thereof) all that capital messuage [dwelling house, outbuildings, and grounds] or tenements with the appurtenances situated, lying, and being in Henley Street within the borough of Stratford aforesaid, and all my barns, stables, orchards, gardens, lands, tenements, and hereditaments [any property that can be inherited] whatsoever. . . .

Item. I give unto my wife my second best bed with the furniture. Item. I give and bequeath to my said daughter Judith my broad silver-gilt bowl. All the rest of my goods, chattels, leases, plate, jewels, and household stuff whatsoever, after my debts and legacies paid and my funeral expenses discharged, I give, devise, and bequeath to my son-in-law John Hall, gentleman, and my daughter Susanna, his wife, whom I ordain and make executors of this my last will and testament. . . .

Russ McDonald, *The Bedford Companion to Shakespeare.* Boston and New York: Bedford Books of St. Martin's Press, 1996.

DISCUSSION QUESTIONS

CHAPTER ONE: SHAKESPEARE, THE MAN

1. Why is there a controversy about who wrote the plays attributed to Shakespeare?

2. On which points concerning the authorship of Shakespeare's work does Diana Price disagree with David Bevington and Jonathan Bate?

3. List the strongest arguments in support of Shakespeare as the author of his plays. What evidence do any of the authors offer in favor of Edward de Vere as the possible author?

4. Using the evidence given in this chapter and any outside sources you may have seen, explain whether you believe that Shakespeare wrote the plays commonly attributed to him.

CHAPTER TWO: SHAKESPEARE'S WORKS: "OF AN AGE AND FOR ALL TIME"

1. How can a play be both "of an age" (the product of a particular author who lived and wrote at a particular time in a particular place) and "for all time" (relevant to the concerns of people who live in different countries throughout several centuries)? How well does this statement pertain to Shakespeare's works?

2. According to Martin Wiggins, Robert Greene was right about the kind of talent Shakespeare possessed. What does Robert Greene say about Shakespeare's talent?

3. What is *bardolatry?* What practices, which began during the eighteenth century, are associated with bardolatry?

4. According to Joseph Papp and Elizabeth Kirkland, why is Shakespeare still "alive" today? What twentieth-century values do you think Shakespeare's plays reflect?

CHAPTER THREE: SHAKESPEARE'S LEGACY

1. According to Harold Bloom, how has Shakespeare changed our concept of what it means to be human?

2. What is blank verse? How does Shakespeare use it differently from other writers? Provide examples when explaining your answer.

3. Based on the articles by Ellen T. Harris, John Gross, and Martha Tuck Rozett, explain how Shakespeare's works have influenced other artists.

4. Shakespeare's words are a part of our language, his characters are central to our way of envisioning humanity, and his works permeate our music and literature, so is it possible today to be an original thinker? Or are we all living in Shakespeare's shadow? Explain your answer.

CHAPTER FOUR: SHAKESPEARE PERMEATES POPULAR CULTURE

1. Robert Hapgood, Lynda E. Boose, Richard Burt, and James R. Andreas all address films based on Shakespeare's works. According to them, what are the benefits of these Shakespeare films? What are the drawbacks?

2. What does Graham Holderness think about the way so many people have capitalized on Shakespeare (organizing a two-month long "bardfest," arguing over whether Shakespeare really wrote the plays attributed to him, using lines out of context for advertising, politicizing a teacher's decision against taking schoolchildren to a ballet, placing lines from Shakespeare's *The Tempest* in a subway)? Do you agree with his assessment? Why or why not?

3. What evidence do you see that Shakespeare pervades popular culture? Give as many examples as you can without utilizing those in the articles.

CHRONOLOGY

1564

William Shakespeare is born in the village of Stratford in central England. Noted contemporary writer, Christopher Marlowe, is also born.

1572

Playwright Ben Jonson, who will later become Shakespeare's friend and rival, is born.

1576

London's first public theater, the Theatre, opens.

1582

William Shakespeare marries Anne Hathaway.

1583

Shakespeare's daughter Susanna is born.

1585

Shakespeare's twins, Hamnet and Judith, are born.

1588–1594

Shakespeare writes his first tragedy, *Titus Andronicus*; his first comedies, *The Comedy of Errors, Love's Labor's Lost, The Two Gentlemen of Verona, The Taming of the Shrew*; his two long narrative poems, *Venus and Adonis* and *The Rape of Lucrece;* and his first tetralogy of history plays, *Henry VI*, parts 1, 2, and 3 and *Richard III.*

1592

Robert Greene refers to Shakespeare as an "upstart crow" in his pamphlet *Groatsworth of Wit.*

1594–1600

Shakespeare is listed as a member of the acting company the Lord Chamberlain's Men. He privately circulates his sequence of sonnets, and he writes his best comedies: *A Midsummer Night's Dream, The Merchant of Venice, Much Ado*

About Nothing, The Merry Wives of Windsor, As You Like It, and *Twelfth Night.* During this period he also writes his romantic tragedy *Romeo and Juliet*; his first Roman tragedy, *Julius Caesar*; a history play, *King John*; and the second great tetralogy of history plays, *Richard II, Henry IV,* parts 1 and 2, and *Henry V.*

1596

Shakespeare's only son, Hamnet, dies at the age of eleven.

1597

Shakespeare buys New Place, the largest home in Stratford.

1598

Francis Meres's book of literary observations, *Palladis Tamia: Wit's Treasury,* attests to Shakespeare's growing fame as both a poet and a playwright.

1598–1599

The Globe Theatre opens; Shakespeare owns one-eighth of its profits.

1600–1607

Shakespeare writes what will later be acknowledged as his greatest tragedies: *Hamlet, Othello, King Lear, Macbeth, Timon of Athens,* and *Antony and Cleopatra.* He also writes the problem comedies, *All's Well That Ends Well, Measure for Measure, Troilus and Cressida*; a romance, *Pericles*; and two poems, "The Phoenix and Turtle" and *A Lover's Complaint.*

1603

Queen Elizabeth I dies; James I becomes king of England. Shakespeare's acting company is licensed by the new king and becomes the King's Men.

1608

The King's Men signs a twenty-one-year lease for the use of Blackfriars, an indoor playhouse.

1608–1613

Shakespeare writes his last tragedy, *Coriolanus*; his three best romances, *Cymbeline, The Winter's Tale,* and *The Tempest*; and his last history play, *Henry VIII.* His sonnet cycle is published in 1609.

1611

The King James translation of the Bible is published.

1616

Shakespeare dies.

1623

The First Folio is published. It is the earliest published collection of Shakespeare's thirty-six plays and contains eighteen plays that had not previously appeared in separate quarto editions. Shakespeare's fellow actors Henry Condell and John Hemings supervised the gathering of the plays and publishing rights. Ben Jonson's commendatory poem is prefixed to the First Folio, as are several other commendatory verses.

1625

King James I dies and is succeeded by his son Charles I.

1625–1660

The theaters are closed during the English civil war and the protectorate of Oliver Cromwell. Charles I is executed in 1649. His son, Charles II, is proclaimed king of Scotland in 1649 but is not restored to the English throne until 1660.

1660

The theaters reopen. For the first time, actresses play the female roles in Shakespeare's plays, beginning with the revival of *Othello.*

1709

The first edition of Shakespeare's plays, with scholarly apparatus, is completed by Nicholas Rowe.

1741

A statue of Shakespeare is placed in Poets' Corner in Westminster Abbey.

1750

The first Oxford lectures on Shakespeare are delivered by William Hawkins.

1765

English lexicographer, essayist, poet, and moralist Dr. Samuel Johnson edits Shakespeare's plays. His "Preface" to the volume and his "Notes to Shakespeare" are considered his best writing.

1769

David Garrick's Stratford Jubilee enshrines Shakespeare as Britain's national poet.

1807

Mary Lamb and her brother Charles adapt Shakespeare for children in their *Tales from Shakespeare.*

1808–1819

Poet and critic Samuel Taylor Coleridge delivers seven series of brilliant but disordered lectures on Shakespeare.

1818

Thomas and Maria Bowdler expurgate words and expressions that cannot, with propriety, be read aloud in a family gathering in their ten volume edition of Shakespeare's plays, *The Family Shakespeare.*

1826

Jakob Mendelssohn writes his overture to *A Midsummer Night's Dream.* The complete music appears in 1843.

1850

Charles Dickens's *David Copperfield* is printed; it contains numerous allusions to Shakespeare, as do other works by Dickens and his contemporaries.

1863–1866

The Cambridge/Globe edition of Shakespeare's complete plays becomes the universal standard of reference.

1869

Pyotr Tchaikovsky's symphony *Romeo and Juliet* is performed.

1874

The New Shakspere Society is founded.

1884

Mark Twain's novel *The Adventures of Huckleberry Finn* is published; it includes parodies of *Romeo and Juliet* and of Hamlet's "To Be or Not to Be" soliloquy.

1887

Giuseppe Verdi's opera *Otello* is performed. (*Falstaff,* Verdi's opera version of *The Merry Wives of Windsor,* appears in 1893.)

1890s

Knowledge of Shakespeare is considered the mark of an educated individual in England.

1922

James Joyce's *Ulysses* includes an entire chapter on Shakespeare and Shakespearean criticism; it opens with Stephen Daedalus's famous theory of Hamlet: "He proves by algebra that Hamlet's grandson is Shakespeare's grandfather and that he is himself the ghost of his own father." (Joyce's 1939 novel *Finnegan's Wake* also includes wonderful Shakespeare parodies.)

1935

Sergey Prokofiev's ballet *Romeo and Juliet* is performed.

1938

The Boys from Syracuse, a musical based on Shakespeare's *The Comedy of Errors*, opens.

1940s–1950s

Laurence Olivier becomes the premier Shakespearean actor on stage and in film. His best performances are as the title characters in *Henry V* (1944), *Hamlet* (1948), and *Richard III* (1955).

1948

Cole Porter's musical *Kiss Me, Kate*, based on Shakespeare's *The Taming of the Shrew*, opens. Orson Welles produces his *Macbeth*. (Welles will later produce *Othello* (1951) and *Chimes at Midnight* (1967), which is based on Falstaff's character in *Henry IV*, parts 1 and 2 and *The Merry Wives of Windsor*.)

1957

Leonard Bernstein's *West Side Story*, based on Shakespeare's *Romeo and Juliet* opens. Japanese director Akira Kurosawa's *Throne of Blood*, based on *Macbeth*, opens.

1966

Franco Zeffirelli produces the film *Taming of the Shrew*, starring Richard Burton and Elizabeth Taylor. Polish writer Jan Kott's influential book *Shakespeare Our Contemporary* is translated into English. Tom Stoppard's play *Rosencrantz and Guildenstern Are Dead*, a response to *Hamlet*, is first performed.

1968

Franco Zeffirelli's film *Romeo and Juliet* opens.

1969

Aime Cesaire's play *A Tempest* is first performed.

1971

Roman Polanski's film *Macbeth* opens.

1982

Woody Allen's spoof on *A Midsummer Night's Dream*, called *A Midsummer Night's Sex Comedy*, opens.

1983

Oscar Zarate's serious comic-book version of *Othello* is published.

1984

Laurence Olivier's film *King Lear* opens.

1985

Akira Kurosawa's film *Ran*, based on *King Lear*, opens.

1988

Ann-Marie MacDonald's play *Goodnight Desdemona (Good Morning Juliet)* is performed.

1989

Kenneth Branagh's film *Henry V* begins the Shakespeare-on-film boom of the 1990s.

1990s

The Shakespeare-on-film boom includes Franco Zeffirelli's *Hamlet* (1990), starring Mel Gibson; Peter Greenaway's *Prospero's Books* (1991), a version of *The Tempest*; *Shakespeare, the Animated Tales* (1992); Gus Van Sant's *My Own Private Idaho* (1993), which makes use of the *Henry IV* plays; Kenneth Branagh's *Much Ado About Nothing* (1993); *Renaissance Man* (1994), starring Danny DeVito; Ian McKellan's *Richard III* (1995); Lawrence Fishburn's *Othello* (1995); Marc Norman and Tom Stoppard's *Shakespeare in Love* (1996); Kenneth Branagh's *Hamlet* (1996); Al Pacino's *Looking for Richard* (1996); Trevor Nunn's *Twelfth Night* (1996); Baz Luhrmann's *William Shakespeare's Romeo and Juliet* (1996); Michael Hoffman's *A Midsummer Night's Dream* (1999).

FOR FURTHER RESEARCH

PRIMARY WORKS: PLAYS

Henry VI, parts 1, 2, 3 (ca. 1589–1592)

Titus Andrónicus (ca. 1589–1592)

The Comedy of Errors (ca. 1589–1594)

Love's Labor's Lost (ca. 1588–1597)

The Two Gentlemen of Verona (ca. 1590–1594)

The Taming of the Shrew (ca. 1590–1593)

Richard III (ca. 1592–1594)

King John (ca. 1594–1596)

Romeo and Juliet (ca. 1594–1596)

A Midsummer Night's Dream (ca. 1595)

Richard II (ca. 1595–1596)

The Merchant of Venice (ca. 1596–1597)

Henry IV, parts 1 and 2 (ca. 1596–1598)

Much Ado About Nothing (1598–1599)

Henry V (1599)

Julius Caesar (1599)

The Merry Wives of Windsor (1597–1601)

As You Like It (1598–1600)

Hamlet (ca. 1599–1601)

Twelfth Night (1600–1602)

Troilus and Cressida (1601–1602)

All's Well That Ends Well (ca. 1601–1605)

Measure for Measure (1603–1604)

Othello (ca. 1603–1604)

King Lear (ca. 1605–1606)

Macbeth (ca. 1606–1607)

Timon of Athens (ca. 1605–1608)

Antony and Cleopatra (1606–1607)

Pericles (1606–1608)

Coriolanus (ca. 1608)

Cymbeline (ca. 1608–1610)

The Winter's Tale (ca. 1609–1610)

The Tempest (ca. 1611)

King Henry VIII (1613)

PRIMARY WORKS: POEMS

Venus and Adonis (1592–1593)

The Rape of Lucrece (1593–1594)

The Sonnets (ca. 1593–1603; published 1609)

"The Phoenix and Turtle" (by 1601)

A Lover's Complaint (ca. 1601–1605)

PRIMARY WORKS: COLLECTED EDITIONS

David Bevington, ed., *The Complete Works of Shakespeare.* 4th ed. New York: HarperCollins, 1992.

G. Blakemore Evans, ed., *The Riverside Shakespeare.* 2nd ed. Boston: Houghton and Mifflin, 1997.

BIOGRAPHIES OF SHAKESPEARE

Peter Alexander, *Shakespeare's Life and Art.* New York: New York University Press, 1961.

Gerald E. Bently, *Shakespeare: A Biographical Handbook.* Westport, CT: Greenwood, 1986.

Mark Eccles, *Shakespeare in Warwickshire.* Madison: University of Wisconsin Press, 1961.

Roland M. Frye, *Shakespeare's Life and Times: A Pictorial Record.* Princeton, NJ: Princeton University Press, 1967.

Francois Laroque, *The Age of Shakespeare.* New York: Harry N. Abrams, 1993.

Peter Levi, *The Life and Times of William Shakespeare.* New York: Henry Holt, 1989.

Charlton Ogburn, *The Mysterious William Shakespeare.* McLean, VA: EPM, 1984.

Diana Price, *Shakespeare's Unorthodox Biography.* Westport, CT: Greenwood, 2001.

A.L. Rowse, *Shakespeare the Man.* New York: Harper and Row, 1973.

———, *William Shakespeare: A Biography.* New York: Harper and Row, 1963.

Samuel Schoenbaum, *William Shakespeare: A Documentary Life.* New York: Oxford University Press, 1975.

SHAKESPEAREAN ANALYSIS AND CRITICISM

C.L. Barber, *Shakespeare's Festive Comedy.* Princeton, NJ: Princeton University Press, 1972.

Ralph Berry, *Shakespeare's Comedies.* Princeton, NJ: Princeton University Press, 1972.

Andrew C. Bradley, *Shakespearean Tragedy.* New York: Viking Penguin, 1991.

John Russell Brown, *Shakespeare and His Comedies.* 2nd ed. London: Methuen, 1962.

Lily B. Campbell, *Shakespeare's Tragic Heroes: Slaves of Passion.* New York: Barnes and Noble, 1968.

Edmund K. Chambers, *William Shakespeare: A Study of Facts and Problems.* New York: Oxford University Press, 1989.

William Empson, *Essays on Shakespeare.* Cambridge, UK: Cambridge University Press, 1986.

M.D. Faber, *The Design Within: Psychoanalytic Approaches to Shakespeare.* New York: Science House, 1970.

Walter C. Foreman Jr., *The Music of the Close: The Final Scenes of Shakespeare's Tragedies.* Lexington: University Press of Kentucky, 1978.

Brian Gibbons, *Shakespeare and Multiplicity.* Cambridge, UK: Cambridge University Press, 1993.

Robert G. Hunter, *Shakespeare and the Comedy of Forgiveness.* New York: Columbia University Press, 1965.

———, *Shakespeare and the Mystery of God's Judgments.* Athens: University of Georgia Press, 1976.

Denis J. Huston, *Shakespeare's Comedies of Play.* New York: Columbia University Press, 1981.

G. Wilson Knight, *The Wheel of Fire.* Cleveland, OH: Meridian, 1964.

Clifford Leech, ed., *Shakespeare: The Tragedies: A Collection of Critical Essays.* Chicago: University of Chicago Press, 1965.

Alexander Leggatt, *Shakespeare's Comedy of Love.* London: Methuen, 1973.

———, *Shakespeare's Political Drama: The History Plays and the Roman Plays.* London: Methuen, 1988.

Carolyn R.S. Lenz et al., eds., *The Woman's Part: Feminist Criticism of Shakespeare.* Urbana: University of Illinois Press, 1980.

Maynard Mack Jr., *Killing the King: Three Studies in Shakespeare's Tragic Structure.* New Haven, CT: Yale University Press, 1973.

Bernard McElroy, *Shakespeare's Mature Tragedies.* Princeton, NJ: Princeton University Press, 1973.

Robert Ornstein, *Shakespeare's Comedies from Roman Farce to Romantic Mystery.* Newark: University of Delaware Press, 1986.

Douglas L. Peterson, *Time, Tide, and Tempest: A Study of Shakespeare's Romances.* San Marino, CA: Huntington Library, 1973.

Gerald M. Pinciss and Roger Lockyer, eds., *Shakespeare's World: Background Readings in the English Renaissance.* New York: Continuum, 1989.

M.M. Reese, *The Cease of Majesty.* New York: St. Martin's, 1961.

Irving Ribner, *The English History Play in the Age of Shakespeare.* Rev. ed. New York: Barnes and Noble, 1965.

Bernard Spivack, *Shakespeare and the Allegory of Evil.* New York: Columbia University Press, 1958.

Clarice Swisher, ed., *Readings on the Tragedies of William Shakespeare.* San Diego: Greenhaven, 1996.

Robert W. Uphaus, *Beyond Tragedy.* Lexington: University Press of Kentucky, 1981.

Donald G. Watson, *Shakespeare's Early History Plays: Politics and Play on the Elizabethan Stage.* Athens: University of Georgia Press, 1990.

David Young, *The Action to the Word: Structure and Style in Shakespearean Tragedy.* New Haven, CT: Yale University Press, 1990.

SHAKESPEARE PERFORMED

Jonathan Bate and Russell Jackson, eds., *Shakespeare: An Illustrated Stage History.* New York: Oxford University Press, 1996.

Gerald Eades Bentley, *The Profession of Player in Shakespeare's Time, 1590–1642.* Princeton, NJ: Princeton University Press, 1984.

Anthony Davis, *Filming Shakespeare's Plays: The Adaptations of Laurence Olivier, Orson Welles, Peter Brook, and Akira Kurosawa.* Cambridge, UK: Cambridge University Press, 1988.

Peter Samuel Donaldson, *Shakespearean Films/Shakespearean Directors.* Boston: Unwin Hyman, 1998.

Andrew Gurr, *Playgoing in Shakespeare's London.* 2nd ed. Cambridge, UK: Cambridge University Press, 1996.

Kenneth S. Rothwell and Annabelle Henkin Melzer, *Shakespeare on Screen.* New York: Neal-Schuman, 1990.

SOURCES FOR VIEWPOINTS AND CITATIONS

John F. Andrews, ed., *William Shakespeare: His World, His Work, His Influence.* 3 vols. New York: Charles Scribner's Sons, 1985.

Sylvan Barnet, "Shakespeare: An Overview," in *The Taming of the Shrew.* New York: Signet, 1986.

Jonathan Bate, *The Genius of Shakespeare.* New York: Oxford University Press, 1998.

Tom Bethell et al., "The Ghost of Shakespeare," *Harper's,* vol. 298, no. 1787, April 1999.

David Bevington, ed., *The Complete Works of Shakespeare.* 4th edition. New York: HarperCollins, 1992.

———, ed., *The Taming of the Shrew.* New York: Bantam Books, 1998.

Harold Bloom, *Shakespeare, the Invention of the Human.* New York: Riverhead Books, 1998.

Lynda E. Boose and Richard Burt, eds., *Shakespeare, the Movie.* New York: Routledge, 1997.

Charles Boyce, *Shakespeare A to Z: The Essential Reference to His Plays, His Poems, His Life and Times, and More.* New York: Facts On File, 1990.

Michael Dobson, *The Making of the National Poet.* Oxford, UK: Clarendon, 1992.

Norrie Epstein, *The Friendly Shakespeare.* New York: Viking Penguin, 1993.

John Gross, *After Shakespeare.* New York: Oxford University Press, 2002.

Graham Holderness, ed., *Cultural Shakespeare: Essays in the Shakespeare Myth.* Hatfield, UK: University of Hertfordshire Press, 2001.

Holger Klein and James L. Harner, eds., *Shakespeare and the Visual Arts.* Lewiston, UK: Edwin Mellen, 2000.

Jan Kott, *Shakespeare Our Contemporary.* New York: Anchor Books, 1966.

Francois Laroque, *The Age of Shakespeare.* New York: Harry N. Abrams, 1993.

Harry Levin, introduction to *The Riverside Shakespeare.* 2nd ed. Ed. G. Blakemore Evans. Boston: Houghton and Mifflin, 1997.

Russ McDonald, *The Bedford Companion to Shakespeare.* New York: Bedford Books of St. Martin's, 1996.

Jeffrey McQuain and Stanley Malless, *Coined by Shakespeare.* Springfield, MA: Merriam-Webster, 1998.

Marc Norman and Tom Stoppard, *Shakespeare in Love: A Screenplay.* New York: Miramax Film and Universal Studios, 1998.

Joseph Papp and Elizabeth Kirkland, *Shakespeare Alive!* New York: Bantam Books, 1988.

Martha Ruck Rozett, *Talking Back to Shakespeare*. Urbana, IL: Associated University Presses, 1994.

Gary Taylor, *Reinventing Shakespeare*. Oxford, UK: Oxford University Press, 1989.

Martin Wiggins, *Shakespeare and the Drama of His Time*. New York: Oxford University Press, 2000.

George T. Wright, *Shakespeare's Metrical Art*. Berkeley and Los Angeles: University of California Press, 1988.

WEBSITES

Mr. William Shakespeare and the Internet, http://shakespeare.palomar.edu. Terry Gray at Palomar College in San Marcos, California, offers categories for research (works, life and times, criticism) and numerous links to discussion groups and news groups.

Shakespeare Online, www.shakespeare-online.com. This website focuses on general study materials and essays on Shakespeare.

University of Virginia Library, Shakespeare Resources, http://etext.lib.virginia.edu. This site offers numerous texts of Shakespeare's plays, including playhouse prompt books and the complete First Folio of 1623.

INDEX